THE MONOGRAPH SERIES OF
THE PSYCHOANALYTIC STUDY OF THE CHILD

Monograph No. 4

THE ANALYSIS OF THE SELF

*A Systematic Approach to the Psychoanalytic
Treatment of Narcissistic Personality Disorders*

THE PSYCHOANALYTIC STUDY OF THE CHILD

MONOGRAPH NO. 4

The Analysis of the Self

*A Systematic Approach to the Psychoanalytic
Treatment of Narcissistic Personality Disorders*

By
HEINZ KOHUT, M.D.

INTERNATIONAL UNIVERSITIES PRESS, INC.

NEW YORK

THE MONOGRAPH SERIES OF
THE PSYCHOANALYTIC STUDY OF THE CHILD

Managing Editors

Ruth S. Eissler, M.D. Heinz Hartmann, M.D.†
Anna Freud, LL.D., Sc.D. Marianne Kris, M.D.
Seymour L. Lustman, M.D., Ph.D.

Assistant Editor

Lottie M. Newman

All contributions for publication in the Monograph Series will be by invitation only. The Editors regret that they do not have facilities to read unsolicited manuscripts.

Copyright 1971, by International Universities Press, Inc.
Library of Congress Catalog Card Number: 70-143392

Seventh Printing, 1983

For B. and G.

CONTENTS

Part II

The Therapeutic Activation of the Grandiose Self

Part III
Clinical and Technical Problems in the Narcissistic Transferences

ACKNOWLEDGMENTS

The psychoanalyst who presents what he hopes to be valid depth-psychological insights must first acknowledge his gratitude to his patients of whose cooperation and increasing self-understanding he is the beneficiary. And secondly he is beholden to his students whose discussions and questions are an invaluable stimulation for a teacher who begins to share his new ideas and discoveries with the younger generation of colleagues. For different though in each case obvious reasons the thanks expressed to these two groups of helpers must be general and the recipients of the gratitude must remain anonymous.

There are others to whom my gratitude can be expressed directly. I owe special thanks to Anna Freud, who read an early version of this study. Her questions stimulated me in many important directions. I am especially grateful to Dr. Marianne Kris for the unfailing support she gave me in pursuing my investigations. I am also grateful to a group of colleagues who gave me their reactions to subsequent versions of the manuscript: Drs. Michael F. Basch, Ruth S. Eissler, John E. Gedo, Arnold Goldberg, George H. Klumpner, Paul H. Ornstein, Paul H. Tolpin, Janice Norton. Dr. Charles Kligerman, moreover, helped me decisively in formulating the title of this book.

I gratefully acknowledge the help of colleagues who consulted with me and candidates whom I supervised. The case material which became thus available to me allowed me to broaden the empirical basis of my presentation. In this respect I owe thanks to Drs. David Marcus, Janice Norton, Anna Ornstein, Paul H. Ornstein.

I want to thank the Editors of the *Journal of the American Psychoanalytic Association,* the *International Journal of Psycho-Analysis,* and *The Psychoanalytic Study of the Child* for permission to use material that first appeared in their publications.

Financial help supporting the preparation of the final manuscript, conscientiously typed by Regina Lieb and Lillian Bigler, came from (a) the Charlotte Rosenbaum Fund through the Student Mental Health Clinic and the Department of Psychiatry of the University of Chicago and (b) the Research Fund of the Chicago Institute for Psychoanalysis.

Finally, I wish to thank Lottie M. Newman for her help with the preparation of the manuscript for publication. Her perceptive advice regarding improvements in form and substance was always in the service of finding the best way of communicating my ideas as clearly as possible. Our cooperation was a most gratifying experience for me.

PREFACE

The subject matter of narcissism, that is, of the cathexis of the self (Hartmann), is a very broad and important one since it can be said with justification that it refers to half of the contents of the human mind—the other half being, of course, the objects. To make a comprehensive presentation of the problems of narcissism would, therefore, be an undertaking of vast proportions which might well surpass the knowledge and skill of any single contributor.

More important even than the magnitude of the task, however, is the fact that a comprehensive presentation presupposes a field that is more or less settled, or the investigation of which seems at least to have reached a plateau. A textbook approach, in other words, is peculiarly fitted to that point in time when a series of significant advances have been made in a specific field and these now require a more detached assessment and integration in the form of a survey which attempts to round out the newly acquired knowledge and to present it in a balanced form. These are not the conditions that prevail with regard to the subject matter of narcissism at the present time.

A deceptively simple but pioneering and decisive advance in psychoanalytic metapsychology, the conceptual separation of the self from the ego (Hartmann); the interest in the acquisition and maintenance of an "identity" as well as in the dangers to which this (pre)conscious mental content is exposed (Erikson); the gradual crystallization of a separate psychobiological existence out of the matrix of the union of mother and child (Mahler); and some detailed, psychoanalytically formulated important clinico-theoretical (Jacobson) and clinical (A. Reich) contributions of recent years—all this work testifies to the increasing interest of psychoanalysts in a subject matter which had tended to be pushed into the background by the vast material contributed to the investigation of the world of objects, i.e., to the developmental and dynamic vicissitudes of the imagoes, or—expressed more in congruence with a central position of the ego's cognitive processes rather than that of the drives within the context of the id—of the representations of objects.

One of the difficulties encountered as one approaches the theoretical problems of narcissism—a difficulty which has become greater by now than the formerly widespread confusion between self cathexis and cathexis of ego functions— is the frequently made assumption that the existence of object relations excludes narcissism. On the contrary, as will be emphasized in the following pages, some of the most intense narcissistic experiences relate to objects; objects, that is, which are either used in the service of the self and of the maintenance of its instinctual investment, or objects which are themselves experienced as part of the self. I shall refer to the latter as *self-objects*.

A few basic conceptual clarifications should be made at the outset. The notions of self, on the one hand, of ego, superego, id, on the other, as well as those of personality and identity, are abstractions which belong to different levels of concept formation. Ego, id, and superego are the constituents of a specific, high-level, i.e., experience-distant, abstraction in psychoanalysis: the psychic apparatus. Personality, although often serviceable in a general sense, like identity, is not indigenous to psychoanalytic psychology; it belongs to a different theoretical framework which is more in harmony with the observation of social behavior and the description of the (pre)conscious experience of oneself in the interaction with others than with the observations of depth psychology.

The self, however, emerges in the psychoanalytic situation and is conceptualized, in the mode of a comparatively low-level, i.e., comparatively experience-near, psychoanalytic abstraction, as a content of the mental apparatus. While it is thus not an agency of the mind, it is a structure within the mind since (a) it is cathected with instinctual energy and (b) it has continuity in time, i.e., it is enduring. Being a psychic structure, the self has, furthermore, also a psychic location. To be more specific, various—and frequently inconsistent—self representations are present not only in the id, the ego, and the superego, but also within a single agency of the mind. There may, for example, exist contradictory conscious and preconscious self representations—e.g., of grandiosity and inferiority—side by side, occupying either delimited loci within the realm of the ego or sectorial positions of that realm of the psyche in which id and ego form a continuum. The self then, quite analogous to the representations of objects, is a content of the mental apparatus but is not one of its constituents, i.e., not one of the agencies of the mind.

Such theoretical clarifications provide a framework for the principal subject matter of this book which attempts to integrate two goals: the description in depth of a group of specific normal and abnormal phenomena within the general realm of narcissism and the understanding of the specific developmental phase which is genetically correlated to them.

Broad as the field of this monograph is, it nevertheless forms only part of a larger study of narcissism. Specifically, this study concentrates almost exclusively on the role of the libidinal forces in the analysis of narcissistic personalities; the discussion of the role of aggression will be taken up separately. On the other hand, this book is a continuation and expansion of a series of studies, published in 1959, 1963 (with Seitz), 1966, 1968. The case material and the conclusions drawn from it, and the conceptualizations contained in these papers, have been used freely throughout the ensuing pages. This monograph constitutes the rounding out and completion of the investigation of the libidinal aspects of narcissism which had been initiated in these earlier essays.

CHAPTER 1

INTRODUCTORY CONSIDERATIONS

The subject matter of this monograph is the study of certain transference or transferencelike phenomena in the psychoanalysis of narcissistic personalities, and of the analyst's reactions to them, including his countertransferences. The primary focus of attention will not be on the schizophrenias and depressions, which are being treated by a number of psychoanalysts with special interest and talent in this field, or even on the milder or disguised forms of the psychoses, which are often referred to as borderline states, but on the contiguous, specific personality disturbances of lesser severity[1] whose treatment constitutes a considerable part of present-day psychoanalytic practice. It is undoubtedly not easy at times to draw a line of demarcation between these conditions and the grave disorders to which they may appear to be related.

During temporary regressive swings in the course of the analysis of some of these patients symptoms might arise which could at first appear to be indicative of psychosis to those who are not familiar with the analysis of severe narcissistic personality disturbances. Yet, strangely, neither analyst

---

[1] Of the different cases referred to in this book only one (patient G.) was psychotic. All the others were active, socially comparatively well-adjusted, and reasonably well-functioning people whose personality disturbance, however, interfered more or less seriously with their capacity to work and to be productive, and with happiness and inner peace.

1

nor patient tends to remain greatly alarmed by these temporary regressive experiences, even though their content (paranoid suspiciousness, for example; or delusional body sensations and profound shifts in self perception), if judged in isolation, would indeed justify the apprehension that a serious break with reality is imminent. But the total picture remains reassuring, in particular the fact that the event which precipitated the regression can usually be identified, and that the patient himself soon learns to look for the transference disturbance (a rebuff by the analyst, for example) when the regressive development is taking place. Once the analyst has become familiar with the patient—and in particular as soon as he has observed that one of the forms of narcissistic transference has spontaneously established itself—he will in general be able to reach the confident conclusion that the patient's central disturbance is not a psychosis, and he will later maintain his conviction despite the occurrence of the aforementioned severely regressive but temporary phenomena in the course of analysis.

How is one to differentiate the psychopathology of the analyzable narcissistic personality disturbances from the psychoses and the borderline states? From what identifiable features of the patient's behavior, or of his symptomatology, or of the analytic process can we derive the sense of relative security experienced by analysand and analyst, despite the presence of some seemingly ominous initial symptoms and of some apparently dangerous regressive swings during the analysis? I am discussing these questions with some reluctance at this point, not only because I trust that the present monograph in its entirety will gradually clarify the issue of differential diagnosis as theoretical understanding and clinical description become integrated in the mind of the reader, but especially in view of the fact that my approach to psychopathology is guided by a depth-psychological orientation which does not lead me toward looking at clinical phenomena according to the traditional medical model, i.e., as disease entities or pathological syndromes which are to be diagnosed and differentiated on the basis of behavioral criteria. For expository purposes, however, I shall now provide an anticipatory summary of the essentials of the pathology of these analyzable patients in dynamic-structural and genetic terms, and outline how the complaints of these individuals can be understood against the background of a metapsychological grasp of their personality disturbance.

These patients are suffering from specific disturbances in the realm of the self and of those archaic objects cathected with narcissistic libido (self-objects) which are still in intimate connection with the archaic self (i.e., objects which are not experienced as separate and independent from the self). Despite the fact that the fixation points of the central psychopathology of these cases are located at a rather early portion of the time axis of psychic development, it is important to emphasize not only the deficiencies of the psychic organization of these patients but also the assets.[2]

On the debit side we can say that these patients remained fixated on archaic grandiose self configurations and/or on archaic, overestimated, narcissistically cathected objects. The fact that these archaic configurations have not become integrated with the rest of the personality has two major consequences: (a) the adult personality and its mature functions are impoverished because they are deprived of the energies that are invested in the ancient structures; and/or (b) the adult, realistic activities of these patients are hampered by the breakthrough and intrusion of the archaic structures and of their archaic claims. The pathogenic effect of the investment of these archaic configurations is, in other words, in

---

[2] It is important to stress that the nature of the psychopathology is not necessarily related to the severity of the disorder. There exist incapacitating clinical conditions (e.g., hysterical fugue states of psychotic proportions) caused by the massive intrusion of infantile object cathexes which overwhelm the reality ego; and there are brief malfunctions of circumscribed portions of the ego (e.g., certain parapraxes) which are due to the effect of narcissistic cathexes. For a telling example of such a narcissistic parapraxis, see Kohut (1970a).

certain respects analogous to that exerted by the instinctual investment of unconscious repressed incestuous objects in the classical transference neuroses.

Disturbing as their psychopathology may be, it is important to realize that these patients have specific assets which differentiate them from the psychoses and borderline states. Unlike the patients who suffer from these latter disorders, patients with narcissistic personality disturbances have in essence attained a cohesive self and have constructed cohesive idealized archaic objects. And, unlike the conditions which prevail in the psychoses and borderline states, these patients are not seriously threatened by the possibility of an irreversible disintegration of the archaic self or of the narcissistically cathected archaic objects. In consequence of the attainment of these cohesive and stable psychic configurations these patients are able to establish specific, stable narcissistic transferences, which allow the therapeutic reactivation of the archaic structures without the danger of their fragmentation through further regression: they are thus analyzable. It may be added at this point that the spontaneous establishment of one of the stable narcissistic transferences is the best and most reliable diagnostic sign which differentiates these patients from psychotic or borderline cases, on the one hand, and from ordinary transference neuroses, on the other. The evaluation of a trial analysis is, in other words, of greater diagnostic and prognostic value than are conclusions derived from the scrutiny of behavioral manifestations and symptoms.

The following two typical dreams may provide us with an anticipatory understanding of the nature of the narcissistic transferences in the analysis of narcissistic personality disturbances, in particular of the fact that the specific psychopathology which is mobilized in the transference does not threaten the patient with psychotic disintegration.

Dream 1: The patient is in a rocket, circling the globe, faraway from the earth. He is, nevertheless, protected from an uncontrolled shooting off into space (psychosis) by the invisible, yet potently effective pull of the earth (the narcissistically cathected analyst, i.e., the narcissistic transference) in the center of his orbit.

Dream 2: The patient is on a swing, swinging forward and backward, higher and higher—yet there is never a serious danger of either the patient's flying off, or of the swing uncontrolledly entering a full circle.

The first dream was dreamed almost identically by two patients who are not otherwise mentioned in the present work. The second dream was dreamed by Miss F. at a point when she felt anxious because of the stimulation by her intense archaic exhibitionism, which had become mobilized through the analytic work. The narcissistic transference protected the first two patients against the danger of potential permanent loss of the self (i.e., against schizophrenia), a danger which had arisen in consequence of the mobilization of archaic grandiose fantasies during therapy. In the second case the narcissistic transference protected the patient against a potentially dangerous overstimulation of the ego (a [hypo] manic state)—an overstimulation that had become a threat as a result of the mobilization of archaic exhibitionistic libido during analysis. The transference relationship to the analyst which is portrayed in these dreams is in all three instances an impersonal one (the impersonal pull of gravity; the patient being connected to the center of the swing)—a telling rendition of the narcissistic nature of the relationship.

Although the essential psychopathology of the narcissistic personality disturbances differs substantially from that of the psychoses, the study of the former contributes nevertheless to our understanding of the latter. The scrutiny of the specific, therapeutically controlled, limited swings toward the fragmentation of the self and the self-objects and the correlated quasi-psychotic phenomena which occur not infrequently in the course of the analysis of narcissistic personality disturbances offers, in particular, a promising access to the understanding of the psychoses—just as it may be fruitful to examine, in depth and in detail, the reaction of a few malignant or near-malignant cells within the healthy tissue of the organism, rather than to approach the problem of carcinoma by concentrating exclusively on patients who are dying of widespread metastases. Thus, while this monograph is not concerned with the psychoses and borderline states, I shall now make a few statements about the perspective gained on these severe forms of psychopathology in the light of the analyzable disorders with which I am dealing.

As is the case with the narcissistic personality disturbances, the psychotic disorders should not only (and perhaps not even predominantly) be examined in the light of tracing their regression from (a) object love via (b) narcissism to (c) autoerotic fragmentation and (d) secondary (delusional) restitution of reality. Instead it is especially fruitful to examine the psychopathology of the psychoses—in harmony with the assumption that narcissism follows an independent line of development—in the light of tracing their regression along a partly different path which leads through the following way stations: (a) the disintegration of higher forms of narcissism; (b) the regression to archaic narcissistic positions; (c) the breakdown of the archaic narcissistic positions (including the loss of the *narcissistically cathected* archaic objects), thus the fragmentation of self and archaic self-objects; and (d) the secondary (restitutive) resurrection of the archaic self and of the archaic narcissistic objects in a manifestly psychotic form.[3]

The last-mentioned stage is only fleetingly encountered during the analysis of narcissistic personality disturbances;

[3] For a recent approach to the metapsychology of the psychoses see Arlow and Brenner (1964). In contrast to the thesis advanced here, these authors believe that the psychoses (and thus, by implication, also the narcissistic personality disturbances) can be adequately elucidated by explaining the symptoms and the behavioral disturbances of the psychotic patient as the outgrowth of his conflicts and defenses, i.e., in essence, within the frame of reference of the metapsychology of the transference neuroses.

but the relevant ephemeral phenomena permit the observation of details which are hidden in the rigidly established pathological positions in the psychoses. It is, for example, particularly instructive to compare the cohesive archaic narcissistic configurations (the grandiose self and the idealized parent imago) (a) with their regressively altered forms as they are moving toward fragmentation, and (b) with their restitutive counterparts when the rigid and chronic condition of a more or less overt psychosis has established itself.

Details of some of the patient's experience of hypercathected disconnected fragments of the body, of the mind, and of physical and mental functions can, for example, be observed during the temporary therapeutic regressions from the cohesively cathected grandiose self, and from the idealized parent imago, which may not be accessible in the corresponding regressions in the psychoses where the communicative capacity becomes severely disturbed and self-observation is either diminished or grossly distorted. Through the mild regressive oscillations, however, which occur during the analysis of narcissistic personality disturbances we gain access to many subtleties of these regressive transformations. We can see in detail, and study comparatively leisurely, the various disturbances in body sensation and self perception, the degeneration of language, the concretization of thought, and the splitting off of formerly synthetically cooperating thinking processes, as well as the observing ego's reaction to the temporary fragmentation of the narcissistic configurations (see Diagram 2 in Chapter 4 for a survey of some of the oscillations which occur during the analysis of these disorders). And it is especially fruitful to compare the relatively healthy archaic narcissistic configurations (the grandiose self; the idealized parent imago) with their psychotic counterparts (delusional grandiosity; the "influencing machine" [Tausk, 1919]).

The decisive differentiating features between the psychoses and borderline states, on the one hand, and analyzable cases of narcissistic personality disturbance, on the other, are the following: (1) the former tend toward the chronic abandonment of the cohesive narcissistic configurations and toward their replacement (in order to escape from the intolerable state of fragmentation and loss of archaic narcissistic objects) by delusions; (2) the latter show only minor and temporary oscillations, usually toward partial fragmentation, with at most a hint of a fleeting restitutive delusion. It is very valuable for our theoretical understanding of both the psychoses and the narcissistic personality disturbances to study the similarities and differences between the relatively healthy archaic grandiosity, which the psyche is able to maintain in the latter disorders, and the cold and haughty psychotic delusions of grandeur, which occur in the former; and to compare in the same way the relatively healthy elaboration of a narcissistically cathected omnipotent and omniscient, admired and idealized, emotionally sustaining parent imago in the transferences formed by patients with narcissistic personality disturbance with the all-powerful persecutor and manipulator of the self in the psychoses: the influencing machine whose omnipotence and omniscience have become cold, unempathic, and nonhumanly evil. Last but not least, the examination of the prepsychotic personality from the point of view of the vulnerability of its higher forms of narcissism (rather than only from the point of view of the fragility of its mature relationships to loved objects) can contribute greatly to the understanding of the psychoses and borderline states and will, for example, explain the following two typical features: (1) the precipitating events which usher in the decisive first steps of the regressive movements lie frequently in the area of narcissistic injury rather than in that of object love; and (2) even in some severe psychotic disorders, object love may remain relatively undisturbed while a profound disturbance in the realm of narcissism is never absent.

The following diagram is intended to provide a preliminary outline of the developmental steps of the two major narcissistic configurations and, simultaneously, of their counter-parts, i.e., the waystations of the regressive transformation of these configurations in (a) the narcissistic personality dis-orders and (b) the (schizophrenic-paranoid) psychoses and borderline states.

DIAGRAM 1

Development and regression in the realm of the grandiose self		*Development and regression in the realm of the omnipotent object*	
(1) Mature form of positive self-esteem; self-confidence.		(1) Mature form of admiration for others; ability for enthusiasm.	Normalcy
(2) Solipsistic claims for attention: stage of the grandiose self.		(2) Compelling need for merger with powerful object: stage of the idealized parent imago.	Narcissistic Personality Disorders
(3) Nuclei (fragments) of the grandiose self: hypochondria.		(3) Nuclei (fragments) of the idealized omnipotent object: disjointed mystical religious feelings; vague awe.	
(4) Delusional reconstitution of the grandiose self: cold paranoid grandiosity.		(4) Delusional reconstitution of the omnipotent object: the powerful persecutor, the influencing machine.	Psychosis

The solid arrow indicates the oscillations of the narcissistic configurations in the course of the psychoanalytic treatment of the narcissistic personality disorders (see Diagram 2 in Chapter 4); the dotted arrow indicates the direction of the process of cure in the analysis of these disorders. The alternatingly dotted and interrupted part of the long arrow indicates the still reversible depth of the regression toward psychosis; the interrupted part signifies that depth of the regression toward psychosis at which the psychotic regression has become irreversible.

The regressive psychic structures, the patient's perception of them, and his relationship to them, may become sexualized both in the psychoses and in the narcissistic personality disorders. In the psychoses the sexualization may involve not only the archaic grandiose self and the idealized parent imago, as these structures are fleetingly cathected before they are destroyed (autoerotic fragmentation), but also the restitutively built-up delusional replicas of these structures which form the content of the overt psychosis. It would be an intriguing task to compare the sexualizations in the psychoses, which were first described and metapsychologically elucidated by Freud (1911), with the sexualizations of the various forms of the narcissistic transferences which occur not infrequently in the analysis of narcissistic personality disturbance. The sexualized versions of the narcissistic transference are encountered either (a) early in the analysis, usually as a direct continuation of perverse trends which were already present before the treatment (see here especially the extensive discussion of the sexualization of the idealized parent imago and of the alter-ego or twinship variant of the grandiose self in the case of Mr. A. in Chapter 3); or (b) fleetingly during the exacerbations of the termination phase in the analysis of narcissistic personality disorders (see Chapter 7).

This is not the place for a comprehensive review of the psychoanalytic theory of the formation of hallucinations and delusions in the psychoses. Within the framework of the present considerations, however, it should be stressed that their establishment follows the disintegration of the grandiose self and of the idealized parent imago. In the psychoses these structures are destroyed, but their disconnected fragments are secondarily reorganized, rearranged into delusions (see Tausk, 1919; Ophuijsen, 1920), and then rationalized through the efforts of the remaining integrative functions of the psyche. As a result of the most severe regressive swings in the analysis of narcissistic personality disorders we occasionally encounter phenomena which resemble the delusions and hallucinations of the psychotic. Mr. E., for example, under the stress of an impending separation from the analyst early in treatment, felt temporarily that his face had become the face of his mother. In contrast to the psychoses, however, these hallucinations and delusions are not due to the elaboration of stable pathological structures which the patient erects in order to escape from the unbearable experience of the protracted fragmentation of his body-mind-self. They occur fleetingly at the moment of a beginning partial and temporary disintegration of the narcissistic structures, in response to specific disturbances of the specific narcissistic transference which has become established in therapy.

The evaluation of the role of specific environmental factors (the personality of the parents, for example; certain traumatic external events) in the genesis of the developmental arrest, or of the specific fixations and regression propensities which constitute the core of the narcissistic personality disturbance, will be undertaken later in this study. A brief, genetically oriented remark, however, may at this point help to solidify the conceptual basis of the differentiation between the psychoses and the borderline states, on the one hand, and the narcissistic personality disturbances, on the other. From the genetic point of view one is led to assume that in the psychoses the personality of the parents (and a number of other environmental circumstances) collaborated with inherited factors to prevent the formation of a nuclear cohesive self and of a nuclear idealized self-object at the appropriate age. The narcissistic structures which are built up at a later age must, therefore, be visualized as hollow and thus as brittle and fragile. Given these conditions (i.e., given a psychosis-prone personality), narcissistic injuries may usher in a regressive movement which tends to go beyond the stage of archaic narcissism (beyond the archaic forms of the cohesive grandiose self or of the cohesive idealized parent imago) and to lead to the stage of (autoerotic) fragmentation.

Two elaborations of the preceding statements regarding (a) the dynamic effect, and (b) the genetic background of the prepsychotic (or rather the psychosis-prone) personality will be inserted at this point. The first one is predominantly of clinical importance, the second one is of greater theoretical interest.

The first modification of the dynamic consequences of a specific weakness in the basic narcissistic configurations of the personality concerns a particular mode of defense against the dangerous regressive potential that is associated with the central defect, a defense which usually results in what is referred to as the *schizoid personality*. This defensive organization (which should be included among the borderline states) is characteristically encountered in personalities whose basic pathological propensity is toward the development of psychosis; it is, however, not encountered in patients with analyzable narcissistic personality disturbances. The schizoid defensive organization is the result of a person's (pre)conscious awareness not only of his narcissistic vulnerability, but also, and specifically, of the danger that a narcissistic injury could initiate an uncontrollable regression which would pull him irreversibly beyond the stage of the nuclear, cohesive, narcissistic configurations. Such persons have thus learned to distance themselves from others in order to avoid the specific danger of exposing themselves to a narcissistic injury.

In opposition to the preceding explanation it might be claimed that the retreat of these persons from human closeness is caused by their inability to love and is motivated by their conviction that they will be treated unempathically, coldly, or with hostility. This assumption is, however, not correct. Many schizoid patients who try to keep their involvement with others at a minimum are in fact capable of meaningful contact and do not as a rule suspect others of ill-will toward them. Their distancing is simply an outgrowth of the correct assessment of their narcissistic vulnerability and regression propensity. For this reason it is important for the psychotherapist to realize that the concentration of their often considerable libidinal resources on pursuits which minimize human contact (such as interest and work in the area of aesthetics; or the study of abstract, theoretical topics) rests on a correct evaluation of their assets and weaknesses. The therapist should thus not be a bull in the china shop of the delicate psychic balance of a valuable, and perhaps creative, individual, but should focus his attention on the imperfections in the defense structures; on the imperfections in the existing processes of libido deployment in work, interests, and interpersonal relations; and on the central psychopathology, i.e., the patient's regression propensity. With regard to the latter the focus of therapy should initially be the careful and unhurried investigation of the patient's minor emotional retreats which occur in consequence of minute narcissistic injuries. The subsequent reconstruction of the relevant genetic context, however, which should supplement the investigation of the patient's here-and-now vulnerability, will give further aid to his ego in its struggles for the achievement of greater mastery in this crucial sector of the personality.

In harmony, therefore, with the therapeutic strategy necessitated by the structure of the psychoses which will be discussed shortly, the appropriate therapy for schizoid patients is, in general, not psychoanalysis but a psychoanalytically informed mode of psychotherapy. Psychoanalysis as a form of psychotherapy should, in my opinion, be neither essentially defined by the therapist's application of its theory in the therapeutic situation nor by his providing of insights and explanations—even including genetic ones—which increase the patient's mastery over himself. While all of these features are part of therapeutic psychoanalysis, something else must be added which produces its essential quality: the pathogenic nucleus of the analysand's personality becomes activated in the treatment situation and itself enters a specific transference with the analyst before it is gradually dissolved in the working-through process which enables the patient's ego to obtain dominance in this specific area. Such a process must, however, not be set in motion if the transference regression would lead to a severe fragmentation of the self, i.e., to a chronic prenarcissistic stage in which even the narcissistic bonds with the therapist (which are characteristically established in the analysis of narcissistic personality disorders) are

destroyed. Since the danger of such an untoward development lies indeed at the motivational center of the schizoid
personality, the treatment which is here indicated is not
psychoanalysis per se but a psychoanalytically sophisticated
form of insight therapy which does not require the therapeutic mobilization of a self-fragmenting regression. (These
therapeutic problems are discussed once more, from a different viewpoint, at the end of this chapter.)

The second elaboration of the dynamic-genetic propositions which were given earlier is even more specifically relevant in the present context of comparing the psychoses with
the narcissistic personality disorders than the understanding
of the functions of the distancing attitudes of the schizoid; it
concerns the role of innate, inherited factors in producing
the propensity toward the fragmentation of the self encountered in the psychoses and in producing the propensity toward the maintenance of a cohesive self which exists in the
narcissistic personality disturbances. No definitive statement
concerning the relative importance of inherited factors can,
of course, be made on the basis of psychoanalytic experience.
Yet after one has reconstructed the early environment of a
patient, including especially the psychopathology of his parents, the conclusion seems at times inescapable that the
patient should be more severely disturbed than he, in fact, is.
In other words, one is led in such instances to the assumption
of the existence of innate factors which maintain the cohesiveness of the archaic grandiose self and of the idealized
parent imago despite catastrophic traumas to which the child
was exposed during crucial phases of early development. In
this context one is especially reminded of the well-known
report by Anna Freud and Sophie Dann (1951) which fur-
nishes an impressive example of the discrepancy between the
limited actual pathology of the children investigated and
the severe pathology that would have been expected on the
basis of an extremely traumatic early environment (concentration camp).

Among the patients referred to in the present work, Mr. E., judged on the basis of his traumatic early environment, would similarly seem to be a candidate for a more severe disturbance than the analyzable personality disorder from which he actually suffered.[4] He had been an "incubator baby," separated from his mother for several months. His mother, who had developed malignant hypertension, never felt any closeness to the child after he was brought home. He seemed hardly ever to have been picked up by anybody because he was supposed to be fragile. He was also rejected by his father and never became integrated into the family. Yet despite all these ominous circumstances this patient's psychic organization was not psychotic and the swings toward the disintegration of his cohesive self configuration which occurred during his analysis were temporary and manageable. He seemed, for example, to have been able early in his life to shift his need for tactile stimulation to the visual area. This shift, however, resulted later not only in perverse voyeuristic activities, but also in important sublimatory possibilities in the visual realm. At any rate the visual stimulation seems to have been sufficient to support the nucleus of a self which in general maintained its cohesiveness, or which, after a temporary fragmentation, could at least re-form itself speedily.

Now a few words about certain aspects of the symptomatology presented by the patients who suffer from personality disorders in the narcissistic realm, particularly with reference to the comparison between the (analyzable) narcissistic disturbances and the psychoses and borderline states. What are the manifestations of narcissistic personality disturbances that enable the analyst to differentiate these disorders from the psychoses and borderline states? I mentioned initially that my approach in this area does in general not conform with the traditional medical aim of achieving a clinical diag-

---

[4] See the Concordance of Cases which lists where in this monograph each patient is discussed.

nosis in which a disease entity is identified by clusters of recurring manifestations. But since I have in the foregoing given an outline of the essential psychopathology in metapsychological terms, the symptomatology of the disorders which will be discussed throughout this monograph can be examined not only in terms of its external appearance, but also with regard to its significance.

The symptomatology of patients with narcissistic personality disturbances (as may also be true during certain phases in the psychoses and for certain types of borderline states) tends to be ill defined, and the patient is in general not able to focus on its essential aspects, but he can recognize and describe the secondary complaints (such as work inhibitions or trends toward perverse sexual activities). The vagueness of the patient's initial complaint may be related to the nearness of the pathologically disturbed structures (the self) to the seat of the self-observing functions in the ego. (See in this context Freud's remarks to Binswanger in his letter of July 4, 1912 [Binswanger, 1956, p. 44f.].) The eye, as it were, cannot observe itself.

Despite the initial vagueness of the presenting symptomatology, however, the most significant symptomatic features can usually be discerned with increasing clarity as the analysis progresses, especially as the narcissistic transference in one of its forms comes into being. The patient will describe subtly experienced, yet pervasive feelings of emptiness and depression which, in contrast to the conditions in the psychoses and borderline states, are alleviated as soon as the narcissistic transference has become established—but which become intensified when the relationship to the analyst is disturbed. The patient will attempt to let the analyst know that, at times at least, especially when the narcissistic transference has become disrupted, he has the impression that he is not fully real, or at least that his emotions are dulled; and he may add that he is doing his work without zest, that he seeks routines to carry him along since he appears to be lacking in initiative. These and many other similar complaints are indicative of the ego's depletion because it has to wall itself off against the unrealistic claims of an archaic grandiose self, or against the intense hunger for a powerful external supplier of self-esteem and other forms of emotional sustenance in the narcissistic realm.

In contrast to the analogous phenomena encountered in the psychoses and borderline states, however, these symptoms are here not established rigidly. While unmistakable evidence for the transient character of the patient's symptoms is easily obtained within the framework of an ongoing analysis, it can also be gathered with regard to his reactions outside the analysis and before the analysis was begun, i.e., from a carefully focused scrutiny of the patient's past history. A pervasive hypochondriacal brooding, for example, may suddenly disappear and (usually in consequence of having received external praise or of having had the benefit of interest from the environment) the patient feels suddenly alive and happy and, for a while at least, shows initiative and has a sense of deep and lively participation in the world. These upward swings, however, are generally short-lived. They tend to become the cause of uncomfortable excitement; they arouse anxiety and are then soon again followed by a chronic sense of dullness and passivity, either experienced openly or disguised by long hours of mechanically performed activities. Furthermore, it usually should not be difficult—at least not for the analyst—to recognize the presence of great narcissistic vulnerability which, in addition to the discomfort caused by the aforementioned anxious excitement, is responsible for the fact that the patient's heightened pleasure in himself soon becomes submerged again and that the increased vitality of his actions cannot be maintained long. A rebuff, the absence of expected approval, the environment's lack of interest in the patient, and the like, will soon again bring about the former state of depletion.

The foregoing pages contain an outline of the psychopathology of the narcissistic personality disturbances and of certain clinical features of these disorders which are correlated with their basic psychopathology. The outline was drawn principally by comparing the narcissistic personality disturbances with the psychoses and borderline states, i.e., by contrasting the essential psychopathology of the two classes of psychic disorder and by comparing their clinical manifestations.[5]

The cases with which I shall be concerned, however, pose not only diagnostic difficulties vis-à-vis the psychoses, but also with regard to the other end of the spectrum of psychopathological states, the transference neuroses. And it must be admitted that, because of the complexity of clinical conditions, it is at first often not easy to come to a decision whether a specific case should be regarded as falling in the area of narcissistic disturbances. Narcissistic features are found in the classical transference neuroses; and, conversely, circumscribed mechanisms characteristic of the transference neu-

---

[5] The preceding discussion was focused predominantly on the differentiation of the analyzable narcissistic personality disturbances from (unanalyzable) schizophrenic psychoses, especially from the veiled or fended-off instances of the latter disorders which are often referred to as "borderline cases."

The detailed differentiating comparison of analyzable narcissistic personality disturbances with (unanalyzable) manic-depressive psychosis will not be undertaken at this time, even though certain oscillations during the analysis of narcissistic personality disturbances can indeed be looked upon and studied as minor and fleeting replicas of manic-depressive psychosis. But again, analogous to the conditions that prevail with regard to the comparison with schizophrenic and borderline cases, the patient's ability to maintain a narcissistic transference is correlated to the fact that his archaic exhibitionism and grandiosity remain largely integrated within the total structure of his cohesive grandiose self, and that, similarly, the archaic omnipotence of the aggrandized, transitional self-object remains largely integrated within the total structure of the cohesive idealized parent imago. The swings of hypomanic excitement and of depressive mood which occur in response to the vicissitudes of the therapeutic transference are, therefore, only temporary, and the previous narcissistic balance is speedily re-established. In manic-depressive psychosis, however, the two basic narcissistic structures are only precariously established and tend to crumble under the impact of a variety of traumas. They then become unable to contain the archaic cathexes: the exhibitionism and grandiosity of the grandiose self thus begin to flood the ego (mania) and the omnipotent aggressivity of the idealized parent imago destroys the patient's realistic self-esteem (depression).

roses occur in the narcissistic disorders—be they severe psychoses or mild narcissistic personality disturbances.

The intricacies of mixed forms of psychopathology and the resulting questions of diagnostic classification will be discussed later (e.g., Chapter 7). At this point, however, it must be stressed that although clinically the transference neuroses and the narcissistic disturbances have a number of features in common, the essential pathogenic structures of these two classes of psychic disorders, and thus some of the important presenting manifestations, are not identical. The differences can be stated by referring to the following facts.

In uncomplicated cases of transference neurosis the psychopathology does not primarily reside either in the self or in the archaic narcissistic self-objects. The central psychopathology concerns structural conflicts over (incestuous) libidinal and aggressive strivings which emanate from a well-delimited, cohesive self and are directed toward childhood objects which have in essence become fully differentiated from the self.[6] The central psychopathology of the narcissistic personality disturbances, on the other hand, concerns primarily the self and the archaic narcissistic objects. These narcissistic configurations are related to the causative nexus of psychopathology in the narcissistic realm in the following two ways: (1) they may be insufficiently cathected and are thus liable to temporary fragmentation; and (2) even if they are sufficiently cathected or hypercathected and thus retain their cohesiveness, they are not integrated with the rest of the personality, and the mature self and other aspects of the mature personality are deprived of a sufficient or reliable supply of narcissistic investments.

In uncomplicated cases of transference neurosis the ego reacts with anxiety to the dangers to which it feels exposed when it is threatened by the breakthrough of forbidden (incestuous-oedipal or preoedipal) object-instinctual strivings.

─────────

[6] See Chapter 2 for the differentiation between archaic self-object (a precursor of psychic structure), psychic structure, and true object.

The danger may be experienced either as a threat of physical punishment, or as a threat of emotional or physical abandonment (i.e., as castration anxiety, or as fear of the loss of the love of the object, or as fear of the loss of the object [Freud, 1926]). In the narcissistic personality disturbances, on the other hand, the ego's anxiety relates primarily to its awareness of the vulnerability of the mature self; the dangers which it faces concern either the temporary fragmentation of the self or the intrusions of either archaic forms of subject-bound grandiosity or of archaic narcissistically aggrandized self-objects into its realm. The principal source of discomfort is thus the result of the psyche's inability to regulate self-esteem and to maintain it at normal levels; and the specific (pathogenic) experiences of the personality which are correlated to this central psychological defect lie within the narcissistic realm and fall into a spectrum which extends from anxious grandiosity and excitement, on the one hand, to mild embarrassment and self-consciousness, or severe shame, hypochondria, and depression, on the other.

The patients whose dominant psychopathology lies in the area of the narcissistic personality disturbances may, in addition to the just-mentioned specific psychic discomforts, also appear to be exposed to the fear of the loss of the object, of the loss of the object's love, and to castration anxiety. It may be stated, furthermore—and with a certain degree of justification—that, while castration anxiety is the leading source of discomfort in the transference neuroses, with fear of the loss of the love of the object coming next, and fear of the loss of the object being last (in frequency of occurrence and in importance), in the narcissistic personality disturbances the order is reversed; i.e., the fear of the loss of the object is first in frequency and importance, and castration anxiety is last.

While such a comparative statement is true, it is incomplete and superficial. The preponderance of (1) the shame,

(2) loss-of-the-love-of-the-object, (3) loss-of-the-object experiences in the narcissistic disorders over (a) the guilt, (b) castration-anxiety experiences in the transference neuroses is not just a diagnostic psychological given that cannot be further explained but is a direct consequence of the essential fact that the self-objects which play the central role in the psychopathology of the narcissistic disorders are not equivalent to the objects in the transference neuroses. The objects in the narcissistic personality disturbances are archaic, narcissistically cathected, and prestructural (see Chapter 2). Whether they threaten punishment, therefore, or withdrawal of love, or confront the patient with their temporary absence or permanent disappearance—the result is always a *narcissistic* imbalance or defect in the patient who had been interwoven with them in a variety of ways and whose maintenance of self cohesiveness and self-esteem, and of a reward-providing relationship to aim-channeling ideals, depended on their presence, their confirming approval,[7] or other modes of narcissistic sustenance. In the transference neuroses, however, the analogous psychological events lead to fear of punishment by an object which is cathected with object-instinctual energies (i.e., an object which is experienced as separate and independent), to tensions concerning the fact that one's love is not being responded to, to the possibility of a lonely longing for an absent object, and the like—with only a secondary drop in self-esteem.

How do the foregoing considerations assist us in evaluating the patient's presenting complaints? How, in other words, can we initially establish a psychoanalytic diagnosis in order to adjust our psychoanalytic strategy (the direction of our interpretations) to the particular requirements of the psychological disturbance? How do we recognize that a patient's

---

[7] One might say that in some instances it is not the loss of the love of the object which is responsible for the patient's lowered self-esteem but the loss of the object's admiration.

disturbance lies in the realm of the narcissistic personality disorders and not in the realm of the ordinary transference
neuroses?

The approach suggested earlier with regard to the differentiation between the narcissistic personality disorders, on the
one hand, and the psychoses and borderline states, on the
other, is the appropriate one here too: the differentiation
should primarily be based on the analyst's metapsychological
understanding of the central psychopathology and not on his
scrutiny of surface manifestations.

It is true, of course, that the presence of circumscribed psychoneurotic inhibitions and symptoms (phobias, obsessions,
compulsions, hysterical manifestations) may point in the
direction of transference neurosis, while vague complaints
about depressed mood, lack of zest and initiative in the area
of work, dullness of interpersonal experience, the patient's
uneasiness about his physical or mental state, multiple perverse trends, and the like, will point toward the area of narcissistic disturbance. These overt complaints are, however, not
a reliable guide. Behind a vague complaint about lack of
initiative or zest the analyst may, after a while, at times detect
a well-circumscribed inhibition or phobia; and, even more
frequently, he will discover the presence of diffuse narcissistic
vulnerability, of circumscribed defects in self-esteem or
self-esteem regulation, or of broad disturbances in the patient's system of ideals, despite the fact that he originally
complained of specific inhibitions, of seemingly well-delimited anxieties, and of other disturbances which appeared to
place the disorder into the realm of the transference neuroses.

It must be stressed again that the overt manifestations
presented by the narcissistic personality disorders are not a
reliable guide toward the answer to the crucial diagnostic
question: whether or not to treat the patient psychoanalytically. Yet, having expressed the warning, I shall—before em-
phasizing once more the only reliable solution to the diagnostic
problem—enumerate some of the syndromes encountered in

those cases where the psychopathology of the narcissistic personality is expressed in more circumscribed and colorful syndromes. In such instances the patient may voice the following complaints and present the following pathological features: (1) in the sexual sphere: perverse fantasies, lack of interest in sex; (2) in the social sphere: work inhibitions, inability to form and maintain significant relationships, delinquent activities; (3) in his manifest personality features: lack of humor, lack of empathy for other people's needs and feelings, lack of a sense of proportion, tendency toward attacks of uncontrolled rage, pathological lying; and (4) in the psychosomatic sphere: hypochondriacal preoccupations with physical and mental health, vegetative disturbances in various organ systems.

Although these complaints and syndromes do indeed occur frequently in cases of narcissistic personality disturbance, and although the experienced psychoanalyst may strongly suspect the presence of an underlying narcissistic personality disorder on the basis of the scrutiny of the patient's complaints, the crucial diagnostic criterion is to be based not on the evaluation of the presenting symptomatology or even of the life history, but on the nature of the spontaneously developing transference. Since this monograph in its entirety deals with the specific transferences (or transferencelike structures) which are mobilized during the analysis of narcissistic personality disturbances, the foregoing statement leads us directly into the center of the present examination.

Two correlated questions, however, must now be raised. Do transferences indeed develop in the psychoanalytic treatment of narcissistic personalities? And, if so, what is the nature of the transferences which do occur?

The delimitation and examination of transferences in the narcissistic disorders confront us with a number of basic theoretical issues which go beyond the uncertainties that are due to the complexities of the clinical conditions. If we postulate the existence of transferences in the narcissistic disorders, we can epitomize the relevant problem in the form of the following questions: What is the concept of transference? And is it as suitably employed in theoretical formulations regarding narcissistic structures and their mobilization during psychoanalytic therapy as it is in the analogous formulations regarding transference neuroses?

According to Freud's early, metapsychologically precise definition (1900), the term transference connotes the amalgamation of repressed, infantile, object-libidinal[8] urges with (pre)conscious strivings that are related to objects in the present. The clinical transference can, in this theoretical context, be understood as a specific example of the general mechanism: the analysand's preconscious attitudes toward the analyst become the carriers of repressed, infantile, object-directed wishes. Such transferences (defined as the amalgamation of object-directed repressed strivings with preconscious wishes and attitudes) are present in the narcissistic disorders (and become mobilized during therapy) in those sectors of the personality which have not participated in the specific narcissistic regression. In the present context, however, we are concerned not with the scrutiny of that part of the personality of narcissistically regressed or fixated analysands which exhibits psychoneurotic features but with the questions (1) whether the narcissistic structures themselves (archaic imagery about the self, for example) occur in a state that corresponds, at least to a certain extent, to the state of repression in the transference neuroses; and (2) whether they become amalgamated with preconscious attitudes of the personality, analogous to the dynamic and structural conditions which exist in the transference neuroses.

Having thus indicated the theoretical framework of the problems which we are confronting, I shall at this point put aside the various intricacies of formulating the concept of

8 The concept of narcissism, and thus of narcissistic instinctual investments, had, of course, not yet been formulated by Freud when he defined transference metapsychologically in Chapter VII of *The Interpretation of Dreams*.

transference in its clinical and theoretical sense,[9] and turn to a more clinically and empirically oriented classification of the transferences (or, if it is preferred, transferencelike structures) which occur in the narcissistic disorders and are mobilized during their analysis. I shall briefly outline this classification which I first proposed in an earlier paper (1966a).

The equilibrium of primary narcissism is disturbed by the unavoidable shortcomings of maternal care, but the child replaces the previous perfection (a) by establishing a grandiose and exhibitionistic image of the self: *the grandiose self;* and (b) by giving over the previous perfection to an admired, omnipotent (transitional) self-object: *the idealized parent imago.*

The terms "grandiose" and "exhibitionistic" refer to a broad spectrum of phenomena, ranging from the child's solipsistic world view and his undisguised pleasure in being admired, and from the gross delusions of the paranoiac and the crudely sexual acts of the adult pervert, to aspects of the mildest, most aim-inhibited, and nonerotic satisfaction of adults with themselves, their functioning, and their achievements. To use the name of the most conspicuous or most clearly delimited manifestation of a group or series of developmentally, genetically, and dynamically related phenomena as a term for the whole group or series has become a well-established practice in psychoanalysis since Freud (1921) referred to all libidinal drive elements as sexual ones "*a potiori* and by reason of their origin" (p. 91).[10] It is to be granted

---

[9] For a discussion of the theoretical aspects of these questions see Kohut (1959), Kohut and Seitz (1963). For a discussion of the clinical applicability of these theoretical considerations see Chapter 9, in particular the case of Mr. K.

[10] It is not easy to define the connotation which the term *a potiori* had for Freud when he explained why he had referred to all libidinal forces as sexual ones. Among the many meanings of the term *potior*, "more important" is probably the one which is most relevant in this context. In other words, Freud used the term "sexual" not only for genital sexuality but also for the pregenital drive elements (the precursors of genital sexuality) because genital sexuality was the more important (and thus the better known) of these two related groups of phenomena.

that the practice of using the fact of the genetic and dynamic unity of a variety of phenomena as a basis for unitary nomenclature and concept formation is not without danger. Hartmann (1960), for example, warns against abuses in this area and refers to the logical errors which are responsible for them as "genetic mistake" (p. 93).[11] On the other hand, it is at times of crucial importance to affirm the deep genetic and dynamic unity of a group of seemingly diverse phenomena by subsuming them under the same term, e.g., through naming them *a potiori*. Such a "genetic" term will evoke most compellingly the right kind of meaning in us. In addition, it will mobilize the internal and social resistances which, paradoxically, must become (optimally) engaged in the conceptual field—especially in a science that deals with complex psychological states. It is only through the gradual overcoming of optimally mobilized emotional resistances, however, that in the long run the acceptance of new ideas can be achieved.

The term *grandiose self* will be used henceforth in the present work (instead of the previously employed "narcissistic self") to designate the grandiose and exhibitionistic structure which is the counterpart of the *idealized parent imago*. Since the self is, in general, cathected with narcissistic libido, the term "narcissistic self" may with some justification be looked upon as a tautology. My preference for the term *grandiose self* is, however, based on the fact that it has greater evocative power than the term "narcissistic self," and I am not discarding the latter term primarily on theoretical grounds. *Narcissism, within my general outlook, is defined not by the target of the instinctual investment (i.e., whether it is the subject himself or other people) but by the nature or quality of the instinctual charge.* The small child, for example, invests other people with narcissistic cathexes and thus experiences them narcissistically, i.e., as self-objects. The expected control over

11 For an excellent definition of the term and the concept "genetic fallacy" see Langer (1957, p. 248).

such (self-object) others is then closer to the concept of the control which a grownup expects to have over his own body and mind than to the concept of the control which he expects to have over others. The question whether the subject may at times invest himself with object-instinctual cathexes—such as with unneutralized aggression in the self-mutilations, or with object-libidinal cathexes in the self-estrangement experiences of schizophrenics—will not be discussed in the present study. A degree of investment *of* the subject *by* the subject with neutralized *object*-libidinal attention cathexes is, however, surely achieved in a number of self-observational activities.

More substantial than the terminological questions are those concerned with the developmental and dynamic position of the principal narcissistic configurations. The central mechanisms ("I am perfect." "You are perfect, but I am part of you.") which the two basic narcissistic configurations employ in order to preserve a part of the original experience of narcissistic perfection are, of course, antithetical.[12] Yet they coexist from the beginning and their individual and largely independent lines of development are open to separate scrutiny. Under optimal developmental conditions, the exhibitionism and grandiosity of the archaic grandiose self are gradually tamed, and the whole structure ultimately becomes integrated into the adult personality and supplies the instinctual fuel for our ego-syntonic ambitions and purposes, for the

---

[12] It hardly needs to be emphasized that in the beginning these processes are preverbal and preconceptual and that such paradigmatic sentences as those given above are to be understood in an evocative sense only, like Freud's famous statements concerning the mechanisms active in paranoia (1911, pp. 63ff.). The appropriate description of the central mechanisms which determine the two main streams of the development of narcissism can only be a metapsychological one. It may, nevertheless, be helpful to say that the grandiose self (which corresponds to some extent to Freud's purified pleasure ego [1915a]) has such analogues in adult experience as, e.g., national and racial pride and prejudice (everything good is "inside," everything bad and evil is assigned to the "outsider"), while the relationship to the idealized parent imago may have its parallel in the relationship (including mystical mergers) of the true believer to his God.

enjoyment of our activities, and for important aspects of our self-esteem. And, under similarly favorable circumstances, the idealized parent imago, too, becomes integrated into the adult personality. Introjected as our idealized superego, it becomes an important component of our psychic organization by holding up to us the guiding leadership of its ideals. (For a more exact discussion of this process, see Chapter 2.) If the child, however, suffers severe narcissistic traumas, then the grandiose self does not merge into the relevant ego content but is retained in its unaltered form and strives for the fulfillment of its archaic aims. And if the child experiences traumatic disappointments in the admired adult, then the idealized parent imago, too, is retained in its unaltered form, is not transformed into tension-regulating psychic structure, does not attain the status of an accessible introject,[13] but remains an archaic, transitional self-object that is required for the maintenance of narcissistic homeostasis.

The main lines of thought pursued in this monograph are organized in accordance with the conceptualizations concerning the two basic narcissistic configurations outlined in the preceding summary. The following four topics thus constitute the substance of this investigation: (1) the transferences which arise from the therapeutic mobilization of the idealized parent imago (to be called *idealizing transference*); (2) those which arise from the mobilization of the grandiose self (comprehensively referred to as *mirror transference*); (3) the analyst's reactions (including his countertransferences) which are encountered during the patient's transference mobilization of the idealized parent imago; and (4) those which are encountered during the mobilization of the patient's grandiose self.

A few additional introductory remarks of a more general nature must, however, still be made, and a number of clinical and theoretical topics briefly introduced at this point, before

[13] In this context see the discussion of *transmuting internalization* in Chapter 2.

the detailed and systematic discussion of the specific narcissistic transferences is undertaken.

Let me begin by affirming my conviction, obtained on the basis of clinical observation, that, given the appropriately attentive, but unobtrusive and noninterfering behavior of the analyst (i.e., the analyst's analytic attitude), (1) a movement toward a specific therapeutic regression is initiated in narcissistic personality disorders; and that (2) a corresponding specific transferencelike condition establishes itself[14] which consists of the amalgamation of unconscious narcissistic structures (the idealized parent imago and the grandiose self) with the psychic representation of the analyst which becomes drawn into these therapeutically activated, narcissistically cathected structures.

The most far-reaching regressions, as was pointed out earlier, lead to the activation of experiences of isolated fragments of the body-mind-self and its functions and to the breakup and loss of the archaic narcissistically cathected objects. This *stage of the fragmented self*[15] corresponds to the developmental phase to which Freud (1914) referred as the *stage of autoerotism* (see also Nagera, 1964). That part of the personality which has not participated in the regression will attempt to deal with the central fragmentation. The patient may, for example, try to explain the experience of fragmentation to himself (hypochondriacal brooding) and may attempt to find words to describe it (hypochondriacal complaints [Glover, 1939]). The healthy part of the psyche will also be able to establish a therapeutic bond with the therapist, and it may thus be possible to create a workable therapeutic relationship. The central area of regression, however, i.e., the fragments of the archaic grandiose self as well as the frag-

14 I am here disregarding the resistances which oppose the establishment of the narcissistic transferences; they will be discussed later.

15 If one wishes to stress the inherent progressive developmental potential toward unification and cohesion, one might here also speak, in a variation of Glover's terminology (1943), of a *stage of self nuclei* (Gedo and Goldberg, 1969).

ments of the archaic idealized object, is in essence beyond the reach of the healthy part of the patient's psyche. In other words, while the patient experiences the effects of the regression on the surrounding psyche, the experience of the fragmented body-mind-self and self-object cannot be psychologically elaborated.[16]

What is of crucial importance here is the fact that the central area of pathology cannot enter into stable amalgamations with preconscious thought contents, including the perceptions of the therapist: the central area of the pathology does not become available to the formation of transferences. Although it is thus possible to assist such patients through psychotherapeutic support (including the giving of insight), an analytic situation cannot be established, i.e., the central area of pathology itself cannot enter into a workable transference amalgamation with the (pre)conscious representation of the therapist. As a matter of fact in these cases it is of decisive importance for the psychotherapist to remain clearly differentiated from the core of psychopathology—if he cannot achieve this separation and becomes drawn into the patient's delusions, he loses his tie to the healthy remainder of the patient's psyche and thus his therapeutic leverage. The maintenance of a realistic, friendly relationship with the psychotherapist is thus of crucial importance in the treatment of the psychoses and borderline states, and the current emphasis on the significance of the so-called *therapeutic alliance* or *working alliance* (Zetzel, 1956; Greenson, 1965, 1967) is fully justified with regard to these cases.

In contrast to the situation which prevails in the psychoses and borderline states, however, the disturbances of the thera-

---

16 It is significant that the patient uses negative terms when he tries to describe the experience of the fragments of the body-mind-self or of the self-object. His lips feel "strange," for example; his body has become "foreign" to him; his thinking is now "odd," etc.—all terms which are expressive of the fact that the regressive changes are, in essence, outside the patient's psychological organization. From a developmental point of view one might, therefore, say that these fragments are prepsychological.

peutic motivation which occur in the analysis of the transference neuroses and of the narcissistic personality disorders are, in general, not due to the kind of rupture of the realistic bond between analyst and analysand that would need to be mended actively, e.g., through unusual warmth in the analyst's behavior (see Jacobson, 1967). In most instances the difficulty is a manifestation of an object-instinctual or of a narcissistic transference which, having become a resistance, needs to be brought under the increased control of the patient's ego through insight-providing interpretations. To assign to the patient's nonspecific, nontransference rapport with the analyst a position of primary significance in the analysis of these forms of psychopathology would, thus, in my opinion, be erroneous. Such an error would rest on an insufficient appreciation of the metapsychologically definable difference between unanalyzable disorders (psychoses and borderline states) and analyzable forms of psychopathology (transference neuroses and narcissistic personality disorders).

The transference intrusion of archaic narcissistic investments, with their characteristic demands on and expectations from the analyst, may be erroneously regarded as a component of the current, realistic relationship to the analyst. This outlook would lead logically to such therapeutic activities as wish gratification in the service of a corrective emotional experience, and to persuasion, exhortation, and education. The therapeutic changes in ego functions thus secondarily brought about would rest on the establishment of a transference bondage or on massive identifications with the therapist. These changes, however, forestall the possibility of the full transference reactivation of the archaic narcissistic structures and thus of the attainment of psychological transformations in which the energies that were formerly bound to archaic goals are freed and become available to the mature personality.

In contrast to the psychoses and borderline states, the central psychopathology of the narcissistic personality disorders concerns psychologically elaborated, cohesive, and more or less stable narcissistic configurations which belong to the *stage of narcissism* (i.e., to that step in psychological development which, according to Freud's formulation [1914], follows the stage of autoerotism). I shall in general refer to this phase as the *stage of the cohesive self*. The fragmentation of the body-mind-self and of the self-object precludes the development of transferences concerning the central area of the pathology in the psychoses and borderline states. In the narcissistic personality disorders, however, the therapeutic activation of the specific, psychologically elaborated, cohesive narcissistic configurations becomes the very center of the analytic process. The narcissistic "object" (the idealized parent imago) and the narcissistic "subject" (the grandiose self) are comparatively stable configurations, cathected with narcissistic libido (idealizing libido; grandiose-exhibitionistic libido), which enter into comparatively stable amalgamations with the (narcissistically perceived) psychic representation of the analyst. A degree of cathectic constancy toward an object is thus attained (see Hartmann, 1952)—albeit that of a narcissistically cathected one. The relative stability of this narcissistic transference amalgamation, however, is the prerequisite for the performance of the analytic task (the systematic process of working through) in the pathogenic narcissistic areas of the personality.

Throughout the ensuing discussion it must be kept in mind that neither the grandiose self (and its transference activation) nor even the idealized parent imago (and its therapeutic amalgamation with the psychic representation of the analyst) has the status of objects in the full psychoanalytic meaning of the term since both structures are cathected with narcissistic libido. Within the conceptual framework of social psychology, and to a more limited extent, within a framework of pure perception and cognition, these narcissistic transferences must be considered as object relations; from the depth-psychological point of view, however, which takes into account the nature of the libidinal cathexes (which in turn influences strongly the mode of perception of the narcissistic

object as well as its cognitive elaboration, e.g., what the analysand expects of it), the object is experienced narcissistically. As previously stated, the expected control over the narcissistically cathected subject and its function, for example,
is closer to the concept which a grownup has of himself and
of the control which he expects over his own body and mind
than to the grownup's experience of others and of his control
over them (which generally leads to the result that the object
of such narcissistic "love" feels oppressed and enslaved by the
subject's expectations and demands). A careful scrutiny of
inner experience thus permits the differentiation between
the comparative self and object status of the grandiose self and
the idealized parent imago: the former has subject quality,
the latter is an archaic (transitional[17]) self-object, cathected

---

[17] The characterization of the idealized parent imago as a transitional object is to be understood in a relative sense only, i.e., it is "transitional" by
comparison with the grandiose self and its libidinal cathexis. To be more
exact: within the sequence of the development from (1) the archaic self-object,
via (2) psychic structure, to (3) the true object (see Chapter 2) the idealized
parent imago falls clearly within the category of the archaic self-object (a
precursor of psychic structure) since it performs functions which the child's
psyche will later perform. In other words, the idealized parent imago is still
far from being experienced as an independent object. By comparison with
the grandiose self, however, it may be considered as showing traces of object
features since it is invested with idealizing libido. Idealizing libido, however,
as will be discussed in Chapters 4 and 12, is also employed (albeit in a sub-
ordinate role) by the mature psyche in the libidinal cathexis of true objects
by becoming amalgamated to the fully developed object-libidinal strivings.

Winnicott's well-known description (1953) of the child's inner attitudes toward such "transitional objects" as blankets, etc., approaches the problem of
the archaic object from a viewpoint that differs from mine (see the analogous
discussion of Mahler's formulations in Chapter 8). My metapsychological conceptualizations are in essence based on reconstructions and extrapolations from
the analysis of adults with narcissistic personality disorders. This procedure
appears here to permit a more differentiating grasp of the meaning of the
psychological experience than is offered by the direct approach to the child
since (a) the original experience emerges with undiminished vigor, and (b)
verbal communication concerning it is vastly facilitated. These formulations
thus cover the phenomena which were described by Winnicott and others
(see, for example, Wulff, 1946). The present formulations, however—specifically those concerning the important distinction between (a) the relationship
of the grandiose self with the environment and (b) the relationship of the
idealized parent imago with the environment—go beyond the descriptive empathic level; they supply an explanation of these phenomena in metapsychological terms.

with a transitional form of narcissistic (i.e., idealizing) libido. The analysand's basic psychological attitude, however, is in both transferences an outgrowth of the fact that the position that has been activated is in essence a narcissistic one.

The structure mobilized in the idealizing transference (the idealized parent imago) is quite dissimilar from that mobilized in the mirror transference (the grandiose self). Still, in view of the fact that they are both cathected with narcissistic instinctual energies, it will not be surprising to learn that there are indeed many instances when the differentiation between them becomes difficult. The following sharp differentiation, however, is motivated not only by expository purposes, but it is, indeed, in many instances empirically demonstrable and justified.

PART I

THE THERAPEUTIC ACTIVATION
OF THE OMNIPOTENT OBJECT

CHAPTER 2

THE IDEALIZING TRANSFERENCE

The therapeutic activation of the omnipotent object (the idealized parent imago), which will be referred to as the *idealizing transference,* is the revival during psychoanalysis of one of the two aspects of an early phase of psychic development. It is the state in which, after being exposed to the disturbance of the psychological equilibrium of primary narcissism, the psyche saves a part of the lost experience of global narcissistic perfection by assigning it to an archaic, rudimentary (transitional) self-object, the idealized parent imago. Since all bliss and power now reside in the idealized object, the child feels empty and powerless when he is separated from it and he attempts, therefore, to maintain a continuous union with it.

The psychoanalytic formulation of early experience is difficult and fraught with danger. The reliability of our empathy, a major instrument of psychoanalytic observation, declines the more dissimilar the observed is to the observer, and the early stages of mental development are thus, in particular, a challenge to our ability to empathize with ourselves, i.e., with our own past mental organizations. Under certain circumstances we are, therefore, forced to content ourselves with loose empathic approximations, must avoid the misleading introduction of the description of later psychological states

37

for earlier ones (adultomorphism), and will often have to be satisfied with expressing our understanding in terms that are derived from mechanical and physical analogies which are at a greater distance from the (empathically) observed psychological field than would seem to be desirable. We are thus inclined to say very little about the psychological content of early phases of mental development but instead to focus our attention on the general conditions which prevail in the mental apparatus at that period. In other words, we are describing psychological states with their tension and relief from tension (and the circumstances which give rise to these changes), but in general we do not attempt to identify an (ideational) content of the archaic experience.

On first sight one would feel compelled to apply *in toto* the preceding considerations to the psychological constellations revived in the idealizing transference (and also to the therapeutic reactivation of the grandiose self which will be discussed later); and, insofar as this transference is the reactivation of the rudimentary beginnings of the idealized object, our formulations must undoubtedly concern the psychological state or condition of the child's mental apparatus and not an ideational content which at that early stage is beyond our grasp.

Two interrelated circumstances, however, allow us to comprehend more about the psychological contents of the idealizing transference, and to describe them in greater detail, than would be expectable on the basis of the preceding reflections: (a) the fact that the stream of development which begins with the archaic (transitional) idealized self-object does not vanish when the maturation of the child's cognitive equipment permits him to recognize more and more details of his environment, and when the correspondingly increasing specificity of his emotional responses and the maturation of his drive equipment enable him to love (and to hate) the important figures who surround him, i.e., to invest the childhood images with object-instinctual cathexes;[1] and (b) the tendency of the psychic apparatus to telescope analogous psychological experiences, with the result that the analysand may express the influence of archaic (transitional) self-objects, which have been reactivated in the narcissistic transference, through the recall of memories of analogous later experiences which correspond to the archaic ones.

The small child's idealizations, whether they are directed at a dimly perceived archaic mother-breast or at a clearly recognized oedipal parent, belong genetically and dynamically in a narcissistic context. Although the idealizing cathexes become increasingly neutralized and aim-inhibited (as the child moves toward the beginning of the latency period), they continue to retain their narcissistic character. Since it is especially in the most advanced stages of their early development that the idealizations (which now coexist with powerful object-instinctual cathexes) leave their strongest and most durable imprint on the permanent structure of the personality by participating in the phase-appropriate internalization processes which establish the superego, it is important to keep in mind that their essentially narcissistic qualities have remained unchanged, even at this relatively late stage of their development.

There is no need to emphasize the paramount importance of the early object cathexes (both libidinal and aggressive) for psychological development or to underline the value of studying their vicissitudes, as first undertaken systematically by Freud in his *Three Essays on the Theory of Sexuality*

---

1 My use of the terms object-instinctual and narcissistic libido does not refer to the target of the instinctual investment; they are abstractions referring to the psychological meaning of the essential experience. Thus, the objects which form the basis for the transference relationships discussed here are invested with narcissistic libido. On the other hand (see Chapter 1), the self may occasionally be invested with object-instinctual cathexis; e.g. (a) during objective self-assessment, (b) in incipient schizophrenia when the patient looks at himself in the mirror as if at a stranger.

(1905). The recognition of the fact, however, that the (normal) child responds increasingly to objects which he experiences as separate and independent from himself should not prevent us from acknowledging the persistent presence of narcissistic components in the total fabric of the psyche and from examining the vicissitudes of their development. The idealization of the parental objects of the late preoedipal and of the oedipal periods can thus be fruitfully understood as the continuation of the archaic idealization—and the later idealized object in its various developmental stages as the heir of the archaic one—despite the simultaneous presence of firm object cathexes in the child's relationship to his parents.

Idealization is one of the two main roads of the development of narcissism. Idealizing narcissistic libido not only plays a significant role in mature object relationships, where it is amalgamated with true object libido, but it is also the main source of libidinal fuel for some of the socioculturally important activities which are subsumed under the term creativity, and it forms a component of that highly esteemed human attitude to which we refer as wisdom (Kohut, 1966a). In the present context, however, it must again be stressed that the amalgamation of the idealized aspects of the parent imago with those broad sectors of the parental imagoes which are cathected with object libido exerts a strong and important influence on the phase-appropriate (re)internalization processes and thus on the building up of two permanent core structures of the personality—(a) the neutralizing basic fabric of the psyche, (b) the idealized superego—which are invested with narcissistic instinctual cathexes.

Certain details of these basic internalization processes in the narcissistic realm are important enough to warrant elaboration. While the child idealizes the parent, the idealized constellation is open to correction and modification through actual experience (the child's recognition of the actual qualities of the parents), and the empathic parents' gradual revelation of their shortcomings enables the child during the preoedipal phases to withdraw a part of the idealizing libido from the parental imagoes and to employ them in the building up of drive-controlling structures. The massive (but phase-appropriate) oedipal disappointment in the parent (normally it is, of course, the parent of the same sex as the child who plays the most important role in this context) leads ultimately to the idealization of the superego, a developmental and maturational step which is of great importance in protecting the personality against the danger of narcissistic regression.

Expressed differently, we can say that the phase-appropriate internalization of those aspects of the oedipal objects that were cathected with object libido (and aggression) leads to the building up of those aspects of the superego which direct toward the ego the commands and prohibitions, the praise, scolding, and punishment that the parents had formerly directed toward the child.[2] The internalization of the narcissistic aspects of the child's relationship to the oedipal parents, however, leads to the narcissistic dimension of the superego, i.e., to its idealization. The internalization of the object-cathected aspects of the parental imago transmutes the latter into the contents and functions of the superego; the internalization of the narcissistic aspects accounts for the exalted position which these contents and functions have vis-à-vis the ego. It is from their idealization, however (the narcissistic instinctual component of their cathexes), that the specific and characteristic aura of absolute perfection of the values and standards of the superego are derived; and the omniscience

2 The "ideal self" as formulated by Sandler et al. (1963) also belongs, I believe, in this context; i.e., it is the ideal of what the child should be, as held up to the child by the parents and accepted by the child. See also Lagache (1961), who distinguishes between *l'idéal de moi, le moi idéal,* and *le surmois;* and Nunberg (1932), who distinguishes between an *Idealich* and the *Ichideal.*

and might of the whole structure are also due to the fact that it is partly invested with narcissistic, idealizing libido.[3]

If, in harmony with the preceding considerations, we survey the development of the child's psyche not only with regard to its object cathexes but also with regard to the vicissitudes of its narcissistic sector, we can further recognize that the latter remains vulnerable, and that its development can be disturbed or blocked, far beyond the stage in which the child's overall outlook on his surroundings is still totally or predominantly narcissistic. That stream of narcissism, in particular, which is subsumed here under the term idealized parent imago, thus remains vulnerable throughout the whole span of its crucial early development, i.e., from (a) the stage of the formation of the archaic idealized self-object, to (b) the time of the massive reinternalization of the idealized aspect of the oedipal parental imago. The period of greatest vulnerability ends, therefore, when an idealized nuclear superego has been securely established, since, as stated before, the capacity for the idealization of his central values and standards which the child thus acquires exerts a lasting beneficial influence on the psychic economy in the narcissistic sectors of the personality.

The influence of the child's interactions with his parents on the taming of his object-instinctual drives, on the increasing dominance of his ego over the drives, and on the drive-controlling and drive-channeling aspects of his superego, is well known and does not require our consideration in the present context. The analogous conditions which influence

---

[3] Throughout this book I use such terms as idealizing libido, idealizing cathexis, idealizing narcissism, and idealization of the superego as condensed renditions of the complex relationships described; e.g., in the above paragraph the use of the term idealizing libido, in particular, affirms in each instance a reference to the quality of the essential psychological experience. The term, in other words, refers exclusively to the subjective way in which an external object (the idealized object) or the functions of a psychic agency (the idealized superego) are experienced; it does, of course, not connote an objective existence of perfect and omnipotent figures or psychic agencies outside of the psychic reality of the experiencing subject.

the development of the child's narcissism, however, deserve our attention, specifically at this point as regards the child's idealizations. The modification of the archaic idealizing cathexes (their taming, neutralization, and differentiation) is achieved by their *passage through the idealized self-object;* and the individually specific result of this process will, of course, have been determined in part by the specific emotional responses of the object which the child idealizes. Just as the severity of a superego, however, may establish itself to some extent in independence of the actual harshness of the parents' behavior (or may, paradoxically, even be heightened by their kindness), so also is the trend toward the absolutarian perfection of the superego (its idealization; its ego-ideal dimension) to some extent independent of the parents' behavior and may—an analogous seeming paradox—be occasionally heightened by a parent's unempathic modesty which may traumatically frustrate the child's phase-appropriate need to glorify him. (See Chapter 10 for a discussion of the analyst's corresponding empathic failure to recognize the analysand's need to glorify him.)

Although the child's oedipal and preoedipal objects (in their object-cathected and narcissistic dimensions) exert a decisive influence on the shaping of the adult personality because they leave a permanent imprint on later drive preferences and object choice, their role as precursors of psychological structure may well be regarded as of at least equal importance. Once the nuclear psychological structures have been established (largely at the end of the oedipal period; but an important firming and buttressing of the psychic apparatus, especially in the area of the establishment of reliable ideals, takes place during latency and puberty, with a decisive final step in late adolescence), object loss, be it ever so crushing, will not leave the personality incomplete. It may (in consequence, for example, of sudden and massive object loss incurred in later phases of life) prevent the personality from ever again extending significant libidinal cathexes to new objects; but in general it will not damage the basic structure of the mental apparatus.[4] Traumatic deprivations and losses of objects up to and including the oedipal period (and, to a lesser extent, throughout latency and adolescence), and traumatic disappointments in them, may, however, interfere seriously with the basic structuralization of the psychic apparatus itself.

It should be added that in the context of the preceding considerations the beginning of latency may be regarded as still belonging to the oedipal phase. It constitutes the last of the several periods of peak vulnerability of the small child's psyche. These moments of greatest danger in early childhood during which the psyche is especially susceptible to traumatization correspond to "an as yet insecurely established new balance of psychological forces after a spurt of development" (Kohut and Seitz, 1963, pp. 128f.). If we apply this *principle of the vulnerability of new structures* (cf. Hartmann, who stressed that newly acquired functions "show a high degree of reversibility in the child" [1952, p. 177]) to the superego at the beginning of latency and, in particular, to the newly established idealization of its values and standards and of its rewarding and punishing functions, it will not be surprising to us to learn that clinical experience demonstrates that a severe disappointment in the idealized oedipal object, even at the beginning of latency, may yet undo a precariously established idealization of the superego, may recathect the imago of the idealized self-object, and may lead to a renewed insistence on, and search for, an external object of perfection. Just as a small child may tolerate the first temporary separations from the mother as long as he knows that the mother will be available if his longing should become unbearable, so also can the child in early latency give up the external idealization if the perfect object is still available for temporary swings of recathexis with idealizing libido. And just as a small

---

[4] For a convincing, and moving, discussion of exceptions to the general rule see two articles by K. R. Eissler (1963b, 1967).

child will not tolerate any separation when he fears that the mother might become irretrievably lost, so is the idealization of the superego again given up in early latency when the idealized object seems irretrievably lost during that period. An unusual vulnerability of the psyche in early latency, and its regressive response to traumas occurring at that period, is, of course, not only a function of that present moment but is also determined by the child's earlier traumatic experiences.

In the specific case of the traumatic loss of the idealized parent imago (loss of the idealized self-object or disappointment in it) up to and including the oedipal phase, the results are disturbances in specific narcissistic sectors of the personality. Under optimal circumstances the child experiences gradual disappointment in the idealized object—or, expressed differently: the child's evaluation of the idealized object becomes increasingly realistic—which leads to a withdrawal of the narcissistic cathexes from the imago of the idealized self-object and to their gradual (or, in the oedipal period, massive but phase-appropriate) internalization, i.e., to the acquisition of permanent psychological structures which continue, endopsychically, the functions which the idealized self-object had previously fulfilled. If the child suffers the traumatic loss of the idealized object, however, or a traumatic (severe and sudden, or not phase-appropriate) disappointment in it, then optimal internalization does not take place. The child does not acquire the needed internal structure, his psyche remains fixated on an archaic self-object, and the personality will throughout life be dependent on certain objects in what seems to be an intense form of object hunger. The intensity of the search for and of the dependency on these objects is due to the fact that they are striven for as a substitute for the missing segments of the psychic structure. They are not objects (in the psychological sense of the term) since they are not loved or admired for their attributes, and the actual features of their personalities, and their actions, are only dimly recognized. They are not longed for but are needed in order to replace the functions of a segment of the mental apparatus which had not been established in childhood.

In the realm of narcissism very early traumatic disturbances in the relationship to the archaic idealized self-object and, especially, traumatic disappointments in it may broadly interfere with the development of the basic capacity of the psyche to maintain, on its own, the narcissistic equilibrium of the personality (or to re-establish it after it has been disturbed). Such is, for example, the case in personalities who become addicts. The trauma which they suffered is most frequently the severe disappointment in a mother who, because of her defective empathy with the child's needs (or for other reasons), did not appropriately fulfill the functions (as a stimulus barrier; as an optimal provider of needed stimuli; as a supplier of tension-relieving gratification, etc.) which the mature psychic apparatus should later be able to perform (or initiate) predominantly on its own. Traumatic disappointments suffered during these archaic stages of the development of the idealized self-object deprive the child of the gradual internalization of early experiences of being optimally soothed, or of being aided in going to sleep. Such individuals remain thus fixated on aspects of archaic objects and they find them, for example, in the form of drugs. The drug, however, serves not as a substitute for loved or loving objects, or for a relationship with them, but as a replacement for a defect in the psychological structure.

In the specific regression which takes place in the analysis of such patients the analysand becomes addicted to the analyst or to the analytic procedure, and—although in the metapsychological sense of the word, the term transference may not be fully correct here—one might say that the transferencelike condition which establishes itself in such analyses is indeed the reinstatement of an archaic condition. The analysand reactivates the need for an archaic, narcissistically experienced self-object which preceded the formation of

psychic structure in a specific segment of the psychic apparatus. From the sought-for object, however (i.e., the analyst),
the analysand expects the performance of certain basic functions in the realm of narcissistic homeostasis which his own
psyche is unable to provide.

Disturbances in the relationship with the idealized object
lead to consequences which can be classified by dividing them
into three groups according to the developmental phase during which the main impact of the trauma had been experienced.

1. Very early disturbances in the relationship with the
idealized object appear to lead to a general structural weakness—perhaps a defective or malfunctioning stimulus barrier
—that interferes broadly with the capacity of the psyche to
maintain the basic narcissistic homeostasis of the personality.
A personality thus afflicted suffers from a diffuse narcissistic
vulnerability. (This topic is discussed further in Chapter 3.)

2. Later—yet still preoedipal—traumatic disturbances in
the relationship with the idealized object (or, again, especially, a traumatic disappointment in it) may interfere with
the (preoedipal) establishment of the drive-controlling, drive-
channeling, and drive-neutralizing basic fabric of the psychic
apparatus. A readiness toward the resexualization of drive
derivatives as well as of internal and external conflicts (often
in the form of perverse fantasies or acts) may be the symptomatic manifestation of this structural defect.

I would like to suggest the following hypothesis in explanation of this clinically observable fact. Just as the superego
(see step 3 below) is the massively introjected internal replica
of the oedipal object, so is the basic fabric of the ego composed of innumerable (by comparison with the superego:
minute) internal replicas of aspects of the *pre*oedipal object.
And just as the loving-approving and angry-frustrating aspects of the oedipal object are internalized during the oedipal
period and become the approving functions and positive
goals of the superego, on the one hand, and its punitive func-

tions and prohibitions, on the other, so also are the approving
and the frustrating aspects of the preoedipal object internalized and form the basic fabric of the ego. (In contrast to the
phase-appropriate massiveness of the oedipal internalization
which forms the superego, the basic fabric of the ego is laid
down in minute quantities of internalization which, however, occur on innumerable occasions throughout the whole
preoedipal period.)

The internalization of the narcissistically invested aspects
of the oedipal and preoedipal object takes place according to
the same principle. The massive, but phase-appropriate, withdrawal of narcissistic cathexes from the oedipal object leads
to the internalization of these cathexes and to their attachment to the approving and prohibiting functions of the superego, as well as to its values and ideals—a process which results
in the specific prestige enjoyed by these functions and contents of the superego. The innumerable, small, nontraumatic
disappointments in the perfection of the preoedipal object
(i.e., the increasingly realistic perception of the preoedipal
object) account similarly for the admixture of prestige (and
thus power) enjoyed by each of the minute prohibitions,
admonitions, and approving and guiding foci, which form in
their entirety the drive-channeling and drive-neutralizing
basic fabric of the ego. (Although the detailed discussion of
this specific subject matter cannot be undertaken here, it may
be mentioned that the term "basic fabric of the *ego*" is not
entirely correct since certain layers of the *id* in the "area of
progressive neutralization" participate to some extent in the
drive-channeling and drive-neutralizing functions [see Kohut
and Seitz, 1963, esp. p. 137].)

3. Finally, if the genesis of the disturbance relates to the
oedipal period, i.e., if a disappointment of traumatic proportions concerns the late preoedipal and the oedipal idealized
object—or even as late as the beginning of latency, if the still
partially idealized external counterpart of the newly internalized object is traumatically destroyed—then the idealization

of the superego will be incomplete with the result that the person (even though he may possess values and standards) will forever search for external ideal figures from whom he wants to obtain the approval and the leadership which his insufficiently idealized superego cannot provide.

But we must now digress from the consideration of the specific developmental vicissitudes of the idealized parent imago and turn to a discussion of two topics which are of fundamental significance for the assessment of developmental data in general: (1) the relationship between the formation of psychic structure and the decathexis of object imagoes; and (2) the difference in the psychological significance of (a) archaic (self-)objects and their functions, (b) psychic structures and their functions, and (c) mature objects and their functions.

The relationship between the formation of psychic structure and the withdrawal of object-instinctual and narcissistic cathexes from object imagoes is demonstrated best by pointing out the following three factors which play an important role in the process of structure formation—one that I should like to call *transmuting internalization*.[5]

1. The psychic apparatus must be ready for the formation of the structure, i.e., the psyche must have reached a maturationally preformed receptivity for specific introjects. (The independent emergence of such internally preformed potentialities is referred to by Hartmann [1939, 1950a] as the primary autonomy of the maturational steps of the psyche.)

2. Preceding the withdrawal of the cathexis from the object there is a breaking up of those aspects of the object imago that are being internalized. This breaking up is of great psychoeconomic importance; it constitutes the metapsychological substance of what, in a term that is closer to empathically or introspectively observable experience, is referred to

5 In the context of these formulations see Loewald's approach (1962) and, especially with regard to point (3), see Loewald's (unpublished) paper of 1965 as quoted by Schafer (1968, p. 10n.).

as optimal frustration. The essentials of the process of fractionized withdrawal of cathexes from objects were, of course, first established by Freud (1917a) in the metapsychological description of the work of mourning. Expressed concretely, the withdrawal of narcissistic cathexes takes place in a fractionated way if the child can experience disappointments with one idealized aspect or quality of the object after another; transmuting internalization is prevented, however, if, for example, the disappointment in the perfection of the object concerns the total object, e.g., when the child suddenly recognizes that the omnipotent object is powerless.

3. In addition to the just-mentioned breaking up of specific aspects of the object imago there takes place, in the process of effective internalization (i.e., of internalization which leads to the formation of psychic structure), a depersonalizing of the introjected aspects of the image of the object, mainly in the form of a shift of emphasis from the total human context of the personality of the object to certain of its specific functions.[6] The internal structure, in other words, now performs the functions which the object used to perform for the child—the well-functioning structure, however, has largely been divested of the personality features of the object. Imperfections in this part of the process are well known: the superego, for example, usually shows traces of some of the human features of the oedipal object, and the drive-controlling basic fabric of the psyche may work with specific personalized methods of threat and seduction which are directly derived from characteristics of preoedipal objects and from their specific attitude toward the child's drives.

We can now turn to the second topic of the present general discussion and emphasize that there is a crucial difference between (1) the narcissistically experienced, archaic self-object

[6] See, in this context, Schafer's comprehensive theoretical approach to the problems of internalization in his recent important scholarly contribution [1968], in particular the final phrase of his broad definition [p. 140]: "an identification may acquire relative autonomy from its origins in the subject's relations with dynamically significant objects."

(an object only in the sense of the observer of manifest behavior); (2) the psychological structures (which are built up in consequence of the gradual decathexis of the narcissistically experienced archaic object) which continue to perform the drive-regulating, integrating, and adaptive functions which had previously been performed by the (external) object; and (3) true objects (in the psychoanalytic sense) which are cathected with object-instinctual investments, i.e., objects loved and hated by a psyche that has separated itself from the archaic objects, has acquired autonomous structures, has accepted the independent motivations and responses of others, and has grasped the notion of mutuality.

Although the archaic, narcissistically experienced object and the mature object which is cathected with object libido are both objects in the terms of social psychology, from the point of view of psychoanalytic theory (metapsychology) they are at the opposite ends of a developmental line and of a dynamic continuum. Expressed differently: endopsychic structures such as the superego (and other, less well-delineated configurations within the ego) are in their psychological significance, and in their mode of functioning, less distant from the mature objects of the psyche than the archaic objects which have not yet become transformed into internal psychological structures. The interpersonal view of social psychology; the sociobiological approach of transactionalism; such contrasts as that between "other-directedness" and "inner-directedness" (Riesman, 1950); and even the psychodynamically sophisticated descriptions of those systems of "direct" child observation which employ the basic theoretical framework of social psychology (or of a related framework of social psychobiology) do not take these crucial differences into account. The introduction of their conceptual framework into psychoanalysis would, therefore, impoverish our science by obliterating these fundamental differentiations. The addict's depletion when he is separated from the soothing psychotherapist, the craving to see the therapist as a strong leader figure by those who have not built up a guiding structure of internal values and ideals—these are examples of the therapeutic reactivation of the need for archaic, narcissistically experienced self-objects. As I hope to demonstrate in this study, these archaic, narcissistically experienced self-objects are indeed revived in therapy around the perception of the figure of the therapist, and they form two distinct types of transferences which can be systematically investigated and worked through. They must not be confused with the therapeutic transference revival of the (incestuous) childhood objects (cathected with object-instinctual investments), a revival that takes place in the analysis of the transference neuroses.

After the preceding discussion of certain general aspects of the relationship of the social environment to the formation and function of psychological structure, we can now return to the examination of the specific circumstances which lead to disturbances in those structures that are derived from the idealized parent imago.

In order to avoid the pitfalls of falsifying oversimplification, let me first apply to our specific field the tested postulate that the vicissitudes of normal and abnormal psychological development are in general intelligible only if considered not as due to single incidents in the child's life but as the result of the interplay of a number of etiological factors. Thus, although the traumatic disturbance of the relationship with the idealized object (or the traumatic disappointment in it) can frequently be assigned to a specific point in the child's early development, the effect of specific traumas can usually be understood only when the existence of a state of readiness to be traumatized is also taken into account. The susceptibility to the trauma is, in turn, due to the interaction of congenital structural weaknesses with experiences which antedate the specific pathogenic trauma. Thus the same condition of the interaction of two complementary series of causative factors prevails in the development of narcissism as it does in the development of object love and object aggression.

The idealizing transference, however, which establishes itself spontaneously in analysis refers generally to that specific point of the development of the idealized parent imago —from the earliest, archaic stage of the idealized self-object to that comparatively late stage, just before the consolidation of its final reinternalization (i.e., as the idealization of the superego)—at which the normal development in the realm of the idealized object had been severely disturbed or interrupted. In assessing the idealizing transference, however, we will often realize that the therapeutic revival of comparatively late stages of the idealized parent imago (a preoedipal or oedipal traumatic disappointment of a son in his father, for example) may rest on the deeper basis of an early, inexpressible disappointment in the idealized mother which may have been due to the unreliability of her empathy and her depressed moods, or may be related to her physical illnesses, or her absence or death.

Furthermore, as has been briefly alluded to, the genetic assessment of the idealizing transference is also complicated by a psychological tendency to which I should like to refer as the *telescoping of genetically analogous experiences*,[7] including especially the fact that the psyche may superimpose memories of important but noncritical later (postoedipal) experiences over the specifically pathogenic earlier ones. This overlaying of the memory of the critical period of developmental disturbance by memories of analogous later experiences is a manifestation of the synthesizing power of the mind; it should not be understood as being necessarily in the service of defense (i.e., as being undertaken in order to ward off the recall of the earlier memory), but usually rather as being in the service of the attempt to express the early trauma through the medium of analogous psychic contents that are closer to the secondary process and to verbal communication.

7 This concept is related to but differs from "the telescoping of events" (Greenacre, as quoted by Kris, 1950; Kris, 1956a) which specifically refers to screen memories.

In clinical practice the recall of such memories of later events —they should be called derivatives only if the psychic content of the event has been retained in the unconscious in the form of a verbalizable memory—can thus often be accepted instead of the recall of the earlier ones, even though the analysand's understanding may remain incomplete if the formulation of the genetic reconstruction of the crucial earlier trauma, and of its influence on the later traumatization, is neglected. (The psychoanalytic theorist, however, cannot allow himself a similar looseness; he must try to determine the period in which the specific pathogenic trauma actually occurred.)

As can be derived from the foregoing considerations, the idealizing transference which establishes itself in the analysis of certain narcissistic personality disorders occurs in specific, distinct forms which are determined by the specific point at which the major traumatic fixation took place or at which the further development of idealizing narcissism was blocked. As a group, however, these transferences are not only metapsychologically but also clinically easily distinguishable from the idealizations that are encountered during certain phases of the analysis of transference neuroses. The regularity and orderliness of the features of the basic idealizing transference, its stability, and its central position in the analytic process— in contrast to the protean manifestations and the peripheral position of the idealizations in the analysis of the transference neuroses—are due to the fact that the narcissistic fixation in all the subgroups of the idealizing transference concerns the narcissistic aspects of the idealized object *before* its ultimate internalization, i.e., before the consolidation of the idealization of the superego. Although the idealizations in the transference neuroses are undoubtedly also maintained by a mobilization of narcissistic-idealizing libido, they must be understood as the expression of a nonspecific overestimation of the love object. The love object, however, is here intensely cathected with object libido to which an admixture of narcissistic libido is only secondarily amalgamated during phases of intense positive transference; and the narcissistic investment always remains subordinated to the object cathexes. In other words, the idealization in the transference neuroses is a nonspecific feature of the positive transference, closely akin to that encountered in the state of being in love.

The idealizing transference which establishes itself during the analysis of narcissistic personalities may occur in a variety of more or less circumscribed types. There are therapeutic reactivations of archaic states which hark back to the period when the idealized mother imago is still almost completely merged with that of the self; and there are other instances in which the pathognomonic transference reactivations concern much later points in the development of the idealizing libido and the idealized object. In these latter instances a trauma led to specific narcissistic fixations during a period, from the late preoedipal phase through early latency, when most sectors of the child's relationship to his parents are already fully cathected with object-instinctual energies. Specific traumas, however (such as a sudden, unexpected, intolerable disappointment in the idealized object at this phase), bring about specific pathogenic injuries in the development of idealizing narcissism (or they undo an idealization which had just barely been established), leading to an insufficient idealization of the superego, a structural deficiency which in turn results in a fixation on the narcissistic aspects of the preoedipal or oedipal idealized object. Persons who have suffered such traumas are (as adolescents and adults) forever attempting to achieve a union with the idealized object since, in view of their specific structural defect (the insufficient idealization of their superego), their narcissistic equilibrium is safeguarded only through the interest, the responses, and the approval of present-day (i.e., currently active) replicas of the traumatically lost self-object.

These two types of idealizing transference, i.e., the developmentally most archaic, and the most mature (and a number of others whose fixation points lie between them), not only can be differentiated metapsychologically but also can be recognized clinically on the basis of the distinct and characteristic (transference) pictures which they present during analytic therapy. As mentioned previously, however, the analyst must take into account the fact that the clinical picture may be obscured by the phenomenon of telescoping, i.e., by the mobilization of memories concerning later events which are analogous to the pathogenic one.

Ultimately, it must also be admitted that it is at times not altogether easy to decide whether the narcissistic transferences of certain patients who reinstate the relationship to comparatively late stages of the idealized object are not superimposed on disturbances which concern more archaic narcissistic objects. Thus there exist indeed clinical instances in which it is not possible to assign the psychopathology to a single dominant fixation point. In these cases the idealizing transference may alternatingly be focused on archaic and on oedipal stages of the idealized object.

CHAPTER 3

A CLINICAL ILLUSTRATION OF
IDEALIZING TRANSFERENCE

While the material to be presented is of necessity abbreviated and condensed, I have made no attempt to simplify the structure of the case. It is, on the contrary, my aim to demonstrate how the theoretical guidelines that have been given may aid in the resolution of some of the genetic and dynamic-structural complexities which are encountered in the analysis of narcissistic personalities.

Mr. A., a reddish-blond, freckled man in his mid-twenties, was a research chemist in a large pharmaceutical firm. Although the initial complaint with which he entered analysis was that ever since adolescence he had felt sexually stimulated by men, it soon became apparent that his homosexual preoccupations were not prominent, occupied a rather isolated position in his personality, and constituted only one of the several indications of an underlying broad personality defect. More important than his occasional homosexual fantasies were (a) his tendency toward feeling vaguely depressed, drained of energy, and lacking in zest (with an associated drop in his work capacity and creativity during periods when this mood had overtaken him); and (b) as a trigger to the preceding disturbance, a great (and in the main quite specific) vulnerability of his self-esteem, manifested by his sensitivity to criticism, to lack of interest in him, or to the absence of praise from the people whom he experienced as his elders or superiors. Thus, although he was a man of considerable intelligence who performed his tasks with skill and creative ability, he was forever in search of guidance and approval: from the head of the research laboratory where he was employed, from a number of senior colleagues, and from the fathers of the girls whom he dated. He was sensitively aware of these men and of their opinion of him, attempted to get their help and approbation, and tried to create situations in which he would be supported by them. So long as he felt accepted and counseled and guided by such men, so long as he felt that they approved of him, he experienced himself as whole, acceptable, and capable; and under such circumstances he was indeed able to do well in his work and to be creative and successful. At slight signs of disapproval of him, however, or of lack of understanding for him, or of loss of interest in him, he would feel drained and depressed, would tend to become first enraged and then cold, haughty, and isolated, and his creativeness and work capacity deteriorated.

In the cohesive therapeutic transference which established itself in the analysis, all these reaction propensities were clearly in evidence and permitted the gradual reconstruction of a certain genetically decisive pattern which had occurred repeatedly and had led to the specific personality defects of the patient. Over and over again, throughout his childhood, the patient (who was the youngest of three children: he had a brother ten years older and a sister three years older than he) had felt abruptly and traumatically disappointed in the power and efficacy of his father just when he had (re-)established him as a figure of protective strength and efficiency. As is so frequently the case (see the earlier remarks concerning the telescoping of analogous childhood events), the first memories which the patient supplied—subsequent to the direct (concerning the analyst) and the indirect (concerning various present-day father figures) transference activations of the crucial pattern—related to a comparatively late period in his life. After an adventurous flight via South Africa and South America, the family had come to the United States when the patient was nine years old, and the father, who had been a prosperous businessman in Europe, was unable to repeat his earlier success in this country. Time and again, however, the father shared his newest plans with his son and stirred the child's fantasies and expectations. Time and again, he started a new enterprise in the building up of which he enlisted his son's interest and participation. And time and again he sold out in panic when unforeseen events and his lack of familiarity with the American scene combined to block his purposes. Although these were, of course, memories of which Mr. A. had always been conscious, he had not previously appreciated the intensity of the contrast between the phase of great trust in the father, who was most confidence-inspiring while he was forging his plans, and the subsequent desperate disappointment in the father who not only lost his nerve in the face of unexpected difficulties, but who also reacted with emotional and physical deterioration (depression; a variety of hypochondriacal complaints for which he would often take to his bed) to the impact of the defeat.

Most prominent among the patient's relevant recollections of earlier occurrences of the idealization-disappointment sequence concerning his father were those of the family's last years in Eastern Europe, in particular the recall of two events which affected the family fortunes decisively when the patient was six and eight years old respectively. The father who, during the patient's early childhood, had been a virile and handsome man had owned a small but flourishing industry. Judging on the basis of many indications and memories, it seems to be an established fact that father and son were very close emotionally up to the point of the catastrophe which occurred when the patient was six, and that the son had admired his father greatly. According to family lore, the father even took the son with him to his factory at an early age (according to the patient, already before he was four), explaining details of his business to the boy, and even asking him—playfully, as one may assume in retrospect—for advice concerning various business matters, as he did again later more seriously, in the United States when the patient was an adolescent. Suddenly the threat that the German armies would overrun the country interrupted their close relationship. At first the father was away a great deal, trying to make arrangements for the transfer of his business to another (Eastern European) country. Then, when the patient was six, German armies invaded the country and the family, which was Jewish, fled. Although the father had initially reacted with helplessness and panic, he later succeeded in re-establishing his business, though on a much reduced scale; but as a consequence of the German invasion of the country to which they had escaped (the patient was eight at that time), everything was again lost and the family had to flee once more.

The patient's memories focused on the beginning of latency as the crucial period when the essential structural defect was incurred (see my earlier remarks about the specific significance of early latency in the context of the "vulnerability of new structures," i.e., specifically, of the barely established superego). There is no doubt, however, that later events (his father's failures in the U.S.A.) compounded the damage; and there is similarly no doubt that the child's still earlier experiences—his being subjected to his father's extreme, sudden, and unpredictable mood swings during the preoedipal and oedipal period; and, especially, his exposure during infancy to the unreliability of the empathic responses of his mother—had sensitized him and had caused the vulnerability which (in combination with a modicum of congenital predisposition) accounted for the severity and the permanence of the structural defect set up by the events at the beginning of latency.

To repeat: although the specific pathogenic focus of the

disturbance related to the traumatic devaluation of the father imago at the beginning of latency, there can be no doubt that the traumas which occurred during an earlier period of his life—not remembered but broadly reinstated by the patient's diffuse sensitivity to the analyst; specifically, to even slight imperfections in the analyst's ability to achieve immediate empathic understanding for all shades and nuances of his current experiences and moods—had prepared the soil for the pathogenic effect of the later traumas. The scrutiny of the current behavior of the patient's mother, and of her present-day personality, furnished ample evidence for the conclusion that she was a deeply disturbed woman who, though seemingly calm and quiet (in contrast to the openly overemotional father), tended suddenly to disintegrate with terrible anxiety and unintelligible (schizoid) excitement when she was exposed to pressure. It may thus be assumed that the patient suffered many disappointments in the mother's phase-appropriately required omniscient empathy and power during the first year of his life and that the shallowness and unpredictability of his mother's responses to him must have led to his broad insecurity and narcissistic vulnerability.

The hub of the patient's psychological defect, however, related to the traumatic disappointment in the idealized father imago in early latency. What was the nature of his defect and how can it be described in metapsychological terms? To put the answer in a nutshell: the central defect of his personality was the insufficient idealization of his superego (an insufficient cathexis with idealizing libido of the values, standards, and functions of his superego) and, concomitantly, the strong cathexis of an externally experienced idealized parent imago in the late preoedipal and the oedipal stages. The symptomatic result of this defect was circumscribed yet profound. Since the patient had predominantly suffered a traumatic disappointment in the narcissistically invested aspects of the father imago (the father's idealized power), no transmuting internalization of the idealized object had taken place, but a fixation on a prestructural ideal figure (for whom the patient was forever in search) occurred. The superego did not possess the requisite exalted status and was thus unable to raise the patient's self-esteem. In view of the fact, however, that the patient had not felt equally deprived of those aspects of the father imago that were invested with object-instinctual cathexes, his superego was relatively intact with regard to those of its contents and functions that were built up as the heir to the object-libidinal and object-aggressive dimensions of the oedipal father relationship: the patient possessed values, goals, and standards; and he was in general not inclined to turn to external figures with the implicit or explicit demand that it should be spelled out to him which conduct was right or wrong or to what goals he should aspire. Basically, his nuclear goals and standards were those of his family's cultural background, transmitted to him by his father. What he lacked, however, was the ability to feel more than a fleeting sense of satisfaction when living up to his standards or reaching his goals. He was able to obtain a sense of heightened self-esteem only by attaching himself to strong, admired figures whose acceptance he craved and by whom he needed to feel supported.

Thus, in the transference manifestations of his specific structural defect, he seemed insatiable in two (tyrannically and sadistically asserted) demands that he directed toward the idealized analyst: (a) that the analyst share the patient's values, goals, and standards (and thus imbue them with significance through their idealization); and (b) that the analyst confirm through the expression of a warm glow of pleasure and participation that the patient had lived up to his values and standards and had successfully worked toward a goal. Without the analyst's expression of his empathic comprehension of these needs (verbal confirmation tended to be sufficient; a "play-acting" wish fulfillment, e.g., through direct praise, was neither required, nor would it indeed have been acceptable to this patient), the patient's values and goals seemed trite and uninspiring to him and his successes were meaningless and left him feeling depressed and empty.

Having described the patient's central psychological defect and its consequences, I now turn to three separate, subsidiary areas of the patient's psychopathology which are, however, interconnected both with the primary defect and with each other: (1) the patient's diffuse narcissistic vulnerability; (2) the hypercathexis of his grandiose self which occurred mainly in response to disappointments in the idealized parent imago; and (3) the tendency toward the sexualization of the narcissistically cathected constellations.

1. The manifestations of the patient's *diffuse narcissistic vulnerability* were nonspecific; and the relevant explanatory reconstructions that can be offered are of necessity more speculative and tentative than the hypotheses presented in explanation of the other aspects of his narcissistic personality disturbance. He was extraordinarily sensitive not only to slights—whether they were personal and intentional, or impersonal and accidental—but also to setbacks due to the vicissitudes of external circumstances to which, however, he always tended to react as to a personal injury, intentionally inflicted on him by an animistically experienced world. The broadness and diffuseness of the relevant psychological defect, and the archaism of the experience of the world into which it belonged, point in the direction of disturbances in the patient's early relationship to his mother. And, as indicated previously, the assessment of the personality of his mother supports the contention that the genesis of his diffuse narcissistic vulnerability was related to his mother's personality disturbance, in particular to the unpredictability and unreliability of her empathic responses during his infancy.

In general, the precursor of the idealization of the archaic parent imago, and of the grandiosity of the archaic self, is the infant's experience of an undisturbed primary narcissistic equilibrium, a psychological state whose perfection precedes even the most rudimentary differentiation into the later categories of perfection (i.e., perfection in the realm of power, of knowledge, of beauty, and of morality). The mother's responsiveness to the child's needs prevents traumatic delays before the narcissistic equilibrium is re-established after it has been disturbed, and if the shortcomings of the mother's responses are of tolerable proportions, the infant will gradually modify the original boundlessness and blind confidence of his expectation of absolute perfection. Expressed in metapsychological terms: with each of the mother's minor empathic failures, misunderstandings, and delays, the infant withdraws narcissistic libido from the archaic imago of unconditional perfection (primary narcissism) and acquires in its stead a particle of inner psychological structure which takes over the mother's functions in the service of the maintenance of narcissistic equilibrium, e.g., her basic soothing and calming activities; and her providing physical[1] and emotional warmth and other kinds of narcissistic sustenance. Thus, as continues to hold true for the analogous later milieu of the child, the most important aspect of the earliest mother-infant relationship is the principle of optimal frustration. Tolerable disappointments in the pre-existing (and externally sustained) primary narcissistic equilibrium lead to the establishment of internal structures which provide the ability for self-soothing and the acquisition of basic tension tolerance in the narcissistic realm.

If, however, the mother's responses are grossly unem-

---

[1] The ability, within certain limits, to regulate skin temperature and to maintain a feeling of warmth appears to be acquired in this way. Narcissistically disturbed individuals tend to be unable to feel warm or to keep warm. They rely on others to provide them not only with emotional but also with physical warmth. Their skin tends to be poorly vascularized and they are unusually sensitive to lowered temperatures ("drafts"). Even persons without excessive narcissistic vulnerability tend, after the immediate shame response (the sudden deployment of disorganized exhibitionistic cathexes) has subsided, to react to narcissistic injuries with vasoconstriction in skin and mucous membranes and are thus, perhaps in consequence of these conditions, more susceptible to infections, especially to the acquisition of the common cold.

pathic and unreliable, then the gradual withdrawal of cathexis from the imago of archaic unconditional perfection is disturbed; no transmuting internalization can take place; and the psyche continues to cling to a vaguely delimited imago of absolute perfection, does not develop the various internal functions which secondarily re-establish the narcissistic equilibrium—either (a) directly, through self-soothing, i.e., through the deployment of available narcissistic cathexes; or, (b) indirectly, via an appropriate appeal to the idealized parent—and remains thus relatively defenseless vis-à-vis the effects of narcissistic injuries. The behavioral manifestations of this state vary widely, of course, depending, among other factors, on the extensiveness and severity of the mother's faulty response. In general, however, one can say that they consist in a hypersensitivity to disturbances in the narcissistic equilibrium with a tendency to react to sources of narcissistic disturbance by mixtures of wholesale withdrawal and unforgiving rage.

Two general statements can be made about the genesis of narcissistic vulnerabilities and fixations.

(i) The interplay between inherited psychological propensities and the *personality* of the parents (especially of the mother) is of vastly greater importance than the interplay between hereditary factors and gross traumatic *events* (such as the absence or death of a parent), unless the gross external factors and the parents' personality disturbances are related (as, for example, when there is divorce of the parents, or in the case of a parent's absence due to mental illness or of his or her loss due to suicide).

(ii) The most specific pathogenic elements of the parents' personalities lie in the realm of their own narcissistic fixations. In particular, we find that, during the earliest phases, (a) the mother's self-absorption may lead to a projection of her own moods and tensions onto the child and thus to faulty empathy; (b) she may overrespond selectively (hypochondriacally) to certain moods and tensions in the child which correspond to her own narcissistic tension states and preoccupations; (c) she may be unresponsive to the moods and tensions expressed by the child when her own preoccupations are not in tune with the child's needs. The result is a traumatic alternation of faulty empathy, overempathy, and lack of empathy, which prevents the gradual withdrawal of narcissistic cathexes and the building up of tension-regulating psychic structures: the child remains fixated on the whole early narcissistic milieu.

Not only does the mother's narcissistic personality organization thus account for the child's early acquisition of narcissistic fixations and vulnerabilities, it also accounts for the fact that the child remains included in the parental narcissistic milieu far beyond the time when his psychological organization is still in tune with such a relationship. The father's personality, however, may, in the later phases, be of decisive influence with regard to the severity of the ensuing personality disturbance: if he, too, because of his own narcissistic fixations, is unable to respond empathically to the child's needs, then he compounds the damage; if, however, his personality is a firmly demarcated one and if he is able, for example, to let himself first be idealized by the child and then to allow the child gradually to detect his realistic limitations without withdrawing from the child, then the child may turn toward his wholesome influence, form a team with him against the mother, and escape relatively unscathed.

Having presented these general considerations, I return to the specific case of Mr. A. The early milieu provided by his mother's psychopathological personality not only was the breeding place in which his diffuse narcissistic vulnerability originated, it also contributed in two ways to the genesis of those aspects of the patient's psychopathology in the narcissistic realm which were acquired in later childhood: (a) through the formation of early narcissistic fixations the child's resilience vis-à-vis narcissistic disturbances became diminished, and he responded to the narcissistic traumas of later periods by the development of further fixations rather than by the building up of tension-regulating psychological structures; and (b) the early and continuing disappointment in the perfection of the mother led to the result that the child was unable to imbue her sufficiently with narcissistic idealizing cathexes, the father imago became correspondingly over-idealized, and the vicissitudes of the idealized father imago had thus a greater traumatic impact on the child's psyche than might otherwise have been the case.

2. Continuing the survey of the patient's subsidiary areas of psychopathology, I now turn to the examination of his *propensity toward a reactive hypercathexis of the grandiose self* in response to disappointments in (or rejections by) the idealized analyst, or indirectly, in response to idealized figures outside the clinical transference.

Swings from the therapeutic activation of the idealized parent imago (idealizing transference) to a transient hypercathexis of the grandiose self are among the most common occurrences in the analysis of narcissistic personalities. The usual clinical manifestations of this event are: coldness toward the formerly idealized analyst; a tendency toward primitivization of thought and speech (ranging from a hint of being stilted to the gross use of neologisms); and attitudes of superiority with an increased tendency toward self-consciousness, shame, and hypochrondriacal preoccupations. These behavioral and symptomatic changes attest to the fact that the reactive hypercathexis of the grandiose self concerns in general rather primitive stages of this psychological configuration, an outgrowth of the regressive nature of the defensive move, in contrast to the cohesive therapeutic reactivation of more mature stages of the grandiose self which is encountered in most instances of primary mirror transference[2] (see Chapter 6).

2 For another clinical illustration of the reactive hypercathexis of the archaic grandiose self, see the episode in the analysis of patient G. described in Chapter 4.

In the analysis of Mr. A., reactive swings toward a hyper-cathexis of the grandiose self occurred not infrequently. They were characterized by the appearance of grandiose schemes (such as unrealistic stock market transactions or research projects), accompanied by emotional coldness, speech mannerisms (in particular, the affected use of isolated words of Spanish which he had learned at the age of nine), and hypochondriacal preoccupations. There were stages, however, when the hypercathexis of his grandiose self was not just the fleeting result of a defensive reaction: for varying periods, especially during the first few years of his long analysis, his grandiose-exhibitionistic tensions were, indeed, nonreactively employed in the formation of a more or less stable mirror transference. The reactive as well as the primary hypercathexis of the grandiose self were predominantly related to early oedipal fixation points: specifically to those junctures when the father was suddenly gone and the child had for a while the fantasy that he was in charge and that he was ruling the roost. These fantasies, however, had to give way abruptly, especially since the atmosphere of general anxiety in the precarious world situation did not permit their playful conscious and preconscious elaboration—often a precursor of later successful sublimations[3]—with the support and the cooperation of friendly adults.

The hypercathexis of the grandiose self played a significant role not only at the beginning of the analysis, but also, in a specific context, during the later phases. When, as a result of several years of analysis, the patient's functioning had improved, when his self-esteem had risen, and when his capacity to react adequately to successes and failures had become more reliable, he would often, and for prolonged periods, have a feeling of unreality about himself and his life which could not be completely accounted for by the newness of the adjustment. It was only when he recalled again the old fantasies

[3] For an apparently beneficial instance of adult cooperation with a child's grandiose fantasy, see Eissler (1963, pp. 73ff.).

of being a grownup while in reality he was still a child, and when he understood how they interfered with his ability to accept himself as an effective adult—it was only then that the sense of magic and unreality began to recede from the experience of his present fuller life.

3. The metapsychological assessment of the patient's psychic disturbance will now be rounded out by a discussion of the third subsidiary area of psychopathology: his tendency toward *sexualization of the pathological narcissistic constellations.*

The subject matter of the relationship of the perversions (and also of the addictions and delinquencies) to the narcissistic personality disorders deserves greater attention than I can devote to it within the confines of this study. It is true, of course, that the manifest syndromes of perverse (and related) activity can dominate the personality to such an extent, can enslave the ego so profoundly, and bring about secondarily such widespread regressions that the narcissistic disturbance which had occupied the primary and central position in the web of the psychopathology is well-nigh covered up and hidden from sight. It is, nevertheless, my impression that specific circumscribed disturbances in the narcissistic realm are usually the nucleus of these widespread disorders. The case of Mr. A., whose perverse symptomatology was comparatively mild, lends itself particularly well to demonstrating the relationship between (a) the circumscribed primary narcissistic disturbance; (b) an early ego defect which is correlated to it; and (c) the sexualization of the narcissistic disturbance.

Mr. A.'s homosexual tendencies had not exerted a widespread secondary effect on the ego or led to diffuse drive regression. Yet, as mentioned initially, it was the presence of homosexual preoccupations which either had prompted the patient to seek analysis or had, at any rate, served as a focal point for his motivation. He had never engaged in homosexual activities and—apart from some sexually tinged, playful wrestling in adolescence and the buying of "physical culture" magazines which contained photographs of athletic men—his homosexual preoccupations were consummated only in fantasy, with or without masturbation. The objects of his homosexual fantasies were always men of great bodily strength and of perfect physique. His own fantasied activity consisted in maintaining a quasi-sadistic, absolute control over these men. In his fantasies he manipulated the situations in such a way that, even though he was weak, he was able to enslave the strong man and to make him helpless. Occasionally he achieved orgasm and a feeling of triumph and strength at the thought of masturbating a strong and physically perfect man and of thus draining him of his power.

Clinically speaking, the homosexual fantasies receded long before there was an equally manifest improvement in the other aspects of the patient's psychopathology: the fantasies recurred only during periods of stress. Subsequently they were replaced by occasional memories of fantasies which had lost their sexual connotation; they were called homosexual "fears" by the patient, i.e., he experienced them only in the context of a distant apprehension that they might return to plague him again. Ultimately even these "fears" disappeared almost completely.

The sexualization of the patient's defects was due to a moderate weakness in his basic psychic structure, resulting in an impairment of its neutralizing capacity. Since the basic neutralizing structures of the psyche are acquired during the preoedipal period, the defect in neutralization must already have been present when the central trauma (the traumatic loss of the idealized parent imago) occurred at the beginning of latency. The insufficiency of neutralization resulted in a sexualization of the patient's relationship to his narcissistically invested objects in these areas: (a) the sexualization of his idealized (oedipal) father imago (on which he had remained fixated and which he needed because he lacked a firmly idealized superego); (b) the sexualization of the mirror image of his hypercathected grandiose self (on which he had remained fixated and which he needed because he lacked a securely cathected (pre)conscious image of the self); and (c) the sexualization of his *need* for idealized values and reliable self-esteem, as well as of the psychological *processes* (internalization) by which ideals and self-esteem are acquired.

The patient's homosexual fantasies can thus be understood as sexualized statements about his narcissistic disturbance, analogous to the theoretical formulations of the analyst. The fantasies stood, of course, in opposition to meaningful insight and progress since they were in the service of pleasure gain and provided an escape route from narcissistic tensions. A degree of tension tolerance had indeed first to be acquired before the patient could assimilate what he was learning about himself. Still, in view of the fact that the sexualization of his narcissistic tensions was not deeply rooted and that its manifestations had in effect made him more aware of the presence of psychopathology for which he needed treatment than the other aspects of the narcissistic disturbance which could be disavowed more easily, a direct interpretation of the meaning of his sexual fantasies was not unprofitable. In fact, such interpretations were often very useful—particularly in retrospect, after the homosexual fantasies had largely subsided—in supporting the insights obtained from the scrutiny of other areas of disturbed psychological functioning.

Parallels could thus be drawn in later stages of the analysis (i) between (a) his insistent demand for the approval of his values and goals by various father figures (including especially the analyst) and (b) his previous fantasies of pursuing physically powerful men; and (ii) between (a) his reactive grandiosity, arrogance, and superiority and (b) the princely demeanor and behavior of some of the young men who had once been a source of sexual excitement. (iii) References to the orgastic experience of gaining strength by draining it from fantasied imagoes of external perfection—the fantasies of subjugating strong, handsome men and, through masturbating them, draining them of their strength—could be interpreted, in retrospect, as sexualized statements concerning the nature of his psychological defect and of the psychological functions which had to be acquired. Suffering from the absence of a stable system of firmly idealized values, and thus of one of the important sources of the internal regulation of self-esteem, he had in his sexual fantasies replaced the inner ideal with its sexualized external precursor, an athletic powerful man; and he had substituted for the enhancement of self-esteem which is experienced by living up to the example of one's idealized values and standards, by the sexualized feeling of triumph, as he robbed the external ideal of its power and perfection and thus in his fantasy acquired these qualities for himself and achieved a temporary feeling of narcissistic balance.[4]

It must, however, be stressed that, in general, the direct interpretation of the content of the sexual fantasies is not an optimal approach in the analysis of such cases, and that it should at first be demonstrated to such patients that the sexualization of their defects and needs serves a specific psycho-economic function, i.e., it is a means for the discharge of intense narcissistic tensions. Even the retrospective use of the contents of the sexual fantasies in support of insights obtained from the scrutiny of nonsexualized material has to be handled with tact and caution since the patient who has overcome a tension-evading habit (which is akin to an addiction) may feel that the analyst is stirring up old temptations by evoking the former sexualization of his conflicts.

No hard and fast rule can be laid down in this area. The skill and experience of the empathic analyst will have to guide him in deciding (1) whether he should avoid putting

---

[4] The presence of an unconscious fellatio fantasy in which swallowing the magical semen stands for the unachieved internalization and structure formation might well be assumed at this point. It never emerged into consciousness, however—perhaps correlated to the fact that active (sadistic) mastery and control tended to retain dominance over passive (masochistic) psychological solutions even when the patient was under severe emotional pressure.

an unnecessary burden on a patient who has barely become capable of abstaining from the sexualization of his defects and needs, and who is just beginning to move toward new and more reliable modes of achieving a narcissistic equilibrium through nonsexualized insights and through the building up of psychological structure; or (2) whether a more firmly established equilibrium allows the broadening of insights by a retrospective survey which includes the former sexual manifestations of the personality disturbance. The tendency toward a regressive escape through perverse sexual pleasures is brought into an intelligible context through such a retrospective survey, and the patient's control over his regressive tendencies is increased.

CHAPTER 4

CLINICAL AND THERAPEUTIC ASPECTS OF THE IDEALIZING TRANSFERENCE

As we have seen, the idealizing transference plays a pivotal role in the psychoanalytic therapy of certain narcissistic disorders and it occupies the limelight for prolonged periods— or at least during some crucial phases—in the analysis of a number of narcissistic personalities. It is important to comprehend the essential difference between the idealizations which occur in the analysis of narcissistic personalities (i.e., the idealizing transference in the narrow sense of the term) and the idealizations that are commonly encountered in the analysis of the transference neuroses.

The idealizations in the narcissistic disorders may derive either from the activation of archaic and transitional or of comparatively mature stages in the development of the idealized parent imago; the specific pathogenic fixation, however, was always established prior to the ultimate completion of the transmuting internalization of the idealized parent imago, i.e., before the point in development when the formation of an idealized superego has become irreversible. The idealizations encountered in the transference neuroses, on the other hand, are derived from psychological structures that were acquired at the end of the oedipal phase and during later stages of psychological development.

Two forms of idealization are seen in the transference neuroses: (a) in one, as has been pointed out, the idealization is present as an admixture to object love (of whatever kind) which has been activated in the transference; it is analogous to the idealizations which characteristically accompany the state of being in love; (b) in the other it occurs as the result of the projection of the analysand's idealized superego onto the analyst. Although the idealizations which occur in the transference neuroses may seem to resemble the idealizations occurring in the analyses of the narcissistic disorders, they are in general neither hard to differentiate from them nor difficult to recognize clinically. A theoretical understanding of the different developmental positions of the two kinds of idealization facilitates the recognition of characteristic differentiating phenomenological features which might otherwise escape the observer.

Let me first mention, however, that despite their widespread occurrence inside and outside of psychoanalysis and thus their great practical importance, I will in the present context forego a discussion of the defensive use of idealization, i.e., of (over)idealizations which (emanating from temporary ego attitudes or from chronic characterological positions) buttress secondarily repressions of, reaction formations against, or denials of a structurally deeper lying hostility. Since idealizations of this type are subordinated to hostile attitudes, the answer to the question concerning their narcissistic or object-instinctual nature depends on our evaluation of the supraordinated constellations of hostility. These problems, however, belong not in the context of the distinction between narcissistic idealization and idealization that is amalgamated with object love but to the relationship between narcissism and hostility, i.e., they must be considered in connection with the topic of narcissistic rage.

The idealizing component of object love, on the other hand, is subordinated to the dominant libidinal object cathexes to which it is amalgamated, and the object (in the transference: the incestuous oedipal childhood imago) upon which it is focused is well differentiated from the self, i.e., it is acknowledged as a center of initiative—of independent perception, thought, and action. Thus the (fantasied) transference interactions with the object contain elements of mutuality (fantasies of giving and receiving a baby, for example), and the reactions to disappointments in the object are expressed through anger and intensified longings which are directed toward the rejecting object.

The overestimation of the object with which one is in love is indeed a function of the narcissistic libido which is amalgamated with the object cathexes (analogous to the idealization of the superego which accounts for the exalted station of the contents and functions of this structure). Unlike the narcissistic libido, however, which is mobilized in the idealizing transference, the narcissistic component of a normal state of being in love (and of certain phases of the positive transference) does not detach itself from the object cathexes but remains subordinated to them and does not—with the single exception of the moderately unrealistic overestimation of the object—lose touch with the realistic features of the object. If the idealizing tensions of the lover become so great that they cannot be absorbed by the object cathexes, they may escape as if through a safety valve to feed a spurt of creative activity—even though an adequate poetic talent is surely not at the disposal of every amorous would-be poet. Here, too, however, the lover does not lose touch with reality—again with the exception of the moderately unrealistic overestimation of the love object—despite the fact that his creative activity is nourished by narcissistic-idealizing libido. Unlike the unrealistic features of the love experiences of adolescent schizophrenics, for example, whose bizarre artistic products and distorted perception of the love object are sometimes the first overt sign of their mental illness, the normal lover's poems continue to extol the realistic aspects and features of the beloved.

It may be important to point out here that the clinical position of the idealizing transference is different from the role played in the therapeutic process by the idealizations that are encountered in the transference neuroses. In particular we must not confuse (a) the specific, essential, and strategic role of the idealization of the analyst in the idealizing transference of narcissistic personalities; and (b) the ubiquitous, auxiliary, and only tactical role of the idealization of the analyst in the analysis of the transference neuroses. During certain periods of the analysis of transference neuroses the patient does indeed cooperate with the analyst on the basis of a temporary idealization and of a temporary acceptance of the idealized analyst in place of his own superego. Such a temporary and focal identification forms part of the "positive transference" (Freud, 1912), and it belongs to the important "area of cooperation between analyst and patient" (E. Kris, 1951). There is no question about the great importance of these idealizations and identifications since it is only with their aid that many initial steps of inner exploration can be undertaken which would otherwise be prohibited by the archaic superego of the patient (see, for example, Nunberg, 1937, esp. p. 172). This tactical use of the bond with the leader-hypnotist-therapist in the formation of a therapeutic "group" *à deux* on the basis of the acceptance of the leader-analyst as a psychoanalytic ego ideal (Freud, 1921) is, however, a nonspecific phenomenon. To be sure, it constitutes a psychological motive force which may lend decisive support to the patient during stressful periods of the analysis. But this force is at least equally effective in all other forms of psychotherapy, including those whose aims are completely at variance with those of psychoanalysis. It must, therefore, be differentiated from the idealizing transference, which is set into motion and maintained by the mobilization of the idealized parent imago. The manifestations of this analytically reactivated psychological configuration, however, are not auxiliary to the central psychoanalytic task, but they themselves constitute the therapeutically activated center of the pathogenic structures in the patient and thus, in the analysis of narcissistic personalities, the very essence of the analytic work.

A few words will suffice with regard to the well-known idealizations of the analyst which occur in consequence of superego projections. The characteristic features of this idealization are derived from the fact that the wisdom and power with which the analysand credits the idealized therapist resemble the system of idealized standards and values from which the projection arose. These transference projections, furthermore, are temporary, and they do not constitute the center of a basic therapeutic constellation, as is the case in the idealizing transference. They arise at specific junctures in the analysis of transference neuroses, namely, at those times when an unconscious superego-ego conflict begins to be mobilized, and when the analysand—in a defensive move, or as a first step toward the conscious acceptance of the presence of the conflict—experiences the commands of his idealized superego as coming from without, i.e., specifically, as coming from the analyst. In this context the analyst tends to be seen predominantly as an ideal figure in a world of standards and values, and rejections by him are, therefore, in general reacted to by the patient with feelings of guilt and of moral unworthiness.

VARIETIES OF IDEALIZING TRANSFERENCE

The most easily recognizable varieties of the idealizing transference (such as the prevalent transference mode of Mr. A.) relate genetically to disturbances during the later stages of the development of the idealized parent imago, especially just before, during, or immediately after the time when normally the idealized parent imago is introjected and the idealizing libido is employed in the idealization of the superego. If these normal processes of gradual (or massive but phase-appropriate) decathexis of the idealized parent imago are severely disturbed or blocked, then the idealized parent imago is retained, it becomes repressed or otherwise inaccessible[1] to the influences of the reality ego, which would still bring about the withdrawal of the idealizing cathexis, and its gradual (or massive, but phase-appropriate) transmuting internalization is prevented.

As can be regularly ascertained, the essential genetic trauma is grounded in the parents' psychopathology, in particular in the parents' own narcissistic fixations. The parents' pathology and narcissistic needs contribute decisively to the child's remaining excessively and protractedly enmeshed within the narcissistic web of the parents' personality until, for example, a sudden withdrawal of the parent, or the child's sudden desperate recognition of how far out of step his emotional development has become, confronts him with the insuperable task of achieving the wholesale transmuting internalization of a chronic narcissistic relationship from which he had formerly unsuccessfully tried to extricate himself. Occasionally a dramatic external event—such as the death or the prolonged absence of a parent, or a parent's illness or helplessness, as well as severe illnesses of the child which all at once demonstrate the parents' limited power—appears to be the main cause of the relevant childhood disturbance. But these events can only rarely, if ever, explain by themselves the ensuing pathological fixations; they are usually the last, overt link in a chain of frequently unobtrusive yet decisive

[1] Frequently the persistent imago of the archaic, prestructural idealized parent imago is not only kept in repression (i.e., separated from the ego by a horizontal split in the psyche), but it also maintains itself within the realm of the ego itself, akin to the conditions described by Freud (1927) for the fetishist (i.e., separated from the reality ego by a vertical split in the ego). This topic will be further pursued in Chapter 7, where the concepts of "vertical" and "horizontal" splits in the psyche are also discussed in detail.

psychological antecedents. They must be understood in the context of the parents' personality and of the history of the parents' whole relationship with the child prior to the external event that became the seed around which the child's psychopathology crystallized. The complexity of the pathogenic interplay between parent and child and the limitless varieties of its forms defy the attempt of a comprehensive description. Yet in a properly conducted analysis, the crucial pattern will often emerge with great clarity, and its detailed understanding constitutes an important, at times decisive step in the analysand's progressive mastery of his fears when the seemingly fixed narcissistic patterns are being loosened.

Mr. B., for example, whose analysis was conducted by a colleague (a woman) in regular consultation with me, established a specific narcissistic transference in which he felt merged with the idealized analyst. The therapist's attention effectively counteracted the tendency toward the fragmentation and discontinuity of the patient's self experience, solidifying his self-esteem and thus secondarily improving his ego functioning and efficiency. To any impending disruption of this beneficial deployment of narcissistic cathexes that was provided by his relationship with the analyst, he reacted at first with great apprehension, followed by a decathexis of the narcissistically invested analyst (accompanied by intense oral-sadistic rage) which seriously threatened the cohesiveness of his personality. Then followed a typical reactive hypercathexis of a primitive form of the grandiose self, with cold and imperious behavior. But, finally (after the analyst had been away for a while), he reached a comparatively stable balance on a more primitive level: he withdrew to lonely intellectual activities which, although he pursued them with less creativity than previously, provided him with a certain sense of mastery, security, and self-sufficiency. In his words, formulated later in the analysis, he "rowed out alone to the middle of the lake and looked at the moon." When the analyst returned, however, and the possibility of re-establishing the

relationship to the idealized self-object offered itself, he reacted with the same apprehension and the mobilization of the
same threatening oral-sadistic rage that he had experienced
when the original narcissistic transference had become "un-
plugged," to use his own significant analogy.

At first I thought that the reaction to the return of the
analyst was a nonspecific one, consisting of two components:
(a) of still unexpressed aspects of the original anger about the
analyst's leaving, which had been kept in abeyance for the
analyst's return, and (b) of a nonspecific rage at having to
give up a newfound balance which—albeit less satisfactory
than the earlier one—protected him against being again
traumatized by the analyst's absences and withdrawals. Although to a certain extent these explanations were correct,
they were incomplete so long as the highly specific genetic
precursor of the current reactions was not taken into account.
The patient was in fact by his reactions describing an important sequence of early events.

The patient's mother had been intensely enmeshed with
him and had supervised and controlled him in a most strin-
gent fashion. His exact feeding time, for example, and, in later
childhood, his eating time, were determined by a mechanical
timer which the mother used as an extension of her need to
control the child's activities—reminiscent of the devices which
Schreber's father employed with his children (see Niederland,
1959a)—and thus the child felt increasingly that he had no
mind of his own and that the mother was continuing to
perform his mental functions long beyond the time when
such maternal activities, empathically performed, are indeed
phase-appropriate and required. Under the impact of the
anxious recognition of the inappropriateness of this relationship, carried forward by maturational pressures, and attempting to surmount his fearful apprehension about striving to
attain greater autonomy, he would in later childhood withdraw to his room, locking the doors, to think his own
thoughts uninfluenced by her interference. When he had

just begun to achieve some reliance on this minimum of autonomous functioning, his mother had a buzzer installed. From then on, she would interrupt his attempts at internal separation from her whenever he wanted to be alone; and she would summon him to her, more compellingly (because the mechanical device was experienced as akin to an endopsychic communication) than would have been her voice, or knocking, against which he could have rebelled. No wonder, then, that he reacted with rage to the return of the analyst after he had "rowed to the center of the lake to look at the moon."

As I have stressed repeatedly, in the vast majority of even the most severe narcissistic personality disturbances, it is the child's reaction to the parent rather than to gross traumatic events in the early biography which accounts for the narcissistic fixations. It must be added, however, that such events in the early life of a child as the absence of a parent (see A. Freud and D. Burlingham, 1942, 1943), or loss of a parent through death, divorce, hospitalization, or his withdrawal because of emotional illness contribute to the narcissistic fixation in a negative sense, i.e., the child is now deprived of the chance of freeing himself from the enmeshment through the gradual withdrawal of narcissistic cathexes which is required for a transmuting, structure-forming internalization. The period which follows the sudden interruption (through an external event) of a child's chronic narcissistic enmeshment with a pathological parent is indeed crucial. It may determine whether the child will make a renewed effort toward maturational progress or whether the pathogenic fixation will now become ingrained. The absence or loss of the pathological parent may be a wholesome liberation if the child's libidinal resources enable him to move forward and, especially if the other parent, or a parent substitute with a special empathic interest in the threatened child, jumps quickly into the breach and permits a temporary re-establishment of the narcissistic relationship as well as its subsequent gradual dissolution. If no substitute is available, however, or if the child's available libidinal resources already were bound too firmly on the pathological parent, then the parent's unavailability contributes to the maintenance and firming of the pathology. The decisive repression of the (archaic) idealized parent imago (or other modes of its inaccessibility, e.g., through a "vertical" split in the psyche) may take place after the external disappearance of the parent; the ensuing fixation on the unconscious, or, as is frequently the case, split-off and disavowed (see Freud, 1925; Jacobson, 1957; Basch, 1968) fantasy of an omnipotent idealized parental figure prevents the gradual or phase-appropriate *transmuting* internalization of the corresponding narcissistic configuration.

A protracted manifest hypercathexis of the idealized parent imago may thus appear in childhood when, during an extended period of separation from a parent, the child is not able to withdraw the idealizing cathexes from him (i.e., when he is not able to see the parent in an increasingly realistic light) and to employ them in the formation of psychic structure. So long as the idealizing fantasies are (pre)conscious and the idealizing libido remains mobile, such occurrences are neither an indication of the existence of current childhood psychopathology nor do they presage a later disturbance. The fantasies about an idealized father spun out by children who were deprived of their fathers during the Second World War belong in this context (see A. Freud and D. Burlingham, 1943; esp. p. 112ff.). The fact that the child endows the "fantasy father" with grandiose features is, I believe, not in the main to be understood in the Adlerian sense (1912), i.e., as an overcompensation meant to counteract the deprivation and to cover a defect. It is rather the fact that the *primarily existing* narcissistic idealization now has no realistic object in relation to which a gradual disillusionment can be experienced. The lack of opportunity to discover the realistic shortcomings of the father accounts for the continuing idealization since decathexis and concomitant structure formation are temporarily delayed. Such fantasies, as noted before, may be formed, consciously elaborated, and temporarily clung to in response to an external deprivation which requires the postponement of a developmental task. The underlying principle, however, which governs the *temporary* conscious elaboration of a hypercathected idealized parent imago is the same as that which determines the acquisition of *permanent* fixations and of *chronic* psychopathology. The decisive difference lies in the fact that in the latter case the idealized parent imago (the fantasy of the omnipotent father, for example) becomes repressed and/or split off. No modification of the fantasy can then take place (nor can it be integrated with the reality ego) without analysis, even if a wholesome parent surrogate should offer itself, or if the parent returns. Unconsciously fixated on an idealized self-object for which they continue to yearn, and deprived of a sufficiently idealized superego, such persons are forever searching for external omnipotent powers from whose support and approval they attempt to derive strength. In analysis, however, these strivings lead to a conspicuous idealization of the analyst (occasionally appearing only after specific resistances against the establishment of the transference have been dealt with); they become available to scrutiny and enable the patient to withdraw the narcissistic cathexes from the repressed idealized parent imago. These processes lead then, simultaneously, not only to a strengthening of the drive-controlling basic structure of the analysand's ego but also, especially, to the idealization of his superego.

Although for purposes of expository simplicity, the preceding instances of idealizing transference were described as related to comparatively late stages of the idealized parent imago, an exact separation of the transference reactivations of the more mature from those of the more archaic forms of this structure cannot be carried out in a neat and orderly fashion without doing violence to the complexity of the actual clinical situation. Thus, although Mr. A.'s idealizing transference, for example, related predominantly to a mature form of the idealized father imago, certain aspects of his personality (referred to previously as the patient's diffuse narcissistic vulnerability) related to an archaic, preverbal need for a perfectly responding, omnipotent, idealized mother-breast and led in the analysis to certain archaic aspects of the idealizing transference which corresponded to an early level of narcissistic fixation. The major aspects of the transference in the case of B., too, were a revival of comparatively late, differentiated aspects of the idealized imago, the hub of the pathology probably relating to a period of maternal depression after a set of twins died shortly after birth when the patient was three years old. Here, too, however, there were significant, very early pathogenic fixation points which concerned the relationship with his pathological mother—she was addicted to barbiturates—during the preverbal stage. In particular there was convincing evidence in the analysis that the unempathic mother, through either insufficient or, at other times, excessive stimulation, had exposed the child to severe traumatization in the tactile sphere.

In view of the telescoping of the earlier forms of idealization with the later ones, I shall dispense with the attempt at an extensive separate discussion of the archaic form of the idealizing transference. It may manifest itself through the expression of vague and mystical religious preoccupations with isolated awe-inspiring qualities which no longer emanate from a clearly delimited, unitary admired figure. Although the manifestations of archaic levels of idealizing transference are thus at times less clear-cut (especially where it merges into the therapeutic activation of the grandiose self), there is never any doubt that a specific emotional bond to the analyst has been formed. Metapsychologically expressed, the regression set in motion by the analytic situation strives toward the establishment of a narcissistic equilibrium, which is experienced as boundless power and knowledge and as aesthetic and moral perfection. (These attributes are still more or less undifferentiated from each other in those instances where the therapeutic regression leads to very early fixation points.) This equilibrium can be maintained as long as the analysand can sustain the feeling that he has become united with the image of the idealized analyst. Once the pathognomonic point of the regression has been reached and a union with the corresponding idealized self-object has been established, the ensuing narcissistic peace leads to a clinical picture of improved functioning. It diminishes the threat of further narcissistic regression—in particular the retreat to the most archaic precursors of the idealized parent imago (e.g., toward a hypomanic fusion with it which is sometimes manifested as a state of quasi-religious ecstasy) or the retreat toward a hypercathexis of the most primitive forms of the grandiose self and, fleetingly, even of the (autoerotic) fragments of the body-self. In addition, there ensues a lessening of the previously present symptomatology which is characteristic for the narcissistic disorders, i.e., of the patient's vague and diffuse depression, disturbed work capacity, and irritability; and of his self-consciousness, shame propensity, hypochondriacal preoccupations, and ill-defined physical discomforts. These symptoms which are manifestations of an instinctual hypercathexis of archaic forms of the grandiose self, with temporary swings toward the (autoerotic) body self, tend to abate early in the analysis because the initial therapeutic activation of the idealized object mobilizes the narcissistic cathexes and deploys them in the idealizing transference.

THE PROCESS OF WORKING THROUGH AND OTHER CLINICAL
PROBLEMS IN THE IDEALIZING TRANSFERENCE

As is the case in the analysis of the transference neuroses, the major clinical problems surrounding the transference can be divided into those which concern the period when the transference is being established and those which concern the period after its establishment, i.e., the period of working through.

Little need be said concerning the first period. Not infrequently the patient becomes aware of inner conflicts activated by certain ego resistances against regression. Anxiety dreams of falling may occur (they appear to be the obverse rendition of flying fantasies); they are encountered especially in patients who are about to develop a reactivation of the grandiose self in a mirror transference (see Part II). And there are early dreams in which the analysand sees himself confronted with the task of climbing a high-soaring majestic mountain and looks apprehensively at the steep path and its treacherous surface in the search for a reliable footing or a secure hold. These dreams occur especially in patients who are about to develop an idealizing transference. No analyst needs to be told, of course, that dreams containing either the dread of falling or the apprehension vis-à-vis a steep mountain may occur in a great variety of psychological situations and express conflicts referring to a variety of developmental levels, including not only the well-known and thoroughly investigated conflicts about phallic assertion and castration fears but also, on the ego level, the nonspecific fear of regression (falling) and the apprehension vis-à-vis a difficult task (mountain). In the analysis of narcissistic personalities, however, such dreams not only give the analyst an early differentiating indication with regard to the type of narcissistic transference that is being mobilized, but their details may also provide him with specific, invaluable clues concerning specific resistances against the establishment of the transference. Is the mobilization of idealizing cathexes, for instance, feared and resisted because the narcissistically invested objects which the child tried to idealize were cold and unresponsive (an icy mountain; a mountain of marble or glass), unreachably distant, or unpredictable and unreliable? Again, there is no need to go into detail since every analyst can easily draw the empirical data from his own relevant case material. In the pre-stages of an idealizing transference there may also appear indications (in dreams and associations, often concerning seemingly abstract, philosophical and quasi-religious preoccupations about questions of existence, life and death) that the patient is afraid of the extinction of his individuality by the deep wish to merge with and into the idealized object.

The analyst should acknowledge the presence of all these resistances and define them to the patient with friendly understanding, but in general he need do nothing further to provide reassurance. He can, on the whole, expect that the pathognomonic regression will establish itself spontaneously if he does not interfere by premature transference interpretations (which the analysand understands as prohibitions or expressions of disapproval) or other deleterious moves. The description of the analyst's proper attitude as given by Freud for the analysis of the transference neuroses also applies in general to the analysis of narcissistic personality disturbances. In order to establish a "proper *rapport*" with the patient, Freud (1913) said, "nothing need be done but to give him time. If one exhibits a serious interest in him, carefully clears away the resistances that crop up at the beginning . . . he will form . . . an attachment and link the doctor up with one of the imagos of people by whom he was accustomed to be treated with affection" (p. 139f.). Certain obvious modifications in Freud's statement would have to be made in order to make it fully applicable to the treatment of narcissistic personality disturbances and, especially, to the establishment of a narcissistic transference. The basic attitude, however, which Freud recommends is as valid here as it is in the transference neuroses.

A number of mistakes which analysts tend to make during this phase will be taken up later in the context of certain typical reactions of the analyst which are prone to occur during the analysis of narcissistic personality disturbances. At this point I wish to emphasize only that an unusually friendly behavior from the side of the analyst, at times justified by the need to create a therapeutic alliance,[2] is no more advisable in the analysis of narcissistic personality disturbances than it is in the analysis of transference neuroses. In the latter case it is experienced as seductive and is likely to produce transference artifacts; in the case of the narcissistic personality disorders it is in general reacted to by the sensitive patient as a patronizing attitude which hurts the analysand's pride, increases his isolation and suspiciousness (i.e., his propensity to retreat toward an archaic form of the grandiose self), and thus interferes with the spontaneous establishment of the patient's specific pathognomonic regression.

The working-through phase of the analysis which relates specifically to the idealizing transference can begin only after the pathognomonic idealizing transference has been established. It is set in motion by the fact that the basic instinctual equilibrium which the analysand's psyche aims to establish initially in the treatment situation and which it attempts to maintain is sooner or later disturbed. In contrast, however, to the vicissitudes of the psychoanalytic process in the transference neuroses, the initial equilibrium in the analytic treatment of the narcissistic disorders is not primarily disturbed by the tensions of unconscious demands that are focused on

[2] The useful concept of a therapeutic (or working) alliance (Zetzel, 1956; Greenson, 1967) has been a healthy reminder to some analysts that the psychological framework which supports the analytic work deserves the analyst's interest and attention. Expressed in different words, it has helped to dispel the notion that the neutrality of the analyst is to be understood in a physicalistic sense rather than psychologically—as, of course, it must be—as average, expectable humane responsiveness. To remain silent when one is asked a question, for example, is not neutral but rude. It goes without saying that—given specific clinical circumstances, and after appropriate explanations—there are moments in analysis when the analyst will not pretend to respond to the patient's pseudorealistic requests but will instead insist on the investigation of their transference meaning.

In this context, however, it must also be said that a concentration on the realistic interactions between analyst and patient may, for some, become an escape route from the analytic work: the interest in the current interactions may begin to serve as a (counter)resistance against the investigation of the central psychoanalytic material, i.e., of the transference. (For further remarks concerning this topic see the discussion in Chapter 8 of the analysand's so-called "positive transference" to, or "rapport" with, the analyst.)

the analyst and by the defenses against them which are mobilized by the ego in the form of resistances against the work of analysis. In view of the fact that the narcissistic equilibrium depends on the analysand's narcissistic relationship to an archaic, narcissistically experienced, prestructural self-object, the disturbance of the equilibrium is here, in essence, caused by certain external circumstances. In the undisturbed transference the narcissistic patient feels whole, safe, powerful, good, attractive, active so long as his self experience includes the idealized analyst whom he feels he controls and possesses with a self-evident certainty that is akin to the adult's experience of his control over his own body and mind. After the sudden loss of the unquestioned control over one's body and mind (in consequence of organic brain damage, for example) most individuals tend to react with specific severe forms of despondency and helpless rage. Analogous reactions occur in the analysis of narcissistic personality disorders. Thus, after he has reached the stage of narcissistic union with an archaic idealized self-object, the analysand responds initially with rage and despondency (which may be followed by a temporary regression to experiences of fusion with the most archaic idealized self-object or to a shift of the narcissistic investments to a hypercathexis of archaic forms of the grandiose self and, fleetingly, even of the autoerotic, fragmented body self) to any event that disrupts his narcissistic control over the archaic parent imago, the analyst.

A detailed examination of the analysand's experience of the narcissistically invested object should provide features which differentiate the analysand's relationship to the idealized object (idealizing transference) from that in which the analyst is experienced as an extension of the grandiose self (mirror transference). And differentiating characteristics do indeed exist. The presence of the idealized self-object is often accepted with the same self-evident certainty with which we accept the presence of the life-sustaining framework of the surrounding air and of the solid ground on which we stand. The analogy between the analysand's relationship with the analyst in the narcissistic transference and the adult's experience of his own body and mind applies thus in general more fully to those cases where the grandiose self has become activated and the analyst is included in the expanded self (mirror transference). Nevertheless, when either one of the narcissistic transferences is interrupted, the patient's reaction tends to be one of having lost control— except, perhaps, for a greater emphasis on the experience of despondency when the idealized object is lost in the transference relationship as compared with a greater emphasis on the reaction of rage when the expanded self has become unavailable.

The foregoing considerations—specifically the fact that, after the pathognomonic therapeutic regression has taken place, the analysand experiences the analyst narcissistically, i.e., not as a separate and independent individual—explain the strategic role played in the course of the analysis not only by the patient's rage, despondency, and regressive retreat when facing extended separations from the analyst (such as the summer vacation) but also by his severe reactions to small signs of coolness from the side of the therapist, or to the analyst's lack of immediate and complete empathic understanding, and, especially, to such apparently trivial external events as minor irregularities in the appointment schedule, weekend separations, and slight tardiness of the therapist. Significantly, and understandably in view of the narcissistic nature of the relationship, the analysand reacts with rage against the therapist even when schedule irregularities and interruptions occur which are undertaken at the request and for the benefit of the analysand. Similar reactions are, of course, also encountered in the analysis of the transference neuroses; they are familiar to all analysts and they play there an important tactical role since, nonspecific though they are in this context, they open not infrequently the transference access to specific vicissitudes of the analysand's infantile object investments. The significance of these occurrences, however, is different in the analysis of the narcissistic personality disorders. Here the patient's reactions to the disturbance of his relationship with a narcissistically experienced object by such events occupy a central position of strategic importance that corresponds to the place of the structural conflict in the psychoneuroses.

Anything that deprives the patient of the idealized analyst creates a disturbance of his self-esteem: he begins to feel lethargic, powerless, and worthless, and, if his ego is not assisted in dealing with the narcissistic disequilibrium by the correct interpretation concerning the loss of the idealized self-object, the patient may, as stated earlier, turn to archaic precursors of the idealized parent imago or may abandon it altogether and shift to reactively mobilized archaic stages of the grandiose self. Such temporary cathectic shifts may be precipitated by seemingly minute narcissistic injuries the discovery of which may put the analyst's empathy and clinical acumen to a severe test. It is in keeping with the narcissistic nature of the patient's relationship to the analyst that, even if we give due consideration to the patient's extreme sensitivity, it is difficult to explain the traumatic impact of the analyst's physical or emotional withdrawal from the analysand in terms of adult logic, or to describe it with the terms of the language of adults. Yet, if the analyst takes into account the nature of the archaic relationship in which the self of the analysand has become grafted onto the omnipotent therapist, he will comprehend that, on the essential level of the therapeutic regression, the patient's reproaches to him concerning a separation are meaningful and justified, even in instances when the separation is realistically minute or when it was initiated by the patient himself.

The archaic nature of the transference accounts, therefore, for certain of the patients' experiences and for the formal characteristics of their reactions, and the analyst must, in general, adjust his empathy to the level of the narcissistic regression. The analyst's grasp of the regressive mode of the interplay with the archaic idealized object must, nevertheless, not induce him to neglect a thorough scrutiny of the precipitating external events or to fail to examine, as accurately as possible, the specific psychological interactions that have set the disturbance of the narcissistic equilibrium into motion.

For example, Mr. G., a severely disturbed twenty-five-year-old man, responded to my announcement that I would be away for a week by an ominous shift of the narcissistic cathexes from the archaic idealized self-object to a primitive form of the grandiose self. Interpretations focused on the meaning of the future separation on the level of object love and narcissism, in their libidinal and aggressive dimensions, were in vain, and the patient remained coldly isolated, near-delusionally superior, and hypochondriacal with a strong paranoid cast. The massive and extensive shift of the instinctual cathexes made it impossible for the patient to lead the analyst toward the crucial event that had precipitated the malignant development. I finally stumbled on the correct insight and thus enabled Mr. G. to examine the significance of his reaction to the separation. What had caused the patient's withdrawal was not my forthcoming absence, but the tone in which I had announced it. The tone, to put it in a nutshell, had been unempathic and defensive. Anticipating a stormy response (such as anxious phone calls in the middle of the night) and bracing myself against it with an unspoken sigh of "Well, here we go again!" I had indeed thought primarily of myself as I made the announcement and had not mobilized the requisite attitude of expectant, neutral readiness to respond empathically to the patient's feelings. It was in reaction to this attitude that the patient had experienced a traumatic disappointment in my empathic capacity which he had previously idealized as limitless,[3] and no progress was

[3] See also the brief description of this episode, and especially of the patient's immediate dream response which depicts his disappointment with the formerly idealized object, the limitlessly empathic analyst, who in the dream had become a breast made out of rubber (Kohut, 1959, p. 471).

made until I could offer my understanding and thus again enable the patient to recathect the idealized self-object.

The preceding illustration exemplifies the existence of countless clinical variations in the analysis of narcissistic disorders; the essence of the curative process, however, can be epitomized in a few comparatively simple principles.

In the analysis of the transference neuroses, we aim at achieving an expansion of the (pre)conscious ego. The increasing dominance of the ego over the infantile aims and desires and the increasing autonomy of the ego's own goal structures are achieved in consequence of the ego's repeated exposure (a) to manageable portions of the repressed libidinal and aggressive strivings which are mobilized as they become focused on the analyst, and (b) to the unconscious mechanisms by which these strivings are fended off. The major work (the overcoming of the most important ego and superego resistances) in the transference neuroses deals with the ego's reluctance to admit the repressed instinctual strivings into its realm. The relinquishment of the childhood objects, however, in the analysis of the typical transference neurosis, is effected almost imperceptively,[4] *pari passu* with the struggle to undo the repressions, and a patient's reluctance to part with the incestuous object (an id resistance) is only occasionally and temporarily the major focus of the analysis. Indeed, should the reluctance to part with the childhood object become the major, and chronic, resistance in the analysis, the analyst will do well to consider the possibility that he is not dealing with an uncomplicated transference neurosis but that narcissistic elements are hiding behind the manifest incestuous object cathexes.

In the analysis of the narcissistic personality disorders, an analogous working-through process is set into motion in

---

[4] I am here disregarding the temporary regressions which are characteristic for the beginning of the terminal phase of the analysis of transference neuroses in which the patient recathects once more his demands for the incestuous transference objects before he finally resigns himself to the fact that they are indeed unobtainable.

which the repressed and/or split-off (here: narcissistic) strivings with which the archaic self-object is invested are guided
into contact with, and are ultimately brought under the
dominance of, the reality ego. In contrast to the conditions
which prevail in the analysis of transference neuroses, the
major part of the working-through process in the analysis of
narcissistic personality disturbances does not concern the
overcoming of ego and superego resistances against the undoing of repressions. Although such resistances also occur
here, including the well-known nonspecific narcissistic resistances[5] (see, e.g., Abraham, 1919; and W. Reich, 1933),
and although there are in addition specific ego resistances (motivated by shame and by hypochondriacal apprehensions as
well as by anxiety concerning hypomanic overstimulation)
which oppose the mobilization of the narcissistic cathexes and
of their recognition, the essential part of the working-through
process concerns here the ego's reaction to the loss of the
narcissistically experienced object.

The working-through process in the idealizing transference
thus differs decisively from that which occurs in the analysis

5 Such nonspecific narcissistic ego resistances tend to occur in the earlier
parts of analyses in both transference neuroses and narcissistic personality
disturbances. A typical example is the following. After a session in which I
demonstrated to patient O. that he was reacting to a forthcoming separation
with a lowering of his moral and aesthetic standards and with a neglect of
his body self, the patient responded in the subsequent hour by criticizing my
technique, my choice of words, etc., in a superior, yet indeed most skillful
and objective way in which realistic perceptions of my shortcomings were put
to a specific defensive use. (It might be mentioned here that a prior analysis
seems to have come to grief because this resistance was not analyzed but was
treated by friendly exhortations, admonishments, and the like, probably employed in the service of maintaining the therapeutic alliance.) Headway in
overcoming the resistance could be made, however (and first glimpses of
significant genetic material could simultaneously be obtained), when—after
accepting the realistic aspects of the patient's critique with as much good
humor as I was able to muster—the patient's attempt to wound the analyst's
self-esteem could be shown to be a "turning from passive into active" or a
kind of "identification with the aggressor." The patient demonstrated by his
behavior (and the careful scrutiny of his method gave access to an increasing
understanding of what he felt) that he experienced my interpretations (and,
in essence, the whole process of analysis) as a painful insult, i.e., as a well-
nigh unbearable narcissistic injury.

of the transference neuroses. In the transference neuroses defenses are removed, object-instinctual investments are given access to the ego, and the result is an improved arrangement of psychological structures, e.g., an increased dominance of the ego over the drives and the defenses. An analogous process also takes place as a first step in the working-through process of the analysis of narcissistic personality disorders as the split-off and/or repressed narcissistic cathexes and the narcissistically cathected prestructural self-object are given access to the reality ego. The essential working-through process, however, aims at the gradual withdrawal of the narcissistic libido from the narcissistically invested, archaic, object; it leads to the acquisition of new psychological structures and functions as the cathexes shift from the representation of the object and its activities to the psychic apparatus and its functions. In the specific case of the idealizing transference the working-through process concerns, of course, specifically the withdrawal of idealizing cathexes from the idealized parent imago and, concomitantly, (a) the building up of drive-regulating structures in the ego, and (b) the increased idealization of the superego.

Various aspects of the present discussion concerning the metapsychology of the therapeutic process in the analysis of narcissistic personalities apply not only to the mobilization of the idealized parent imago in the idealizing transference but also to the therapeutic reactivation of the grandiose self in the mirror transference (see Part II). The psychoeconomic principles which determine the course and speed of the analysis are identical for both of these major forms of narcissistic transference. The developmental and dynamic-structural position of the two reactivated narcissistic configurations, however, are different, and the important temporary regressive and progressive swings which occur in the transference as a result of the patient's reactions to the analyst are, therefore, also not the same.

Diagram 2 outlines, in a schematic form, the temporary regressions which occur characteristically during the working-through process. (The return to the relative equilibrium of the transference would, of course, have to be indicated by a reversal of the arrows.)

DIAGRAM 2

SCHEMA OF THE TYPICAL REGRESSIVE SWINGS WHICH OCCUR DURING THE ANALYSIS OF NARCISSISTIC PERSONALITY DISORDERS

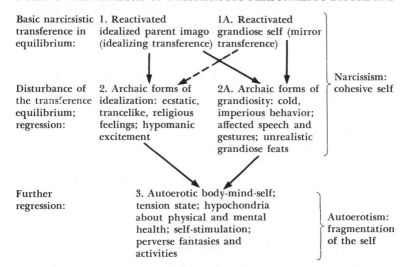

Basic narcissistic transference in equilibrium:

1. Reactivated idealized parent imago (idealizing transference)

1A. Reactivated grandiose self (mirror transference)

Disturbance of the transference equilibrium; regression:

2. Archaic forms of idealization: ecstatic, trancelike, religious feelings; hypomanic excitement

2A. Archaic forms of grandiosity: cold, imperious behavior; affected speech and gestures; unrealistic grandiose feats

Narcissism: cohesive self

Further regression:

3. Autoerotic body-mind-self; tension state; hypochondria about physical and mental health; self-stimulation; perverse fantasies and activities

Autoerotism: fragmentation of the self

All the arrows indicating the direction of the regressive swings which occur during the working-through process are solid, which indicates that the occurrence of the specific process has been substantiated by numerous clinical observations. The swing from 1A to 2, however, is marked by a broken line. I have only recently, and for the first time, encountered the regular occurrence of this specific psychological event during the analysis of a patient in whom the activation of the grandiose self seems to constitute the basic transference. In view of the fact, however, that this analysis, though in an advanced state, is not yet completed, I hesitate to claim with absolute certainty that the presenting mirror transference may not be masking an underlying idealization (as appears to be the case, for example, with certain types of juvenile delinquents referred to in Chapter 7).

In the idealizing transference the working-through process thus concerns the following typical sequence of events: (1) the patient's loss of the narcissistic union with the idealized self-object; (2) the ensuing disturbance of the narcissistic balance; (3) the subsequent hypercathexis of archaic forms of either (a) the idealized parent imago or (b) the grandiose self; and, fleetingly, (4) the hypercathexis of the (autoerotic) fragmented body-mind-self.

Over and over again will the analysand experience these regressive swings after suffering a disappointment in the idealized analyst. But he will be enabled to return to the basic idealizing transference with the aid of the appropriate interpretation. Here, even more than in the analysis of the transference resistances in the transference neuroses, the repeated analysis of the same or of similar experiences is required, and the ego's (often very narrow) scope in tolerating the (therapeutic) narcissistic deprivations must be assessed correctly. If the repeated interpretations of the meaning of separations from the analyst on the level of the idealizing narcissistic libido are not given mechanically, but with correct empathy for the analysand's feelings—sometimes in particular for what appears to be his lack of emotions, i.e., his coldness and retreat in response to separations (see especially position 2A in Diagram 2)—then there will gradually emerge a host of meaningful memories which concern the dynamic prototypes of the present experience. Here, as in the analogous phases of the working-through process in the mirror transference, new memories will emerge, and memories that have always been conscious will become intelligible in the light of the present transference experiences.

The patient will, for example, recall lonely hours during his childhood in which he experienced intense voyeuristic preoccupations (the child's searching through the drawers in an empty house) and engaged in perverse activities (a boy's putting on his mother's underwear). These activities will then become intelligible when they are understood not so much as sexual transgressions that are undertaken while external surveillance is lacking but rather as attempts to supply substitutes for the idealized parent imago and its functions by creating erotized replacements and through the frantic hypercathexis of the grandiose self. Viewed metapsychologically the deeply frightening feelings of fragmentation and deadness which the child experiences are a manifestation of the fact that, in the absence of the narcissistically invested self-object, the cathexis is withdrawn from a cohesively experienced self and regressive (autoerotic) fragmentation and hypochondriacal tensions now threaten the child (see position 3 in Diagram 2). The various perverse activities in which the child engages are thus attempts to re-establish the union with the narcissistically invested lost object through visual fusion and other archaic forms of identification.

The patient may furthermore often remember, and gratefully understand, how he tried to revive the feeling of a cohesive self by a variety of self-applied stimuli: putting the face against the cold floor in the basement; looking in the mirror to reassure himself that he is there and that he is whole; smelling a variety of substances, and smelling his own body odor; various oral and masturbatory activities; and the (often grandiose and dangerous) performance of various athletic feats (jumping from high places, climbing over rooftops, etc.) in which flying fantasies were being enacted by the child, in order to reassure himself about the reality of his physical existence (see position 2A in Diagram 2) in the absence of the omnipotent self-object. Adult analogues (during the weekend, for example, when the analyst's integrating attention is withdrawn) are intense voyeuristic preoccupations, the temptation to steal (shoplift), and recklessly speedy drives in the car. Less uncontrolled, less unrealistically grandiose, and thus less dangerous, are the long restless walks which the patient undertakes in order to gain reassurance about being alive and whole through sexualized sensory and proprioceptive stimulation. The meaningful recall of the relevant childhood memories and the ever-deepening understanding of the analogous transference experiences converge in giving assistance to the patient's ego, and the formerly automatic reactions become gradually more aim-inhibited and are more under the control of the ego. During transitional phases the patient will give evidence of the fact that his increasing insight has led to greater ego dominance, e.g., by changing from dangerous perverse peeping acts to socially acceptable artistic activities (photography, watercoloring, etc.) and from being driven toward the undertaking of endless lonely and desperate walks to socially integrated forms of athletic or artistic body stimulation in sports and musical activities. Whatever the behavioral details of the changes may be, there is no question that they are due to the fact that the working-through process leads to the accretion of psychic structure, just as happens in the transference neuroses as the result of the analogous analytic work.

Not only is the ego's sublimatory ability increased (as evidenced by the patient's changing external attitudes); the ego also demonstrates in the transference that it has acquired increasing tolerance for the analyst's absence, for a break in the routine of the appointments (regularity of appointments with the analyst always becomes equivalent to the analyst's continuous presence), and for the analyst's occasional failure to achieve immediately a correct empathic understanding. The patient learns that the idealizing libido (admiration and esteem) need not be immediately withdrawn from the imago of the idealized self-object, that the tension of longing for the absent idealized self-object can be tolerated, and that the painful, and at times dangerously isolating, regressive shifts of the narcissistic cathexes to the archaic forms of the idealized self-object and grandiose self and to the fragmented (autoerotic) body-mind-self can be prevented. Concomitant with the increase in the ability to maintain a part of the investment of the self-object with idealizing cathexes, despite the external separation from it, there is an enhancement of the processes which lead to transmuting internalizations (i.e., the object can be relinquished and the analysand's psychic organization acquires the capacity to perform some of the functions which had previously been performed by the object).

The patient's ability to maintain object cathexes in the nonnarcissistic sectors of his personality may also improve when his narcissistic fixations have been loosened, and the idealizing component of mature forms of object investments may thus become increasingly capable of absorbing some of the narcissistic energies that had become mobilized in the analysis of the narcissistic sector. The essential therapeutic progress in the analysis of the archaic investments of the idealized object imago, however, occurs in consequence of the transmuting internalization of the narcissistic energies as the idealized self-object is relinquished. It leads to the redistribution of the narcissistic energies in the personality itself, i.e., (a) to the strengthening and expanson of the basic neutralizing structure of the psyche and thus, secondarily, to increased drive control and increased capacity for deinstinctualization; (b) to the formation of ideals or to their strengthening; and (c) to the acquisition of a number of more highly differentiated psychological attributes which utilize the narcissistic instinctual energies that have become available to the patient.

PART II

THE THERAPEUTIC ACTIVATION OF
THE GRANDIOSE SELF

CHAPTER 5

TYPES OF MIRROR TRANSFERENCES: A CLASSIFICATION ACCORDING TO DEVELOPMENTAL CONSIDERATIONS

The idealizing transference discussed in Part I constitutes the therapeutic revival of that aspect of a developmental phase in which the child attempts to save the original narcissism by giving it over to a narcissistically experienced omnipotent and perfect self-object. Under favorable circumstances the child gradually faces the realistic limitations of the idealized self-object, gives up the idealizations, and *pari passu* makes transmuting reinternalizations. In these not only the genesis from the original narcissistic source is still recognizable, they also may bear the individual imprint of the real parental object through which the narcissistic configurations had passed before they became reinternalized. Thus the content of the oedipally internalized values and ideals of the superego (and the specific mode of the preoedipally internalized drive-controlling basic structure of the ego) are decisively influenced by the specific values and ideals held by the parents (and by the favored modes of drive control employed by them, such as seductiveness or threats); the specific absolutarian flavor, however, of the central, idealized values of the superego and the almost unalterable condition of the ego's central armamentarium of drive control and drive discharge

105

are manifestations of the fact that these structures are descendants of the child's original narcissistic state and are thus the carriers of some of that absolute perfection and power which were characteristic of their ancestral archaic organization. If the optimal transmuting internalization of the idealized self-object is interfered with, then, as demonstrated in the preceding chapters, the idealized object is retained as an archaic prestructural object, is revivable in analysis in the cohesive form of the idealizing transference, and the process of reinternalization which was traumatically interrupted in childhood can now be taken up again during the analysis.

In analogy to the cohesive therapeutic revival of the idealized self-object in the idealizing transference, the grandiose self is therapeutically reactivated in the transferencelike condition for which the term *mirror transference,* despite its insufficient inclusiveness, will usually be employed. The mirror transference and its precursors thus constitute the therapeutic revival of that aspect of a developmental phase (roughly corresponding to the condition which Freud referred to as the "purified pleasure ego") in which the child attempts to save the originally all-embracing narcissism by concentrating perfection and power upon the self—here called the grandiose self—and by turning away disdainfully from an outside to which all imperfections have been assigned.[1]

Although the detailed reconstruction of the sequence of developmental stages on the basis of analytic material is fraught with uncertainties, no observational material known to me opposes the view favored by theoretical considerations

[1]Later analogues with which these two major narcissistic configurations of early life can be compared (but with which they are by no means identical) are: (1) the phenomenon of social, racial, or national prejudice in which the ingroup, the center of all perfection and power, corresponds to the grandiose self, while everything imperfect is assigned to the outgroup (see Kaplan and Whitman, 1965; Whitman and Kaplan, 1968); (2) the relationship of the true believer to his God (see Jones, 1913) in which the figure of the perfect and omnipotent God, with whom the powerless and humble believer wants to merge, corresponds to the ancient omnipotent self-object, the idealized parent imago.

that the creation of the idealized self-object and of the grand-iose self are two facets of the same developmental phase, or, in other words, that they occur simultaneously. I believe that the tendency to assume that the grandiose self is the more primitive of the two structures rests on the same prejudice which assigns to object love, without qualification, the su-premacy over narcissism. Objectively, however, the original narcissism not only is a precursor of object love but also undergoes itself an important development in two directions of which the grandiose self and the idealized parent imago are more or less simultaneous way stations. The theoretical recognition of the parallelism of these streams of development does, however, not imply that in all individuals the develop-mental emphasis is equally distributed in all three directions. On the contrary, it is just the fact that in certain persons the major emphasis (and the major pathology) lies in the direc-tion of the development of the grandiose self which accounts for their establishing a mirror transference in analysis, while others who have their major fixation points around the ideal-ized self-object or around early sexual objects develop an idealizing transference or a transference neurosis.

Under favorable circumstances (appropriately selective pa-rental response to the child's demands for an echo to and a participation in the narcissistic-exhibitionistic manifestations of his grandiose fantasies) the child learns to accept his real-istic limitations, the grandiose fantasies and the crude exhi-bitionistic demands are given up, and are *pari passu* replaced by ego-syntonic goals and purposes, by pleasure in his func-tions and activities and by realistic self-esteem. Analogous to the development of the idealized self-object, the outcome of the development of the grandiose self is determined not only by the features of the child's own narcissism but also by cer-tain features of the important personalities who surround the child. The final ego-syntonic goals and purposes, the pleasure in the self and its functions, and healthy self-esteem are thus influenced by two sets of factors: (1) A person's ultimate goals and purposes, and his self-esteem, carry the imprint of the relevant characteristics and attitudes of the imagoes (transformed into psychological functions by the process of transmuting internalization) of the persons against whom the child's grandiose self had been reflected or whom the child had accepted as extensions of his own greatness. Thus the specific goals and purposes which frequently determine the later major directions of one's life are often derived from identifications with the very figures who originally had been experienced as extensions of the grandiose self. (2) Our ultimate goals and purposes and our self-esteem, however, also carry the earmark of the original narcissism which infuses into the central purposes of our life and into our healthy self-esteem that absoluteness of persistence and of conviction of the right to success which betrays that an unaltered piece of the old, limitless narcissism functions actively alongside with the new, tamed, and realistic structures. If the optimal development and integration of the grandiose self is interfered with, however, then this psychic structure may become split off from the reality ego and/or may become separated from it by repression.[2] It is then no longer accessible to external influence but is retained in its archaic form. In analysis, however, it becomes remobilized in the cohesive form of the mirror transference, is again and again brought under the influence of the reality ego, and the process of its gradual modification which was traumatically interrupted in childhood can now be taken up again.

The gradual recognition of the realistic imperfections and limitations of the self, i.e., the gradual diminution of the domain and power of the grandiose fantasy, is in general a precondition for mental health in the narcissistic sector of the personality. But there are exceptions to this rule. A persistently active grandiose self with its delusional claims may severely incapacitate an ego of average endowment. A

[2] Compare the discussion of the analogous conditions pertaining to the idealized parent imago in Chapter 4, n. 1.

gifted person's ego, however, may well be pushed to the use of its utmost capacities, and thus to a realistically outstanding performance, by the demands of the grandiose fantasies of a persistent, poorly modified grandiose self. Churchill may have been such a person (see my discussion of the influence of a persistent infantile flying fantasy [1966a]); Goethe may be another example (see Eissler's [1963a] description of the early circumstances which reinforced the child's belief in the magical power of his wishes and his imagination); and Freud's (1917c) famous—essentially autobiographical?—remark concerning the later successes of the firstborn son of a young mother clearly belongs in the same context.

A parody of the relationship between a persistent greatness fantasy and the ego of an unusually gifted person is not infrequently encountered during the analysis of narcissistic personalities whose major fixation is on the grandiose self. Because of a persistence of old convictions concerning their omniscience such patients are often unable to ask for information (in a new city, for example, they will walk for miles rather than ask for directions) and they are unable to admit a lacuna in their knowledge. When they are asked, for example, whether they have read a certain book, their grandiose self, with its persistent omniscience, forces them to say yes—sometimes with the indirectly beneficial result that they now have to rush and quickly read the book (a good prognostic sign!)—in order to pull reality achievement after the magical claim. That such incidents, if handled seriously and unaggressively and not prematurely humorously by the analyst, can be of great analytic benefit goes probably without saying. Lying as a symptom (pseudologia fantastica), on the other hand, has to be evaluated carefully since variations in the relationship between the narcissistic structures and the patient's ego account for important differences in diagnosis and prognosis.

With regard to the content of the lies, the propensity toward pseudologia can be subdivided as follows: (a) it may be due to the pressure of the grandiose self, in which case the lies ascribe some great achievements to the self of the liar; or (b) it may be due to the pressure of the need for an idealized object, in which case the lies ascribe some great achievements, great monetary or intellectual possessions, or high social status to another person who occupies a position of leadership (is a parental figure) vis-à-vis the patient. (In their comparatively most undisguised form the falsifications concern the person's actual father or other relatives of the parental generation.)

Concerning lies which are due to the ego's inability to maintain its reality organization under the pressure of fantasies created by the need for an idealized object, the following misunderstanding which occurs frequently during the analysis of narcissistic personality disturbances must be mentioned. Repeating in the analysis what he has also been wont to do in his everyday life, the patient will attribute to others an achievement which he has indeed brought about through his own ability and effort (cf. the clinical example supplied by E. Kris, 1951, esp. p. 22). A variety of dynamic conditions may, of course, play a role in the production of such a syndrome. (At times it may even serve predominantly the simple warding off of a potentially traumatic psychoeconomic imbalance, akin to the fending off of compliments which is a common occurrence that is familiar to everyone.)

In the course of analytic treatment, however, this syndrome is most often considered by analysts to be the result of a structural conflict with the superego—analogous to the dynamic situation of the so-called negative therapeutic reaction —and is interpreted as such to the patient. (For example: "You felt guilty about surpassing your father, therefore you attribute to him something that in fact was achieved by you.") The situation is different, however, in those narcissistic personalities who have suffered the traumatic loss of the idealized parent imago in childhood and who, in consequence of this loss, are afflicted with a specific structural defect in the form of the insufficient idealization of the superego. The fact that the analysand attributes his own deed to someone else is in these instances due not to his guilt but to his yearning for an omnipotent archaic object to whom he wants to attach himself. Accordingly, the resistance with which the patient opposes the interpretative dissolution of his pseudologia is motivated by his fear of losing the narcissistic sustenance which he derives from the aggrandized object that he has created in fantasy.

Whatever the basic constellation which underlies the pseudologic syndrome, i.e., whether it is motivated by the pressure of the grandiose self or by the search for an idealized parent imago, the analyst who has become experienced in the treatment of narcissistic personality disorders will be able to predict with a good deal of accuracy the way by which the transformation of the pathological material will take place. The lies will gradually become fantasies; then ambitious plans and fanciful ideals; and finally, if the analysis is successful, they will have become replaced by reasonable action patterns and goals. During a typical transitional phase, which occurs frequently midway on the road toward full integration, the patient presents the former lies as quasi-jokes, both in the psychoanalytic situation and in his daily life. These jokes often arouse a degree of annoyance in the analyst who is not familiar with this specific line of therapeutic development; and the analyst will thus be inclined to call the seemingly still delinquent ego of the patient to the task of truthfulness and realism. As usual, however, the educative approach and a critical attitude are not favorable. On the contrary, the analyst should welcome the fact of the patient's temporary straddling between half-joking lies and half-lying jokes as a sign of progress on the road toward the ego's mastery of the pressure which is exerted on it by unmodified grandiose fantasies concerning the self or by fantasies concerning an omnipotent archaic object. The analyst's dissatisfaction with the degree of functional ego dominance which has been achieved by the patient not only tends in general to interfere with further progress but may even undo the progress which has already been made.

These considerations are especially important in the evaluation of a patient's analyzability, not only as regards the ordinary analysand but also in the assessment of applicants for psychoanalytic training. Disregarding the transitional cases for the purposes of exposition, there is a vast difference between (1) those whose ego has succumbed to the pressures of the grandiose self and has become addicted to lying and other forms of delinquency and (2) those whose ego struggles valiantly to live up to the assertions of the grandiose self concept on which they have become fixated, but who under the intense pressure of the grandiose self will in circumscribed segments of reality, or in moments of sudden imbalance, confuse grandiose imagination with reality. Such people often have real gifts since (a) the fixation on the original fantasies about themselves may have been the result of exaggerated and unrealistic parental response to real endowment, and (b) the persistent demand of the grandiose self forced the developing ego to respond with unusual performance. Be that as it may, it is important to keep in mind that some patients will present themselves for therapeutic or training analysis with an initial symptomatic lie or a corresponding delinquent act, i.e., a form of behavior which constitutes the first, testing, transference revelation of the hidden grandiose self. It is of decisive influence with regard to the development of the analysis that the analyst respond analytically to this behavior, i.e., recognize it and state truthfully that its significance is still unknown. If such patients (candidates) are rejected off-hand (which is rare), or, as happens more frequently, if the analyst—justified by the supposed need to establish immediately a clear-cut realistic and moral relationship between himself and the patient—responds with open disapproval or the demand for the correction of the symptomatic act, then some potentially creative people with good analytic prognosis

will be weeded out. As stated earlier: the crucial differentiation can usually not be made immediately; the analyst needs
time to observe the full interplay between the greatness assertions of the grandiose self and the response of the ego. The
reality ego's intermittent confusion by the assertions of the
grandiose self, however, is indeed found among talented and
capable people, and the systematic analysis of these pressures
in an initial setting of benevolent acceptance constitutes as
usual the appropriate atmosphere. I might add that, according to my experience, it is particularly hard for those analysts
who have been older siblings to accept this policy as valid
since their own early prestige fixations (their own grandiose
self) often crystallize around their ethical superiority over
the (delinquent) younger ones.

     It would be rewarding to study the specific influence ex-
erted by the personality of the older sibling within the fabric
of society. The channeling of a variety of pregenital and
genital rivalrous, jealous, and envious feelings into attitudes
of moral and intellectual superiority is especially pronounced
in girls who were faced with the birth of a brother during
early latency. They attempt to overcome the narcissistic blow
by an attitude of contempt toward, and of moral and intellectual superiority over, the new arrival and their achievements
in school—and the parental response to their successes in the
realm of athletic, intellectual, and cultural pursuits—become
inordinately important to them. Such women may later develop into responsible, socially concerned, intellectually and
culturally ambitious persons who struggle valiantly to overcome their resentment against younger men and to transform
it into attitudes of protection and guidance toward them. To
the work of an analyst such women often bring significant
assets in the realm of moral firmness and intellectual ability.
Their difficulties, as might well be expected, lie in the area
of unresolved hostility toward younger sibling figures and,
what is more important because it can be more easily rationalized, they tend toward the substitution of what seems

to them the all-too-passive attitude of the analyst (who is content to assist the patient in removing the obstacles that stand in the way of liberating his own personality, his own potentialities, and his own initiative) by the more active stance of the educator, admonisher, and guide.

Leaving these details we return now to our principal topic. The cohesive therapeutic reactivation of the grandiose self in analysis occurs in three forms; these relate to specific stages of development of this psychological structure to which the pathognomonic therapeutic regression has led: (1) The archaic *merger through the extension of the grandiose self;* (2) a less archaic form which will be called *alter-ego transference* or *twinship;* and (3) a still less archaic form which will be referred to as *mirror transference* in the narrower sense.

THE MERGER THROUGH THE EXTENSION OF THE GRANDIOSE SELF

In its most archaic form the cognitive elaboration of the narcissistically cathected object is least in evidence: the analyst is experienced as an extension of the grandiose self and he is referred to only insofar as he has become the carrier of the grandiosity and the exhibitionism of the analysand's grandiose self and of the conflicts, tensions, and defenses which are elicited by these manifestations of the activated narcissistic structure. In metapsychological terms, the relationship to the analyst is one of (primary) identity. From the sociological (or sociobiological) point of view we may call it a merger (or a symbiosis) if we keep in mind that it is not the merger with an idealized object (as striven for and temporarily established in the idealizing transference) but an experience of the grandiose self which first regressively diffuses its borders to include the analyst and then, after this expansion of its limits has been established, uses the relative security of this new comprehensive structure for the performance of certain therapeutic tasks. It is for this stage *par excellence* that the repeatedly adduced analogy between the experience of the narcissistically cathected object and the adult's experience of his own body and mind and their functions is most appropriate (although the flavor of this specific experience of the narcissistically cathected object does not entirely vanish from the other forms of the remobilization of the grandiose self). Since, in this revival of the early stage of primary identity with the object, the analyst is experienced as a part of the self, the analysand—within the sector of the specific, therapeutically mobilized regression—expects unquestioned dominance over him. The target of this archaic mode of narcissistic libidinal investment—in the analytic situation: the analyst —experiences this relationship in general as oppressive and he tends to rebel against the unquestioning absolutarianism and tyranny with which the patient expects to control him.

THE ALTER-EGO TRANSFERENCE OR TWINSHIP

In a less archaic form of the activation of the grandiose self the narcissistically cathected object is experienced as being like the grandiose self or as being very similar to it. This variant of the transference activation of the grandiose self will be referred to as the alter-ego transference or the twinship. Dreams, and especially fantasies, referring to a relationship with such an alter ego or twin (or conscious wishes for such a relationship) are frequently encountered in the analysis of narcissistic personalities. The pathognomonic therapeutic regression is characterized by the fact that the patient assumes that the analyst is either like him or similar to him, or that the analyst's psychological makeup is like, or is similar to, that of the patient.

THE MIRROR TRANSFERENCE IN THE NARROWER SENSE

In the most mature form of the therapeutic mobilization of the grandiose self the analyst is most clearly experienced as a separate person. He is, however, important to the patient only, and accepted by him only, within the framework of the needs generated by the therapeutically reactivated grandiose self. It is this form of the analytic reactivation of the grandiose self for which the term mirror transference is most accurate. In this narrower sense of the term the mirror transference is the therapeutic reinstatement of that normal phase of the development of the grandiose self in which the gleam in the mother's eye, which mirrors the child's exhibitionistic display, and other forms of maternal participation in and response to the child's narcissistic-exhibitionistic enjoyment confirm the child's self-esteem and, by a gradually increasing selectivity of these responses, begin to channel it into realistic directions. As was the mother during that stage of development, so is now the analyst an object which is important only insofar as it is invited to participate in the child's narcissistic pleasure and thus to confirm it. Occasionally, though only very rarely, there also occur dreams during the analysis which portray a relationship (of the self) with someone who is seen as through a mirror (the analyst as the reflector of the grandiose self). Although conceivably such dream pictures may also occur in the analysis of a transference neurosis and simply symbolize the analytic process of self-scrutiny, I have never observed them except in cases in which a major part of the instinctual investment of the grandiose self was in the process of becoming mobilized in relationship to the therapist. The mirror relationship and its significance are at times also clearly, though indirectly, portrayed by the patients' fantasies, free associations, and products of sublimation,[3] but undisguised fantasies of looking at oneself in the mirror do not seem to be produced by analysands even at the peak of the therapeutic activation of the grandiose self. Such fantasies may not occur because the situation can be enacted and rationalized easily by the patient's looking at himself in the

[3] For a striking clinical example, see the case of Mr. E.

mirror in reality. (For a thoughtful discussion of the psychological significance of the mirror, see Elkisch, 1957).

The most significant relevant basic interactions between mother and child lie usually in the visual area: the child's bodily display is responded to by the gleam in the mother's eye. It must, however, be noted here that in many instances of mirror transference in which the need for the analyst's echoing, approving, and confirming plays a central role in the working-through process, the appearance of the undisguised urge to be looked at usually occurs—more or less sexualized—as a temporary regressive phenomenon after more aim-inhibited wishes for attention and understanding have been frustrated. In certain patients who establish a mirror transference, furthermore, the visual area is often clearly overburdened by cathexes channeled into it after the failure of other modes of interaction (e.g., archaic oral and tactile) in the realm of the child's narcissistic needs. The acceptance of the child's body (especially of the oral and peri-oral region [Rangell, 1954] by tactile responses leads under favorable circumstances to a basic equilibrium in the realm of the narcissistic cathexis of a cohesive body self. If the mother, however, recoils from the child's body (or cannot tolerate lending her own body to the child for his narcissistic enjoyment through the extension of his narcissistic cathexes to include the mother's body), then the visual interactions become hypercathected and, by looking at the mother and by being looked at by her, the child attempts not only to obtain the narcissistic gratifications that are in tune with the visual sensory modality but also strives to substitute for the failures that had occurred in the realm of physical (oral and tactile) contact or closeness.

Patient E., for example, whose mother had been chronically ill and depressed during his childhood was afraid of looking at the analyst for fear of overburdening him by his gaze. The gaze, however, was the carrier of the wish to be held and carried by the mother (and most likely also to suck on her breast), and he feared that the fulfillment of this wish would be the sick mother's undoing.

The auditory modality may, on the other hand, take over for the visual one when there is a defect in the visual area. Such an instructive variant is unmistakably portrayed in a movie of blind children in the nursery by Burlingham and Robertson (1966). It contains the touching scene in which a blind girl responds with undisguised narcissistic delight when she suddenly recognizes that it is her own musical performance that is played back to her via a tape recorder. Here the tape recorder fulfills the function of a mirror.

We may thus conclude that the mother's exultant response to the total child (calling him by name as she enjoys his presence and activity) supports, at the appropriate phase, the development from autoerotism to narcissism—from the stage of the fragmented self (the stage of self nuclei) to the stage of the cohesive self—i.e., the growth of the self experience as a physical and mental unit which has cohesiveness in space and continuity in time.[4] The experience of isolated mental and physical functions, however, which precedes the stage of the cohesive self (the stage of narcissism) must, of course, not be considered as morbid but be regarded as appropriate to this earlier phase of development. It should not be forgotten, furthermore, that the capacity to enjoy single parts of the body and their function as well as single mental activities continues after the cohesiveness of the self experience has been firmly established. In these later stages, however, adults as well as children can enjoy the component parts and functions of their body and mind because they feel secure that these body parts and their functions belong to a firmly established total self, i.e., that there is no threat of fragmentation. Yet we know that children also enjoy games in which body parts are again isolated—counting toes, for example: "This little piggy went to market, this little piggy stayed home, this little

4 In this context see E. Jacobson (1964) who speaks of the "development of object and self constancy" (p. 55).

piggy ate roast beef, this little piggy had none, and this little piggy cried wee-wee all the way home." Such games seem to rest on the setting up of slight fragmentation fears at a period when the cohesiveness of the self has not yet become totally entrenched. The tension, however, is kept in bounds (like the separation anxiety in the peek-a-boo game [Kleeman, 1967]), and when the last toe is reached, empathic mother and child undo the fragmentation by uniting in laughter and embrace.

The sense of the reality of the self (see Bernstein, 1963), which is the manifestation of its cohesiveness due to its firm cathexis with narcissistic libido, leads not only to a subjective feeling of well-being but secondarily also to an improvement of the functioning of the ego, which can be objectively ascertained in a number of ways, e.g., by assessing the results of a patient's increased capacity for work and increased work efficiency when the cohesiveness of the self experience has been strengthened. On the other hand, patients will often attempt to counteract the subjectively painful feeling of self fragmentation by a variety of forced actions, ranging from physical stimulation and athletic activities to excessive work in their profession or business.[5] The misleading impression that a psychosis had been precipitated by overwork (see, for example, D. P. Schreber, 1903) is based on the fact that the patient, sensing the rapid and dangerously increasing fragmentation of the self which precedes the overt outbreak of the psychosis, attempts to counteract it by frantic activity.[6]

[5] Sexual activity, too, ranging from certain kinds of masturbatory practices resorted to by children who are suffering from a chronic narcissistic depletion to the need for the incessant, self-reassuring performance of sexual exploits by certain Don Juan types, has the aim of counteracting a sense of self depletion or of forestalling the danger of self fragmentation. Much of the sexual activity of adolescents, who, especially during the later part of this transitional period, are exposed to the revival of the frightening childhood experiences of self depletion and self fragmentation, also serves primarily narcissistic purposes; i.e., even relatively stable adolescents undertake it, mainly in order to enhance self-esteem.

[6] For additional remarks concerning the reciprocal influences between efficiency of ego functions and cohesiveness of the self, see Kohut (1970a).

Many of the most severe and chronic work disturbances of our patients, it may be added here, are in my experience due to the fact that the self is poorly cathected with narcissistic libido and in chronic danger of fragmentation, with a secondary reduction of the efficacy of the ego. Such people are either chronically unable to work at all, or (since their self is not participating) they are able to work only in an automatic way (as the isolated activity of an autonomous ego, without the participation of a self in depth), i.e., passively, without pleasure and without initiative, simply responding to external cues and demands. Occasionally even the patient's awareness of this rather frequent type of work disturbance in narcissistic personality disorders comes about only in the course of a successful analysis. The patient will one day report that his work has changed, that he is now enjoying it, that he now has the choice whether to work or not, that the work is now undertaken on his own initiative rather than as if by a passively obedient automaton, and, last but not least, that his approach has now some originality rather than being humdrum and routine: a living self in depth has become the *organizing center of the ego's activities* (Hartmann, 1939, 1947).

While a relationship to an empathically approving and accepting parent is one of the preconditions for the original establishment of a firm cathexis of the self, and while in analysis disturbances in this realm are once more open to correction, the opposite sequence of events (the movement from a cohesive self to its fragmentation) can often be observed both in analysis and in a child's interplay with his pathogenic parents. The fragmentation of the self can, for example, be studied in patients who, with the aid of the analyst's presence and attention, have tentatively re-established a feeling of the cohesiveness and continuity of the self. Whenever the mirror transference cannot be maintained (in whichever of its three forms it had established itself), the patient feels threatened by the dissolution of the narcissistic unity of the self; he begins to experience the regressively re-instated hypercathexis of isolated body parts and mental functions (elaborated as hypochondria) and turns to other, pathological means (such as perverse sexual activities) in or-der to stem the tide of regression. Occasionally patients will report parental behavior which seems to them to be sadisti-cally designed to counteract a feeling of pleasure in their in-tegrated self and bring about a painful sense of fragmen-tation.

Patient B., for example, remembered from his childhood the following destructive reaction of his mother. When he would tell her exuberantly about some achievement or ex-perience she seemed not only to be cold and inattentive but, instead of responding to him and the event that he was de-scribing, would suddenly remark critically about a detail of his appearance or current behavior ("Don't move your hands while you are talking!" etc.). This reaction must have been experienced by him not only as a rejection of the particular display for which he needed a confirming response but also as an active destruction of the cohesiveness of his self experi-ence (by shifting attention to a *part* of his body) just at the most vulnerable moment when he was offering his total self for approval.

The empathic analyst will—knowingly or intuitively—heed this example and realize that there are indeed moments in an analysis when even the most cogent and correct inter-pretation about a mechanism, a defense, or any other detail of the patient's personality is out of place and, for instance, unacceptable to the patient who seeks a comprehensive re-sponse to a recent important event in his life, such as a new achievement or the like. The cold voices, it may be added, which the paranoiac often reports as commenting on aspects of his behavior, details of his looks, etc., are perhaps to be understood not only as the criticism of a projected superego but also as the projected expression of a feeling of fragmenta-tion which arose as the result of the patient's insufficiently developed or declining psychic capacity to maintain a solid cathexis of the self.

Whatever the developmental vicissitudes of the instinctual investment of the self in the major psychoses and whatever the genetic and dynamic basis of its disturbance in these serious disorders—in the treatment of the group of narcissistic personality disturbances with which the present study deals, the fluctuations of the cathexis of the self are correlated to the state of the narcissistic transference. The three forms of the transference reactivation of the grandiose self, which, as was discussed before, correspond to three different developmental stages of the grandiose self, can be identified by their different clinical manifestations. Since the oldest form consists in the transference re-establishment of an ancient identity with the object through the extension of the grandiose self, the transference object has hardly any separateness, and object elaborations in the associative material are either absent or very scanty and inconspicuous. Because of the fact that the alter-ego transference (twinship), in which not a primary identity but a likeness (similarity) with the object is established, corresponds to a more mature developmental phase than that from which the merger transference takes its origin, object elaboration in the associative material is more in evidence and a degree of separateness of the object is predicated by the analysand. Since, finally, the separateness of the object is cognitively most clearly established in the mirror transference in the narrower sense of the term, object elaborations are here the most abundant. The object, however, is even here still cathected with narcissistic libido; and it is reacted to only insofar as it contributes to (or interferes with) the maintenance of the analysand's narcissistic homeostasis.

Despite these significant differences, however, I shall make little effort to identify the specific form of the grandiose self that has been mobilized and frequently refer to all of its manifestations as mirror transference. Since the manifestations of the mirror transference in the stricter sense of the term are clearly the best known and most easily identifiable products of the therapeutically mobilized grandiose self, this term (used *a potiori*) is most evocative with regard to the whole group of related relevant phenomena. The important issue is, after all, not the specific mode of the transference interplay by which the analyst becomes involved in the mobilization of the patient's grandiose self but the fact that the transference brings about the (re-)establishment of a cohesive and durable narcissistic object relationship which, on the whole, antedates the full development of the child's object love, and at any rate is independent of the stage of development reached by the latter. It is relatively unimportant whether the patient uses the analyst (in the merger) as an extension of his own (split-off and/or repressed) archaic greatness and exhibitionism, whether he experiences him (in the alter-ego transference) as the separate carrier of his own (repressed) perfection, or whether he demands from him (in the mirror transference) an echo and a confirmation of his greatness and an approving response to his exhibitionism. The main therapeutic benefit which accrues from the transferencelike condition established by the activation of the grandiose self is that it enables the patient to mobilize and maintain a working-through process in which the analyst serves as a therapeutic buffer and enhances the gradual harnessing of the ego-alien narcissistic fantasies and impulses.

One further, and last, set of arguments in favor of using the term mirror transference for the whole group of transference phenomena that are the expression of the therapeutic mobilization of the grandiose self: it may well be that the mirror transference in the narrower sense is the only one that corresponds, at least in approximation, to a recognizable developmental phase, while the silent merger with the analyst through the extension of the analysand's grandiose self and the alter-ego transference (twinship) are reinstatements of regressive positions taken in early childhood (preoedipally) after the failure of the mirror stage. Although there exist undoubtedly normal developmental stages of primary identity with the object and of a primary relationship with an alter-ego-self (occurring either earlier than the mirror stage or overlapping its beginnings), the clinical transference apparently reinstates not these primary forms but their secondary appearance in childhood after the failure of the mother's mirror functions. (The relationship is similar to that encountered in compulsive neurosis where the anality that is defended against is not the revival of the original anal stage but the reactivation of the regressive return to anality in early latency after the retreat from shattering oedipal castration anxieties.)

It is hard to reconstruct the child's experience of the object in his primary identity with it and in his primary alter-ego (twinship) relationship to it. These stages occur very early, i.e., before any verbal communications could assist our empathy. The mirror stage, however, continues into the verbal stage and the interactions between parent and child are, therefore, more open to our empathic understanding, even in their preverbal beginnings (cf., for example, Trollope's description of "Baby Worship" as quoted in Kohut, 1966a). The secondary, regressively taken precursors of the later merger and twinship transference, however, are more accessible in childhood, and memories of frightening childhood loneliness with near-delusional mergings into others, and about imaginary playmates and transitional objects with alter-ego features, are not infrequently obtained in the analysis of adults.

It must be admitted that even the purest forms of mirror transference in the narrower sense of the term encountered in the analysis of narcissistic personality disturbances are not direct replicas of a normal developmental phase. They, too, are regressively altered editions of a child's demands for attention, approval, and for the confirmatory echoing of its presence, and they always contain an admixture of the tyranny and overpossessiveness which betrays a heightening of oral-sadistic and anal-sadistic drive elements produced by intense frustrations and disappointments. The mirror transference in the stricter sense of the word is, nevertheless, closer to being a therapeutic reinstatement of a normal phase of development than the merger and the twinship and, in a correctly conducted analysis, the latter two tend to change gradually into the former, and the mirror transference tends to become more and more akin to the normal developmental phase; i.e., the sadistic elements diminish and the demands for affection and response take on the vigor, and approximate giving the pleasure, which is encountered in the corresponding phase-appropriate interactions between parent and child.

The three types of the therapeutic reactivation of the grandiose self not only correspond thus to different stages of the development of this psychological structure, but they are also distinguishable by their clearly different clinical manifestations. Yet, despite their developmental and phenomenological differences, the dynamic clinical effect of the three subtypes of the transference reactivations of the grandiose self is the same: (1) in all three forms the analyst becomes the figure around whom a significant degree of object constancy in the narcissistic realm can be established, however primitive the object may be; and (2) with the aid of this more or less stable narcissistically invested object, the transference contributes, in all three of its forms, to the maintenance of the cohesiveness of the self of the analysand.

That the analyst can be enlisted in the support of this cohesively cathected structure is an expression of the fact (a) that, genetically, the formation of an (often only precariously maintained) cohesive grandiose self was indeed achieved to a certain extent during childhood; and (b) that the listening, perceiving, and echoing-mirroring presence of the analyst now reinforces the psychological forces which maintain the cohesiveness of this self image—archaic and (by adult standards) unrealistic though it may be.

CLINICAL EXAMPLES

The efficacy of the mirror transference in fostering the cohesiveness of the self can be demonstrated best by adducing clinical examples in which the threat of deeper psychological regression disturbs the established transference equilibrium. By contrasting the mirror transference in this way with regressive states of greater psychological primitiveness, it will be easier to demonstrate its own specific psychological content and effect. Analogous to the insight-providing and thus therapeutically invaluable, controlled, temporary swings toward the disintegration of the idealized parent imago when the idealizing transference is disturbed,[7] we encounter such regressive states as a consequence of a disturbance of the mirror transference. Their metapsychological essence is the temporary fragmentation of the narcissistically cathected, cohesive (body-mind) self and the temporary concentration of the instinctual cathexes on isolated body parts, isolated mental functions, and isolated actions, which are then experienced as dangerously disconnected from a precariously maintained or crumbling self.

The disturbance of the equilibrium of the mirror transference, with the ensuing threat of fragmenting regression, will now be illustrated with the aid of specific cases.

Mr. B. had been in analysis with a colleague (a woman) for three months. The patient, a college instructor in his late twenties, had sought analysis ostensibly because of sexual disturbances and the breakup of his marriage. Despite the seemingly circumscribed nature of his presenting symptoms, however, he suffered from a vague and widespread personality disturbance, experienced alternatingly as severe states of tension and as a feeling of painful emptiness, both at the borderline of physical and psychological experience. In addition,

---

[7] See the discussion of this topic in Chapter 3; see also the case of Mr. G. in Chapter 4.

the patient felt threatened by sudden upsurges of intense, tantrumlike rage.

Within a few weeks after the beginning of the analysis (and without any undue activity from the side of the analyst) the patient began to experience the analysis as very soothing. He described it as being "like a warm bath" (a meaningful simile, based on the experience that the external, yet enveloping, temperature regulation provided by a warm bath has the effect of restoring the bather's narcissistic equilibrium and, by the gently physical stimulation which it supplies, to increase the sense of the cohesiveness of the body self). In the course of each analytic hour, and progressively during each week as he appeared to accumulate the effect of consecutive sessions, his tensions and the feeling of painful emptiness subsided, and the patient reported that his work improved and that he felt, and was, vastly more productive. During the weekends, however, the tension increased considerably, he began to worry over his physical and mental functions, had dreams of violence and threatening destruction, and was prone to react with sudden rage to minor irritations. But he was already beginning to realize that his tensions were related to being separated from the analyst (even though he was overtly still mainly preoccupied with the concern that his former wife would forget him or would not be thinking of him).

During an analytic hour in this period he experienced suddenly an intense feeling of wholeness, well-being, heightened self-confidence, and a subsiding of his tension and inner emptiness after a statement by the analyst which contained the phrase, "As you told me about a week ago." The patient expressed intense pleasure that the analyst could remember something that he had said in a previous hour, and the analyst got the distinct impression from the patient's response that the cohesiveness of the patient's self experience—here, in particular, along a time axis—was supported by the fact that he was listened to, empathically responded to, and remembered (i.e., that the analyst's mirror functions enabled the patient to cathect a reactivated grandiose self with narcissistic libido).

It may be added here that many patients with narcissistic personality disturbances complain of a feeling of fragmentation, consisting specifically of a sense of separation of their self experience from their various physical and mental functions. The fleeting fragmentation of an as yet unreliably cathected self when a patient, as a consequence of therapeutic progress, becomes absorbed in external pursuits is rather frequently encountered temporarily in the later phases of successful analyses of narcissistic personality disturbances. The greater cohesiveness of the self which has been achieved in the analysis brings about an improvement of various ego functions, leading to the channeling of interest toward vocational and interpersonal aims. Fascinated by the novel experience, the patient may have lost himself in a particular pursuit when he suddenly becomes aware of anxious hypochondriacal preoccupations concerning his physical and especially his mental functions. These tensions, however, tend to disappear quickly when—at first with the aid of the analyst's interpretations, and later spontaneously—the patient comprehends that the condition is due to the fact that his self had temporarily become deprived of its cohesive narcissistic cathexis which had been uncontrolledly siphoned into his actions.

Patient M., for example, a thirty-year-old man (in analysis with a student, a woman, under supervision with the author) had, despite reasonable external success in his profession, experienced his work as nonfulfilling and had engaged in a variety of restless social pursuits designed to obliterate an oppressive sensation of inner emptiness. In the analysis he became aware of his intense exhibitionism which had remained unresponded to in his childhood. The working-through process allowed him increasingly to consolidate his nuclear grandiose self, and he was able not only to indulge in exhibitionistic fantasies (playing the violin to a large, imaginary audience, for example) but also to devote himself to his regular work (which indeed provided him with a stage for the fulfillment of exhibitionistic wishes in a socially acceptable form) with more and more initiative and zest. During a transitional period, however, he was subject to attacks of anxiety both when he played the violin and when he allowed himself to become absorbed by his regular work. In each instance the detailed scrutiny of the experience revealed that the anxiety was due not only to a threatening hypomanic stimulation in consequence of the intrusion of his as yet relatively untamed exhibitionism, but even more to a sense of loss of self (a decathexis of the self with the threat of its renewed fragmentation) as he abandoned himself to his activities and aims, i.e., invested them with narcissistic libido. These anxiety experiences, however, occurred only during a limited transitional period. Later he became able to combine the narcissistic investment of cherished self-syntonic activities and self-syntonic goals with that enhancement of self cohesiveness which is the usual accompaniment of the successful exercise of a person's ego functions.

The specific junctures in the course of analysis (such as the one described during the analysis of Mr. M.), when self cathexis is in danger of becoming absorbed by the patient's newly invested pursuits, must be distinguished from the chronic psychological condition which compels people to be engaged in action at all times, since they are able to feel alive only in their activities. Their actions are not seen by them as the outgrowth of their plans, purposes, goals, and ideals (they are not based on a stable self experience), but they are a substitute for the self. A similar symptom, the existence of which is often recognized only during analysis, consists in the fact that the patient does not experience himself as cohesive along a time axis. Initially such patients often complain that they cannot remember the content of their analytic sessions from one day to the next. This impression tends to persist subjectively even though it can be shown to be objectively incorrect since the patient may in fact remember the preceding sessions. By contrast, such patients (e.g., Mr. B.) begin to feel subjectively whole and complete (including the sense of their continuity in time) when the analyst gives evidence of remembering the patient's earlier accounts and feeling states—a clear sign that the analyst (in the mirror transference) has begun to fulfill an important (pre)structural function in the maintenance of the cohesiveness of the patient's self.

The episode from the analysis of Mr. B. exemplified the function of the mirror transference in reinforcing the cohesiveness of the reactivated self along the time axis. The following clinical vignette (which also occurred early in analysis) constitutes another, especially instructive, illustration of a temporary regressive fragmentation of the therapeutically reactivated grandiose self. This episode, however, demonstrates not a threat to the cohesive experience of the self in time (i.e., to the experience of the self as a continuum), but a threat to its current cohesiveness in breadth and depth.

Mr. E. was a graduate student in his late twenties. Although he had originally sought therapy because of the breakup of his marriage, he soon revealed a variety of other difficulties, in particular a tendency toward a variety of perverse fantasies and practices. The details of his psychopathology and of his loosely knit personality structure will not be discussed here. Suffice it to say that he sought relief from painful narcissistic tension states by a number of perverse means in which the inconstancy of various superficially cathected objects and the protean quality of his sexual goals were indicative of the fact that he could trust no source of satisfaction, and that he could not even commit himself to the means by which he hoped to obtain pleasure and reassurance. As the (narcissistic) transference began to develop, however, it became clear that voyeuristic-exhibitionistic aims played a specific role in his perversions and that he would turn to the attempt to gain satisfactions in this area when he felt otherwise threatened by rejection.

At this point I shall not enter into a discussion of the specific genetic determinants of which certain glimpses could be obtained during the analysis (see, however, Chapter 1). I shall restrict myself here to a brief report of the patient's experience on a particular weekend during an early phase of his long analysis. Although the patient was already beginning to realize that separations from the analyst[8] upset his psychic equilibrium, he did not yet understand the nature of the specific support which the analysis provided. During earlier weekend separations he had attempted to counter the vaguely perceived inner threat by employing a variety of remedies. He had turned to the relatively unafflicted realm of intellectual pursuits, for example; and there had been an upsurge of homosexual and heterosexual preoccupations and involvements which usually ended up in dangerous voyeuristic activities in public toilets during which he achieved a feeling of merger with the man at whom he gazed. In the course of this weekend, however, he was able, through an act of artistic sublimation, not only to spare himself these cruder means of protection against the threatened dissolution of the self, but also to explain the nature of the reassurance he was receiving from the analyst. During this weekend, the patient painted a picture of the analyst. The key to the understanding of this artistic production lay in the fact that in it the analyst had neither eyes nor a nose—the place of these sensory organs was taken by the analysand. On the basis of this evidence (there was abundant additional material, past and present, which corroborated this interpretation) the conclusion could be reached that a decisive support to the maintenance of the patient's narcissistically cathected self image was supplied by the analyst's perception of him: in the mirror transference the analyst was experienced by this patient as the (narcissis-

8 This analysis was carried out by a senior student at the Chicago Institute for Psychoanalysis under regular supervision by the author.

tic) libidinal cement which counteracted and prevented the tendency to fragmentation. The patient felt whole when he thought that he was acceptingly looked at by an object that substituted for an insufficiently developed endopsychic function: the analyst provided a replacement for the lacking narcissistic cathexis of the self.

A matter of conceptual clarification, which was already alluded to previously in a theoretical context, may be usefully re-introduced at this point and reviewed against the background of the preceding clinical material; namely, one has to distinguish between (a) the cohesion of the patient's self image (the wholeness of the reactivated grandiose self), which he could maintain with the aid of the analyst's presence, i.e., of the analyst's real or imagined unifying perceptions and responses, and (b) the unity and cohesion of the patient's ego and its functions.

Although the two concepts are on different levels of abstraction (the conception of the self being nearer to introspective or empathic observation; that of the ego being further from it), one may say that the experience of a unitary self, in consequence of a reliable narcissistic cathexis of the self image, is an important precondition for a cohesively functioning ego; that, by contrast, the absence of such a cathexis tends to lead to disordered ego functions; and, finally, that the narcissistic cathexes of a mirror transference may remedy the disturbance of the ego, i.e., improve ego functions via the intermediate step of supplying cohesiveness to the self. (For a discussion of the mutual relationship between ego and self, see Kohut, 1970a.)

CHAPTER 6

TYPES OF MIRROR TRANSFERENCES: A CLASSIFICATION ACCORDING TO GENETIC-DYNAMIC CONSIDERATIONS

The preceding classification of the transferences which arise in consequence of the therapeutic remobilization of the grandiose self was based on developmental considerations. In this chapter I shall discuss the types of the mirror transference that are related not so much to (congenitally pre-formed?) maturational stages of the grandiose self but rather to external factors active in the (childhood) past and in the current (therapeutic) environment. Specifically, I shall now delimit three different ways—(1) primary; (2) secondary; (3) reactive—in which the mirror transference (in the comprehensive meaning of the term) establishes itself in analysis, and indicate how these different modes of its emergence are related (a) to the vicissitudes of the grandiose self during childhood and (b) to certain current experiences in the setting of the clinical transference. The therapeutic mobilization of the grandiose self may thus arise either directly (*primary mirror transference*), or as a temporary retreat from an idealizing transference (*reactive remobilization of the grandiose self*); or in a transference repetition of a specific genetic sequence (*secondary mirror transference*).

133

There is no need for a lengthy separate discussion of the primary mirror transference since this form constitutes the usual mode of the clinical appearance of the transference remobilization of the grandiose self. Suffice it to repeat then, as emphasized in other places, that, given the appropriate, noninterfering, attitude of the analyst, the primary mirror transference will establish itself spontaneously in the analysand. The specific type of the transference (whether merger, alter-ego transference, or mirror transference in the narrower sense) is determined by the pathognomonic fixation point. And the specific fears which the patient experiences while the transference establishes itself (such as fear of uncontrollable regression expressed in falling dreams; fears of uncontrolled overstimulation by the reactivated primitive exhibitionism; fear of loss of contact with reality due to the upsurge of grandiose fantasies; etc.) are related to the specific type of the transference which is being set in motion. The same, of course, holds true for the specific resistances which, motivated by the patient's specific apprehension, will oppose the establishment of the transference. The careful observation of the mixture of tentative transference manifestations, and of the specific fears and resistances which are related to them, is of great value to the analyst since it may give him clues concerning not only the genesis of the pathology but also the specific dynamic interplay between central grandiosity and exhibitionism, on the one hand, and surrounding personality structures, on the other, which are often not discernible with equal clarity in the later stages of the analysis.

If the analysand's fears cause him unwarranted discomfort or if they protractedly interfere with his ability to attempt to re-engage (the interest of) the archaic self-object in the remobilized grandiose self, then it is helpful for the analyst to explain the significance of the initial impasse to the patient. Such explanations cannot, of course, contain specific genetic material, and the communication of intuitively established genetic reconstructions by the analyst should be avoided since they tend to be experienced by the patient as an invitation to establish a nonspecific, defensive, archaic relationship with an omniscient object. If the analyst, however, restricts himself to giving the patient a friendly clarification of the dynamics of the current situation, then the patient will see that the analyst is familiar with the type of disorder from which he suffers, he will feel more secure, and his anxiety and the correlated resistances will diminish.

THE REACTIVE MOBILIZATION OF THE GRANDIOSE SELF

Despite the great practical importance of the reactive mobilization of the grandiose self, there is also no need for its detailed discussion in the present context. Its position—as a way station, or as a turning point—in the typical regressive swings which occur during the analysis of narcissistic personality disorders was depicted diagrammatically in Chapter 4 (position 2A, Diagram 2, p. 97), and its manifestations in the course of treatment are illustrated by clinical examples (see cases G. in Chapter 4 and L. in Chapter 10) which demonstrate some of the consequences of the analyst's faulty responses in reaction to an idealizing transference.

The retreat from an idealizing transference to a (reactive) mobilization of the grandiose self concerns a tactical detail of the analytic process which is, in essence, not different from the familiar temporary regressions that follow certain frustrations of object libido in the analysis of transference neuroses. These typical cathectic shifts take place within the broader context of a narcissistic transference—the term transference (or, specifically, mirror transference) is, however, not a suitable one for the clinical manifestations of the reactive mobilization of the grandiose self. What ensues under such circumstances is hardly ever a positive therapeutic deployment of the grandiose self but a rapid hypercathexis of an archaic grandiose self image which is rigidly defended by hostility, coldness, arrogance, sarcasm, and silence (position 2A in Diagram 2). In a number of instances the regression which follows the disappointment in the idealized object does not stop at the level of archaic narcissism but moves further toward the hypercathexis of the autoerotic, fragmented body-mind-self with painful experiences of hypochondriacal worry and archaic shame (position 3 in Diagram 2). Between the retreat positions of archaic narcissism (2A) and autoerotism (3) we occasionally encounter ephemeral manifestations of near-delusional merger fantasies associated with the patient's uncertainty concerning his identity.

Such primitive identifications, intermingled with hypochondriacal worries, were, for example, not infrequently experienced by Mr. E. (Chapter 5), who, at moments when he was disappointed in the analyst, felt that he was taking on the bodily or facial features of his dead mother. This primitivization of the looking-merging expression of his unfulfilled oral-tactile yearnings and of his wish for aim-inhibited tenderness and empathy (from a maternal figure) occurred even in advanced stages of his analysis, i.e., at periods when he had already become capable of the sustained performance of creative sublimatory activities which had replaced the primitive visual merging of his voyeuristic perversion (see the discussion of this phase of Mr. E.'s analysis in Chapter 12).

Ominous as the manifestations of these regressive states would seem to be, in most instances neither analyst nor patient became unduly alarmed by them. There are rare exceptions, it is true (see, for example, the case vignette referring to Mr. G. in Chapter 4, in which the severity of the regression and the intensity of the anal drive elements with the corresponding paranoid attitude were indeed alarming); but in the vast majority of the cases of the type of pathology with which this study is concerned these regressions are clearly a part of the therapeutic process and are soon accepted by the patient as grist for the mill of the insight-producing work which leads to the gradual expansion and strengthening of his ego.

These regressive swings are neither preventable nor are they indeed therapeutically undesirable. Given the analysand's narcissistic vulnerability, they cannot be avoided since no analyst's empathy can be perfect—not anymore than could be a mother's empathy vis-à-vis the needs of her child. And, as stated before, the understanding that is gained from their therapeutic scrutiny is of great value to the patient. The analytic work, however, does not focus on the regressive position itself which constitutes a retreat from a workable narcissistic transference; and the *isolated* interpretation of the content of the manifestations of the archaic grandiose self or of the patient's hypochondriacal worries and shame experiences would thus be fruitless and a technical error. Once the dynamic context of the current transference swing has been clarified, there is no need to avoid the empathic reconstruction of the childhood feelings which correspond to those which accompany the temporary regressive position in the analysis. Thus an analogy between the patient's present hypochondriacal concerns and the vague health worries of a lonely child who feels unprotected and threatened can be drawn, facilitating the patient's grasp of the deeper meaning of his present condition as well as of its genetic roots. The primary task of the analyst, however, at these junctures, is still the recognition of the total therapeutic movement, and his interpretations must focus primarily on the traumatic event that precipitated the retreat.

THE SECONDARY MIRROR TRANSFERENCE

In most instances the mirror transference evolves gradually from the beginning of treatment (primary mirror transference); in a number of cases, however, it is preceded by an initial brief phase of idealization. The significance of the secondary mirror transference is less apparent than that of the reactive mobilization of the grandiose self; and the genetic connotations of its appearance, in particular, require examination.

During a limited initial period in the analysis of certain, otherwise apparently self-centered or self-absorbed, narcissistic personalities, the temporary presence of an idealizing transference is unmistakable. Even if this idealizing attitude of the patient is not disturbed by premature interpretations, or by other active or passive interferences from the side of the analyst, it often disappears quickly, to be replaced by clear signs in the patient's behavior and his free associations which indicate that a shift from the mobilization of the idealized object to that of the grandiose self has taken place and that a mirror transference (in the form of any of its three developmentally determined subtypes) has become established. This then persists throughout the long span when the systematic working-through processes focus on the integration of the remobilized grandiose self. The initial idealization of the analyst must usually be understood as the manifestation of a specific intermediate step on the backward path of the analysand's not yet completed therapeutic regression. In such instances we see, in the patient's dreams and memories, the images of figures whom he admired and idealized in his early life, although their emergence is clearly related to his current attitude toward the analyst; or we encounter the patient's direct expression of consciously experienced admiration for the analyst.

A clinical example of the first kind of idealization (images of admired figures in early dreams) preceding a secondary mirror transference will be adduced later in the context of the discussion of the tendency of some analysts (at times due to a mobilization of their countertransference) to respond with erroneous or premature or otherwise faulty interpretations when they are idealized by their patients. This case, Miss L. (Chapter 10), almost certainly constitutes an example of a fleeting idealizing transference attitude (as expressed indirectly) in the initial dreams of an analysis. In this case the idealization reinstated a short-lived attempt at organizing an onrush of threatening narcissistic tensions through the idealization of an admired priest in early adolescence. A stalemate in the analysis, which occurred in consequence of a mistake by the analyst, delayed not the continuation of an idealizing transference but the channeling of the exhibitionistic demands of the grandiose self into a workable mirror transference.

A clinical example of the second kind of idealization (direct expression of conscious admiration for the analyst) preceding a secondary mirror transference is contained in the extensive account (related, however, primarily in a different context) of the analysis of Mr. K. (Chapter 9). During a brief, early period in this patient's analysis he had openly expressed great admiration for the analyst and had idealized the analyst's appearance, behavior, and physical and mental capabilities. The brief idealization repeated an abortive idealizing attempt during the patient's childhood (he was about three and a half years old at the time) directed toward his father. When, after the birth of a brother, the attitude of the patient's mother suddenly changed from uncritical admiration to critical rejection of him and his demands for attention, the child attempted to deal with his intense narcissistic frustration by setting up his father as an admired idealized image to whom he could attach himself. This attempt failed, however, for a number of reasons, especially because the patient's father despite considerable external successes seems to have been afflicted with a specific, severe disturbance of his self-esteem which made him unable to accept the role his son had tried to assign to him. Thus, instead of allowing the child to glorify him and to obtain a sense of narcissistic gratification and balance by attaching himself to the admired figure, the father rejected the child's admiration and belittled and criticized his wish to set up an identificatory attachment.

The child's attempts to create an idealized father imago

were thus short-lived, and he retreated toward attitudes and activities designed to bring about the revival of the narcissistic balance that had been characteristic of an earlier period in his life. He now attempted to enhance his self-esteem through the reinstatement of the old grandiosity and exhibitionistic display that had once been fostered by his mother. Specifically he turned toward an enactment of grandiose and exhibitionistic pursuits in the form of athletic activities, which persisted into his adult life and became the nodal point of his later successes and failures. The details of this patient's instructive personality development will not be presented at this point. The present vignette of a genetically crucial period in his early life is given only in order to clarify how the specific sequence of the establishment of his narcissistic transference in analysis (an initial period of idealization, followed by a secondary mirror transference) repeated a sequence of events in his childhood (the brief attempt at idealization which was followed by a return to the hypercathexis of the grandiose self).

Whether expressed openly or in disguise, directed at the analyst or indicated by allusions to him, metapsychologically these fleeting idealizations constitute the revival of a forward step in one of the important developmental directions of narcissism which had not been successfully completed in childhood: namely, of the attempt to establish a reliably idealized parent imago as a precursor to the achievement of its internalization in the form of the idealized superego. Thus, unlike the temporary swings from the idealized parent imago to the grandiose self which occur later in therapy (reactive mobilization of the grandiose self), the shift from the mobilization of the idealized parent imago to that of the grandiose self repeats in these cases a specific sequence from the childhood of the analysand: (a) the tentative idealization of a childhood object; (b) a (traumatic) interference with the idealization; and (c) (a return to) the hypercathexis of the grandiose self. Neither the brief period of idealization nor the ensuing spontaneous shift toward the grandiose self must be disregarded since it is this total sequence which constitutes the essential transference repetition of the crucial psychological events from the past. The analyst must, therefore, neither reject the initial idealization nor attempt to prolong it artificially.

The clinical significance of the idealization of the therapist which precedes the establishment of a secondary mirror transference is threefold.

1. The idealization of the therapist may be taken as a specific test to which the patient exposes the therapist early in their encounter (see Chapter 10).

2. The idealization of the therapist may be evaluated as a favorable prognostic sign since, in these cases, the working-through process opens two roads to the remobilized narcissistic cathexes: (a) it provides the opportunity for a therapeutic transformation of the grandiosity and exhibitionism of the archaic grandiose self into realistic ambitions and self-esteem; and (b) during late phases of treatment when a renewed idealization of the analyst (secondary idealizing transference) has taken the place of the (secondary) mirror transference, it provides the opportunity for a therapeutic transformation of an idealized parent imago into internalized ideals.

3. The fact, finally, that there is in these cases, during the phase of the establishment of the therapeutic regression, a temporary standstill in the retrogressive movement of the narcissistic libido at the stage of idealization may also be taken as the announcement of an important therapeutic aim; as if an unreached developmental goal of childhood were briefly illuminated early in therapy before it again disappears from sight.

Occasionally, though less regularly and conspicuously, an idealizing transference may also establish itself during the later phases of an analysis that has been characterized by the presence of a mirror transference from the beginning of treatment (primary mirror transference). In such cases—as well as, of course, in all cases of secondary idealizing transference which follow a secondary mirror transference—the working-through process consists of two phases: an earlier one in which the mirror transference is the focus of analysis; and a later one (secondary idealizing transference) in which the analytic work deals with the now cohesively emerging idealization.

CHAPTER 7

THE THERAPEUTIC PROCESS IN
THE MIRROR TRANSFERENCES

What is the goal and what is the content of the specific work-ing-through processes which are set in motion during the analysis of the grandiose self? As in the earlier discussion of the working-through process in the idealizing transference, it is best to begin by comparing the working-through process which focuses on the grandiose self in the mirror transference with the well-known analogous therapeutic action in the transference neuroses.

The crucial therapeutic agent in the psychoanalytic treat-ment of the transference neuroses is the interpretation of the unconscious object-directed strivings (and of the defenses against them) which have been mobilized in the treatment situation and which use preconscious imagery about the analyst as the central vehicle for the formation of transfer-ences. The process of working through, i.e., the ego's repeated encounter with the repressed strivings and its confrontation with the archaic methods which it uses in fending them off, leads to expansion of the realm of ego dominance, the goal of psychoanalytic therapy.

Analogous to the incestuous object investments which be-come remobilized in the analysis of the transference neuroses, the grandiose self which is activated in the mirror transfer-ence had not been gradually integrated into the reality-oriented organization of the ego but had, in consequence of pathogenic experiences (e.g., of prolonged enmeshment with a narcissistic mother, followed by traumatic rejection and disappointment) become dissociated from the rest of the psychic apparatus. The exhibitionistic urges and grandiose fantasies thus remain isolated, split off, disavowed, and/or repressed, and are inaccessible to the modifying influence of the reality ego.

I cannot here enter into an extended discussion of the disadvantages as well as the advantages (in adaptation) which accrue to the growing personality from a dissociation and/or repression of the grandiose self but will mention only the two main psychic dysfunctions which are related to it: (1) the tensions produced by the damming up of primitive forms of narcissistic-exhibitionistic libido (the heightened tendency to hypochondriacal preoccupation, self-consciousness, shame, and embarrassment), and (2) the lowering of the capacity for healthy self-esteem and of ego-syntonic enjoyment of activity (including *Funktionslust* [Bühler]) and success which is due to the fact that the narcissistic libido is tied to the unrealistic unconscious or disavowed grandiose fantasies and to the crude exhibitionism of the split-off and/or repressed grandiose self and thus unavailable to the ego-syntonic activities, aspirations, and successes which surround the (pre)conscious self experience.

If, for example, a person's narcissistic libido is bound to a repressed unmodified flying fantasy, he may be deprived not only of the feeling of well-being that emanates from healthy locomotion but also of the enjoyment of goal-directed action and of "the soaring of the imagination" (Sterba, 1960, p. 166), i.e., of sublimated thought-action. The flying fantasy, it may be added here, appears to be a frequent feature of unmodified infantile grandiosity. Its early stages are common to both sexes and are probably reinforced by ecstatic sensations while the small child is being carried by the omnipotent idealized self-object; its later stages, however, concern, in the boy, the blissful experiences which surround the lifting up of the penis during the first erections (Greenacre, 1964). Flying dreams and fantasies are, of course, ubiquitous and occur in many varieties.[1]

The essential aspect of the working-through processes in the mirror transference involves the mobilization of the split-off and/or repressed grandiose self and the formation of preconscious and conscious derivatives which penetrate into the reality ego in the form of exhibitionistic strivings and of grandiose fantasies. Analysts are, in general, familiar with the mobilization of the later stages of the grandiose self when its grandiosity and exhibitionism are amalgamated with firmly established object-directed strivings. Specific environmental situations during the child's oedipal stage foster this type of grandiosity, which is in these instances experienced within the framework of (and subordinated to) object-libidinal strivings. If the child has no realistic adult rival, for example, because of the death or absence of the parent of the same sex during the oedipal phase; or if the adult rival is depreciated by the oedipal love object; or if the adult love object stimu-

---

[1] The irrational fear of heights (acrophobia) is, as I could ascertain through psychoanalytic observation in two cases, at least in some instances not constructed according to the model of a psychoneurotic symptom (i.e., as symbolic castration anxiety in reaction to the mobilization of an incestuous wish [see, in this context, Bond, 1952]), but is due to the mobilization of the infantile, grandiose belief in one's ability to fly. To be specific: the unmodified grandiose self urges the ego to jump into the void in order to soar or sail through space. The reality ego, however, reacts with anxiety to those portions of its own realm which tend to obey the life-threatening demand.

The essential psychopathology which accounts for these instances of acrophobia is paralleled by that which forms the metapsychological substratum of certain cases of motion sickness (see Kohut, 1970a). In other words, the propensity of certain individuals to develop motion sickness is also not constructed like a hysterical symptom, i.e., the symptom does not arise in consequence of the fact that the exposure to rhythmical motion revives the experience of prohibited infantile sexual stimulation, but it arises in consequence of the repetition of a disturbance of the secure merger with the idealized self-object —for example, in the form of a person's exposure to an external situation (such as being in a car with an unempathic driver) which resembles the unempathic way in which the idealized object carried the child who attempted to gain psychological stability and security through merging into it.

lates the child's grandiosity and exhibitionism; or if the child is exposed to various combinations of the preceding constellations, then the phallic narcissism of the child and the grandeur which are appropriate to the early oedipal phase are not exposed to the confrontations with the child's realistic limitations that are phase-appropriately experienced at the end of the oedipal phase and the child remains fixated on his phallic grandiosity.

The various (often, but not always, deleterious) symptomatic results of such fixations are well known, such as the counterphobically exaggerated display of many so-called phallic personalities (speed racers, daredevils, etc.) where an anxious ego disavows an early acquired recognition that the oedipal exaltation was unrealistic and, denying its intense castration anxiety, asserts its invulnerability vis-à-vis realistic danger and requires a continuous supply of admiration and acclaim for its reassurance.

The ego's insecurity in such instances of fixation on early oedipal grandiosity, however, is hardly ever simply due to the unrealistic nature of the claims and aspirations of the phallic grandiose self. As a matter of fact, psychologically uncomplicated fixations of this type lead at times to the result that the ego attempts to live up—nondefensively, i.e., not primarily in order to bring about reassurance against the threats of castration anxiety—to the demands of the phallic grandiosity, which in turn, with luck and endowment, may bring about realistically valuable achievements.

In most instances, however, the nexus of causative circumstances is more complex. For example, behind the imagery concerning the relationship of a boy's grandiose self with a depreciated father (in the girl, with a depreciated mother) lies regularly the deeper imago of the dangerous, powerful rival-parent, and, as stated before, the defensive oedipal narcissism is principally maintained to buttress the denial of castration anxiety.

Not only is it important to realize that the oedipal grandiosity of the child is a defensive one; it is also noteworthy that behind the depreciating attitude of the oedipal love object (the mother in the case of the boy) toward the oedipal rival (the father) and the manifest preference for the (thus over-stimulated) child (the son), there is in the oedipal love object (mother) regularly a covert attitude of admiration and awe toward her own oedipal love object (the mother's father). Thus the mother who overtly belittles the adult male (i.e., the boy's father) and who appears to prefer the boy harbors a deep admiration, mixed with awe and fear, toward the unconscious imago of her own father. The son participates in the mother's defensive belittling of his father and elaborates this emotional situation by spinning out grandiose fantasies; he senses, however, the mother's fear of the strong male figure with the adult penis and realizes (unconsciously) that her exaltation of him, the son, is maintained only so long as he does not develop into an independent male. In other words, he functions as a part of his mother's system of defenses.

The bulk of the cases, however, with which this study is concerned, deals not with the results of the fixation on oedipal grandiosity (characterized by the admixture of strong object cathexes and the presence of castration fears) but with instances in which the major fixations are fastened to earlier points in the development of the child's narcissism. Disregarding the structural complexities which occur when phallic fixations are evaded by a display of defensively regressive infantile attitudes or when early fixations are presented through the medium of later (e.g., oedipal) experiences ("telescoping"), I now turn to the examination of the content and the position of the prephallic grandiose self and of the analytic work that is concerned with it.

The aim of the analysis is, of course, the inclusion into the adult personality (the reality ego) of the repressed or otherwise nonintegrated (isolated, split-off, disavowed) aspects of the grandiose self, whatever its developmental position, and the harnessing of its energies in the service of the mature sector of the ego. The primary central activity in the clinical process during the mirror transference thus concerns the patient's revelation of his infantile fantasies of exhibitionistic grandeur. The raising to consciousness, however, and the increasing acceptance of formerly dissociated grandiose strivings by the reality ego, and, as a consequence of the previous steps, the communication of these fantasies to the analyst, proceed in the face of strong resistances.

The content of the grandiose fantasies[2] and the detailed vicissitudes of their painful confrontation with reality during therapy will not be discussed extensively here since the main focus is the transferencelike condition which establishes itself in analysis and, in particular, its psychoeconomic and psychodynamic significance in the clinical process.

In addition, it must be admitted that it is often disappointing for the analyst to behold the apparently trivial fantasy which the patient, after so much time, labor, and intense inner resistance has ultimately brought into the light of day and which, often accompanied by a last burst of intense shame and resistance, he finally describes to the analyst. *Parturient montes, nascetur ridiculus mus.* (The mountains will be in labor, a ridiculous mouse will be born. Horace, *Ars Poetica,* 139.) The disappointment of the analyst (in contrast to the intense emotion which the analysand experiences while he, for the first time, shares his innermost secret with another person and thus, in effect, with himself) may be in part due to the analyst's resistances against the regression which a full empathic resonance with the archaic material would require. The failure of the revelation to make a strong emotional impact on the analyst may, however, also be due to the fact that in the preceding long drawn-out period of working through

2 For a general discussion of the genesis and function of "grandeur and omnipotence fantasies" see the relevant remarks dispersed widely in a number of J. Lampl-de Groot's essays (1965, esp. pp. 132, 218, 236, 269, 314, 320, 352ff.). Concerning typical fantasies, in particular the fantasy of being able to fly, see also Kohut (1966a, p. 253ff. and p. 256f.) for a specific illustration concerning a flying fantasy which became integrated into reality-adapted behavior.

the primary process material has been gradually changed into a secondary process form, has become communicable, so to say, and is now no longer what it once was, even though the patient himself still experiences during its revelation an echo of its former immense power.[3]

True, at times even the content of the fantasy permits an empathic understanding of the shame and hypochondria, and of the anxiety which the patient experiences: shame, because the revelation is at times still accompanied by the discharge of crude, unneutralized exhibitionistic libido; and anxiety because the grandiosity isolates the analysand and threatens him with permanent object loss.

Patient C., for example, had the following dream during a period when he was looking forward to being publicly honored and celebrated: "The question was raised of finding a successor for me. I thought: How about God?" The dream was partly the result of the not altogether unsuccessful attempt to soften the grandiosity through humor; yet it aroused excitement and anxiety, and led, against renewed resistances, to the frightening recall of childhood fantasies in which he felt that he was God.

In many instances, however, the grandiosity which forms the nucleus of the fantasies revealed by the analysand is only hinted at. Patient D., for example, recalled with intense shame and resistance that as a child he used to imagine that he was running the streetcars in the city. The fantasy appeared harmless enough; but the shame and resistance became more understandable when the patient explained that he was running the streetcars through a "thought control" which emanated from his head, and that his head (apparently disconnected from the rest of his body) was way above the clouds while it exerted its magical influence.

3 For a discussion of the changes which unconscious fantasies undergo in the process of becoming conscious and for an indication of the possibility that unaltered primary process fantasies may be "beyond the compass of (the sensory organ) consciousness as are the ultraviolet rays to the eye," see Kohut (1964, p. 200).

In other instances the grandiose fantasy contains elements of a magical-sadistic control over the world; the patient is Hitler, Attila the Hun, etc., and he has large populations under his (magical) control whom he influences as if they were inanimate pieces of machinery. Magical destruction of buildings and cities and their magical rebuilding also play a role, as does, at times, the total dominance over a single other person, who, however, is the only reality that is left in an otherwise empty world. Some patients report the belief that everybody is their servant, slave, or property (patient H.) and that everybody whom the child encountered knows this but does not talk about it; and, similarly (patient G.), there may exist the conviction—not just the fantasy!—(in a patient who, as an adult, was more severely disturbed than the others who are being mentioned here) that everybody in school knew his name, while he did not know theirs—he was Rumpelstiltskin in reverse—and that this circumstance attested to his unique, elevated position among the children, and was not the outgrowth of the simple fact that he was unable to relate to them while they, in reality, knew, of course, each other's names, as well as his. Finally, there is the recurrent theme of being "special," "unique," and very frequently, of being "precious" ("like a very fine instrument," "like a very fine watch"), which appears to be the nodal point of a host of frightening, shameful, and isolating narcissistic fantasies that cannot find more definitive expression than that permitted by these words.

Occasionally the analyst may witness a specific resistance to the full integration of the infantile grandiose fantasy, even after it had been apparently fully recovered and acknowledged. This resistance takes the form of the patient's inability to employ his insight as a stepping stone toward realistic action. Under these circumstances the analyst's interpretations must often focus on the contrast between fantasied greatness and realistic success. He must show that the patient is still unable to tolerate these two facts: (a) that there is a risk of failure in any action, however well prepared it may be; and (b) that the scope of even great realistic successes is limited. The patient, in other words, has mastered the irrational content of his grandiose fantasies, but has not yet transformed his need for omnipotent certainty concerning the results of his efforts and for unlimited success and acclaim into the ego-syntonic attitudes of persistence, optimism, and reliable self-esteem.

Mr. N., a physiologist, had achieved considerable improvement of a broad and deeply ingrained work inhibition during analysis. But he continued to experience severe difficulties when faced with the task of preparing the results of his research for publication. His grandiose fantasies had become sufficiently integrated with his realistic ambitions and action patterns to constitute a solid impetus for his activities while he was carrying out the bulk of his research work. His persistent fixation on the archaic need for certainty of success and for limitless achievement and limitless acclaim, however, still made it impossible for him to reveal his finite achievement, to expose himself to the uncertainty of the response of the scientific community, and to accept the fact that the acclaim he could receive would be at best a limited one.

The encounter with reality of certain aspects of the grandiose fantasy may, however, not only be temporarily blocked by the aforementioned *specific* difficulty, but its rising to consciousness in all its aspects—or its integration with the structure of the ego when it had existed in a split-off state— and the freeing of the exhibitionistic needs which are associated with it, tend *in general* to be opposed by strong resistances. In its oedipal form (phallic grandiosity and phallic exhibitionism) the grandiose self is overshadowed by strong object configurations, and the prominent rivalry tensions and castration fears of this phase may obscure the specific anxieties and resistances that are elicited by the mobilization of the narcissistic aspects of the oedipus complex. In those instances, however, in which the spontaneous therapeutic regression brings about the activation of the prephallic grandiose self—especially of the stage in which the child needs the unqualified acceptance and admiration of his total body-mind-self, approximately during the later part of the oral phase of libido development—the anxieties and defenses which are specifically related to the narcissistic structures are more easily distinguished. True, the presence of oral and anal drive elements is unmistakable; but here it is primarily not the aims of these drives (and even less: specific verbalizable fantasies concerning their objects) but their primitiveness and quantity which cause the apprehension. In other words, the danger against which the ego defends itself by keeping the archaic grandiose self dissociated and/or in repression is the dedifferentiating influx of unneutralized narcissistic libido (toward which the threatened ego reacts with anxious excitement) and the intrusion of archaic images of a fragmented body-self (which the ego elaborates in the form of hypochondriacal preoccupations).

Having stated the principle, I must acknowledge that in the actual clinical situation it is at times not easy to determine quickly and reliably whether the nucleus of the activated pathogenic structures which dominate the transference lies in the realm of prephallic narcissism or of the oedipal phase. The analyst's decision rests (1) on his empathic grasp of the nature of the patient's central anxieties and of the defensive maneuvers which he employs in order to escape from them; and (2) on his theoretical comprehension of the various relationships which may exist between the (prephallic and phallic) narcissistic structures and the structures which relate to the object-invested conflicts of the oedipal period.

As I said before, the central anxiety encountered in the analysis of narcissistic personality disorders is not castration anxiety but the fear of the dedifferentiating intrusion of the narcissistic structures and their energies into the ego. Since the symptomatic results of such intrusions have already been discussed and demonstrated, I shall only enumerate them briefly here. They are: fear of loss of the reality self through ecstatic merger with the idealized parent imago, or through the quasi-religious regressions toward a merger with God or with the universe; fear of loss of contact with reality and fear of permanent isolation through the experience of unrealistic grandiosity; frightening experiences of shame and self-consciousness through the intrusion of exhibitionistic libido; and hypochondriacal worries about physical or mental illness due to the hypercathexis of disconnected aspects of the body and the mind. This listing of the ideational content of the fears which are experienced during the analysis of narcissistic personalities could be expanded and the description of the psychic elaboration of the patient's apprehensions could be refined. Here, however, I would rather draw attention again to a general quality of these anxieties, namely that, on the whole, they tend to be vague and that the ego's primary fear is aroused in response to the quantity of the excitations and to the threat of the archaic nature of the energies which are intruding into its realm.

There is, of course, little difficulty in distinguishing these fears from the phobic retribution anxieties of the oedipal phase when the castration anxiety is experienced more or less directly in the form of the fear of being killed or mutilated by a circumscribed adversary of superior strength. The differentiation becomes more difficult, however, (a) when the oedipal anxieties are expressed in preoedipal symbols; or (b) when a broad, defensive regression to preoedipal levels has taken place in order to escape from the castration fears. Although these complexities do not otherwise belong to the subject matter of this monograph, they must be dealt with insofar as they relate to the differentiation with which we are concerned. Thus, by comparison with the anxieties elicited by the threatened intrusion of narcissistic structures, there is in both of the above-mentioned instances, always, sooner or later, at least a hint of a triangular situation; there is, furthermore, a greater degree of elaboration of the source of the danger (a personal adversary); and finally there is a greater degree of elaboration of the nature of the danger (i.e., the punishment). The differentiation between (a) hypochondriacal worry (elaborated in terms of fears of physical or mental illness) which is due to fears of autoerotic fragmentation, and (b) castration anxiety expressed regressively as fear of disease (or in terms of prephallic drive elements, e.g., fears of being swallowed, eaten, bitten, drowned, poisoned, suffocated by being buried alive, etc.) may serve as an example.

In the first instance, i.e., in the case of the fear of the intrusion of archaic narcissistic cathexes which threaten the cohesiveness of the self, the analyst will obtain the impression that, the longer the analytic work proceeds, the more vague the content of the apprehension will become. The patient may ultimately speak of vague physical pressures and tensions, or of fears of loss of contact, of contentless, stimulating anxious excitement, etc., and he may begin to talk about childhood moments of being alone, of not feeling quite alive, and the like. The opposite, however, will hold true in the second instance, i.e., in the case of regressively elaborated castration fears. The longer the analytic work proceeds here, the more specific the elaboration of the fear will become, and the more circumscribed the sources of the danger. And, finally, if the patient recalls childhood episodes of competition with superior rivals which are followed by experiences of retribution fears, there is then, of course, no doubt about the fact that the activated conflicts belong to the oedipal phase. Due to the regression of oedipal material, on the one hand, and the elaboration and the tendency toward the telescoping of narcissistic and autoerotic tensions with later experiences, on the other hand, the manifest pictures may thus at first seem similar. The therapeutic movement, however, and the underlying flavor of the experience point into opposite directions and allow the differentiation.

With regard to the general organization of a patient's psychopathology, the following relationships may exist between the phallic-oedipal structures in which the child's wounded narcissism plays only a secondary role, and the narcissistic structures (phallic and prephallic) which are the leading pathogenic determinants of a narcissistic transference. (1) Either (a) the narcissistic or (b) the object-transference pathology is clearly predominant; (2) a dominant narcissistic fixation coexists with an important object-transference pathology; (3) a manifestly narcissistic disorder hides a nuclear oedipal conflict; and (4) a narcissistic personality disorder is covered by manifestly oedipal structures. Only careful observation and noninterference with the spontaneous development of the transference will, in many instances, allow the decision with which of these relationships the analysis is dealing. It must also be mentioned, however, that even in some cases of genuine, primary narcissistic fixation, an oedipal symptom cluster (e.g., a phobia) may still emerge, if ever so briefly, at the very end of the treatment and must then be dealt with analytically as in the case of a typical primary transference neurosis.

ACTING OUT IN THE NARCISSISTIC TRANSFERENCES
THE PROBLEM OF THERAPEUTIC ACTIVISM

The asocial nature of the grandiose self accounts for its fundamental resistance to the influence of psychoanalysis, and one of the most important transference resistances encountered during the mobilization of the repressed grandiose self in analysis is thus its deflection from the mirror transference and the employment of its instinctual energies in the syndrome of asocial acting out. Much of the overt and covert delinquent behavior of narcissistic personalities (including the asocial acts which occur during analytic therapy) is therefore neither due to a defect in the superego (except, indirectly, insofar as the insufficient idealization of the superego is related to the fact that the main weight of the narcissistic cathexes is concentrated on the grandiose self), nor is it, in a pattern of uncomplicated impulsivity, simply due to the weakness of the ego vis-à-vis the drives. The acting out of narcissistic personalities is a symptom which is formed in consequence of a partial breakthrough of repressed aspects of the grandiose self. Thus, although usually maladaptive and often destructive, it may nevertheless be regarded as an achievement of the ego which amalgamates the grandiose fantasies and exhibitionistic urges to suitable preconscious contents and rationalizes them, analogous to the process of symptom formation in the transference neuroses.

The relationship between the tendency toward acting out and the mobilization of the grandiose self is a very specific one, i.e., in the analysis of the narcissistic disorders the occurrence of the seemingly alloplastic acting out rather than the formation of the seemingly more autoplastic psychoneurotic symptoms is due to the fact that the therapeutic process brings about simultaneously two important changes from the pretherapeutic psychic equilibrium: (a) the hypercathexis of the grandiose self, and (b) the weakening of the specific defensive mechanisms (repression-countercathexis; dissociation-disavowal) that had prevented the intrusion of the exhibitionistic-grandiose impulses of the grandiose self into the reality ego. The specific reason for the choice of acting out, however, as the pathognomonic emergency symptomatology during a mirror transference which has become temporarily uncontrolled is neither the intensity of the (grandiose-exhibitionistic) impulses, nor the primitiveness of the reverberating instincts (i.e., the frequent occurrence of unneutralized oral demands and oral-sadistic vengefulness), nor the weakness of the ego. The specific determinant of the acting out is the very narcissism of the mental organization which is involved in the sudden breakthrough of the grandiose self. The specific regression to the pathogenic fixation points leads to a lessening of the differentiation between self and not-self and thus to a blurring of the differentiation between impulse, thought, and action. In other words, what appears, on superficial scrutiny, to be alloplastic action is, in reality, not action but the autoplastic activity of a stage of psychological development in which the external world is still cathected with narcissistic libido.

Whatever the nature of a patient's propensity might be to deflect without delay the therapeutically mobilized psychic energies from the psychoanalytic situation itself, this tendency always confronts the analyst with the dilemma whether or not he should or must interfere with the patient's activities. The technical problem whether the analyst must become active and, if so, in what area and to what extent and degree, is, of course, to be evaluated not only with regard to the type of psychopathology, and to the metapsychological structure of the patient's activity which is correlated to it, but also often from the point of view of the practical question whether the danger that the patient might harm himself or others (the threat of suicide, homicide, delinquent and perverse activities which openly invite detection and punishment, etc.) is becoming so great that it must be dealt with. In these latter instances it is best for the analyst not to try to amalgamate the expression of his realistic concern with emergency interpretations, but to state simply and forthrightly that he hopes the patient will not carry out his ominous plans or will stop his hazardous activities. The necessity for such major forceful interference by the analyst, however, arises mainly in instances of borderline psychosis and in the related instances of profound ego defect which results in unbridled impulsivity. In cases of hysterical acting out (which is a dramatizing infantile language), however, the analyst's activity has a different, more strictly psychoanalytic, purpose which can (and should) be explained to the patient while it is being employed. The aim of the analyst's activity (his advice to the patient to stop the dramatizing enactments) is here— analogous to the aim of the technique which Freud suggested to Ferenczi with regard to the analysis of phobias (Ferenczi, 1919)—to channel the unconscious, repressed incestuous drives, and the conflicts about

them, toward a confrontation with the secondary processes of
the ego, i.e., to encourage the formation of verbal fantasy
derivatives in the form of free associations during the analytic
sessions.

All of these aforementioned considerations, especially those
with regard to the analyst's direct expression of concern in
case of danger, will apply at times to certain aspects of the
analysis of instances of acting out in cases of narcissistic personality disturbance. In general, however, the acting out is
here most directly to be understood as a form of communication within a total archaic comprehension of the world that
does not yet allow the distinction between action and thought.
While it is thus at times necessary—and effective!—to alert
the patient's ego that, *in the interest of self preservation,* a
change of activities is indicated, no moral issue must be raised
other than the practical and realistic one that, in view of the
prevailing mores of the times, the patient is putting himself
in jeopardy by his doings.

Apart from calling forth the expressions of realistic concern
from the side of the analyst, however, the actions of the
patient require interpretation, and—in contrast to the content of the acted-out dramatizations of hysterical or phobic
patients—they constitute here a valuable means of increasing
the span of the analysand's ego through insight. Thus, when
patient E. returned to dangerous voyeuristic pursuits in public toilets during separations from the analyst, or when he
felt that the analyst had not understood him, nonmoralizing
interpretations that his wishes for mirroring, approval,
and understanding had regressively deteriorated toward an
enactment of an archaic visual merger not only were effective
in giving him greater control on later occasions when he felt
disregarded or misunderstood, but also led to an ever-deepening grasp of his own personality and to the emergence of
significant relevant memories from his childhood. He recalled, for example, that the first episode of voyeurism in a
public toilet had occurred at a country fair after he had asked

his mother to watch and admire his skill on a high swing. When his mother, who was already severely ill (malignant hypertension) at the time, could not mobilize any interest in his wish to exhibit his prowess, he turned away from her and went to the public toilet. Driven by a force which he understood only now, but for which he could now also recall the appropriate feeling tone, he looked at a man's genitals and, merging into it, felt at one with the power and strength that it symbolized. (In theoretical terms: a regression from a stage corresponding to the mirror transference to that of a merger had taken place.)

The movement of the transference manifestations is in general from the more archaic forms (e.g., merger) to the most advanced position (mirror transference in the narrower sense). Patient E.'s behavior during the weekend separations from the analyst constituted a temporary reversal of this direction in response to the vicissitudes of the clinical transference relationship.

Another example of such a temporary regression from a mirror transference to a merger was furnished to me by a colleague.[4] The episode to be described is in certain respects analogous to the weekend behavior of Mr. E., but there is a decisive difference. Mr. E.'s regression took place *early* in the analysis, before significant structural changes had been achieved, and it involved an overt, dangerous *action*. In the case of Mr. I., the episode took place *late* in a generally successful analysis of a narcissistic personality disturbance and, as a result of the significant structural improvements that had already been achieved by the preceding analytic work, no action was involved and the regression was restricted to expressing itself in the form of a *dream*.

The patient, Mr. I., a twenty-five-year-old industrial employee, had brought old diaries from his childhood to an analytic session and had read them to the analyst. The analyst

[4] This analysis was conducted by a colleague (a man) in regular consultation with me.

reacted with interest to the content of the diaries, but—even though he was not aware of any emotional reserve on his part—he may have responded to the reading of the diaries with less than enthusiasm, feeling perhaps that the patient had put these written records between himself and the analyst; i.e., that the reading constituted an obstacle to the direct and free communication of the patient's thoughts and memories. Be that as it may, the patient, as can be deduced from his subsequent reaction, was disappointed in the analyst's response. In the following night he dreamed a two-part dream: (a) He had gone fishing and had caught a big fish. He brought the fish proudly to his father. But the father, instead of admiring the gift, was critical; (b) he saw Christ on the cross, suddenly slumping; the muscles suddenly relaxing, dying.

In reviewing the session which preceded the dream in the light of the total transference development, the conclusion could be drawn that in it the patient had temporarily retreated from a mirror transference *in sensu strictiori* to an archaic (masochistically experienced) merger. The analyst apparently did not appreciate fully the deep emotional meaning that the reading of the diaries had for the patient which in fact was not a resistance to communication but a true (i.e., analytically valuable) gift. The patient had indeed reached a stage in which formerly secret material from childhood could now be shared. The patient felt that the analyst (as had the patient's narcissistic father in childhood) had responded negatively to the patient's progress. (In analogous instances I have observed a tendency in analysts toward a narcissistic retreat from a patient who has undertaken an important step toward emotional health without the immediate, direct assistance of the analyst.) Thus the patient who had expected an approving acceptance (mirror transference on a differentiated and aim-inhibited level) of his psychological achievement felt rebuffed and retreated to a merger fantasy: Christ in death reuniting with God Father.

(" 'Father, into Thy hands I commit my spirit!' and having said this he breathed his last." Luke, 23, 46). The situation was in fact soon remedied when the analyst interpreted the meaning of this sequence to the patient.

The foregoing clinical vignette concerns a late stage in the successful analysis of a narcissistic personality. There is no doubt that in such instances no more is needed to allow the transference to return to its appropriate, basic level than a correct interpretation, albeit given with a realistic degree of warmth. The question of therapeutic activism, however, is of great importance in the treatment of certain specific types of narcissistic personalities. It was Aichhorn (1936) who, in introducing his active technique for the creation of a thera- peutically effective emotional attachment to the analyst in the treatment of juvenile delinquents, took the pioneering theoretical and technical steps in this area. Anna Freud (1951) described Aichhorn's technique as follows; "Owing to the peculiar narcissistic structure of his personality, the im- postor is unable to form object-relationships; nevertheless he can become attached to the therapist through an overflow of narcissistic libido. But his narcissistic transference will set in only where the therapist is able to present to the impostor . . . a glorified replica of his own delinquent ego and ego- ideal" (p. 55).

In suggesting that the analyst offer himself actively to the patient as an ego ideal, Aichhorn neither differentiated be- tween the ego ideal and its precursor, the idealized parent imago, nor did he assign a separate and special position to the grandiose self. Yet Anna Freud's brief summary of Aich- horn's active technique with these specific cases is quite compatible with the theoretical formulations proposed with regard to the transference conditions that are established in the analysis of a broad spectrum of narcissistic personality disturbances beyond the cases of juvenile delinquency. When, for example, she says that the therapist presents to the im- postor "a glorified replica of his own delinquent ego and ego-ideal," this formulation is partly akin to the differentiation between a transference on the basis of a therapeutically reactivated grandiose self (specifically a twinship or alter-ego relationship to the therapist) and of a transference on the basis of a reactivated idealized parent imago.

The application to Aichhorn's work of the earlier considerations concerning therapeutic activity will be helpful to us in sharpening our theoretical grasp of this technical problem.

There is hardly any doubt that Aichhorn's active techniques which encourage the establishment of a narcissistic transference are unavoidable in the treatment of some types of gross delinquency in general and of juvenile delinquency in particular; these are emergency measures which are required in order to create an emotional bond with the analyst —i.e., a transferencelike focusing of the grandiose self and/or of the idealized parent imago upon him—which will initially keep the patient from leaving the therapy. The evaluation of the active establishment of a transference bond in such cases should, however, in principle, begin with the question whether the actively created transference relates to a (delinquent) grandiose self or to the idealized parent imago. A delinquent's capacity to attach himself to the analyst in open admiration may well indicate that an idealized parent imago and the deep wish to form an idealizing transference were (preconsciously) present, but that they had been denied and hidden. Certain adolescents (or adults who prolong a certain type of adolescence throughout their life) will often proclaim their apparently complete commitment to the grandiose self (preconsciously, because of the embarrassment about the weakness which idealizing attitudes seem to imply to them, or because of their fear of the ridicule to which nonvirile sentimentality might expose them). Behind these preconscious fears of social disgrace, however, lies unconscious fear of a traumatic rejection of their idealizing attitude by the idealized object or the anticipation of a traumatic disillusionment with the idealized object—a dread, in other words, of frustrations in the narcissistic realm which would lead to intolerable narcissistic tensions and to the painful experience of shame and hypochondria.

Although the psychoanalytic treatment of cohesive syndromes of juvenile delinquency of the type treated by Aichhorn is not within the scope of my direct clinical experience, certain conclusions about Aichhorn's methods in establishing a narcissistic transference with such cases can be drawn on the basis of Aichhorn's own clinical descriptions and on the basis of experiences with related disorders. I would thus suggest that the success of Aichhorn's procedure is due to the following circumstances. We assume that the delinquent's basic fixation is on the idealized parent imago and on the central pathognomonic transference propensity which corresponds to this constellation, i.e., the propensity to establish an idealizing transference. Surrounding this nuclear yearning for an idealized object, however, are those layers of the delinquent's personality which not only deny the yearning for the idealized object, and for an idealized superego, but which, on the contrary, make him loudly proclaim his contempt for all values and ideals. Or, expressed in different words, there is a defensive hypercathexis of the grandiose self (perhaps acquired originally after a painful disappointment in an idealized object or the loss of it). The flaunting of omnipotent unrestricted activities and the delinquent's pride in his skill of ruthlessly manipulating his environment serve to buttress his defenses against becoming aware of a longing for the lost idealized self-object, and against the emptiness and lack of self-esteem that would supervene if the continuous elaborations of the delinquent grandiose self, in word and deed, were to cease. If the therapist would offer himself to such a delinquent as an ideal figure in the world of values, he could not be accepted. It was Aichhorn's special skill and understanding for the delinquent that led him to offer himself first as a mirror image of the delinquent's grandiose self. He was thus able to initiate a veiled mobilization of idealizing cathexes toward an idealized self-object without disturbing the necessary protection of the defensively created grandiose self and its activities. Once a bond is established, however, and idealizing cathexes have been mobilized, a working-through process becomes possible and a gradual shift from the omnipotence and invulnerability of the grandiose self to the more deeply longed for omnipotence and invulnerability of an idealized object (and the requisite therapeutic dependence on it) can be achieved.

The specific problems posed by the active mobilization of the grandiose self in the psychoanalytic treatment of narcissistic delinquents (especially adolescents) is not a principal focus of this study. Here we are dealing with the analysis of the ordinary narcissistic personality disorders in which delinquent activities in the usual sense do not dominate the clinical picture. In the analytic treatment of these cases, however, it is not desirable to create a situation in which the analysand's regressive compliance is actively utilized for the purpose of bringing about an idealization of the therapist. The active encouragement of an idealization of the analyst leads to the establishment of a tenacious transference bondage (analogous to the attachments which are fostered by organized religions), bringing about a cover of massive identification and hampering the gradual therapeutic alteration of the existing narcissistic structures. We may well heed Freud's relevant warning that there exists "a temptation for the analyst to play the part of prophet, savior and redeemer to the patient," i.e., to encourage the patient to put the analyst "in the place of his ego ideal," a procedure to which "the rules of analysis are diametrically opposed" (1923, p. 50n.).

Yet, while it is analytically deleterious to bring about an idealization of the analyst by artificial devices, a spontaneously occurring therapeutic mobilization of the idealized parent imago or of the grandiose self is indeed to be welcomed and must not be interfered with.

A few general remarks concerning the so-called passivity of the psychoanalyst during the psychoanalytic treatment may be in order at this point since the opposition of psychoanalysts to assuming a role of leadership vis-à-vis their patients is often mistakenly discussed as if it were a moral issue (cf., for example, Hammett, 1965, esp. p. 32) which could be joined by putting one value system (the analyst's equalitarianism, modesty, and the like) against another (that he ought to acknowledge his unavoidable responsibility as the patient's leader and guide since he should indeed know the answers to some of the patient's problems of living). The choice, however, must be made on the basis of our understanding of what the elements are that constitute the essential factors in the process of the psychoanalytic cure. If the analyst assumes actively the role of "prophet, saviour and redeemer," he actively encourages conflict solution by gross identification, but stands in the way of the patient's gradual integration of his own psychological structures and of the gradual building up of new ones. In metapsychological terms the active assumption of a leadership role by the therapist leads either to the establishment of a relationship to an archaic (prestructural), narcissistically cathected object (the maintenance of the patient's improvement depends thereafter on the real or fantasied maintenance of this object relationship) or to massive identifications which are added to the existing psychological structures. By contrast, psychoanalytic therapy allows transferences to develop spontaneously (including the relations to archaic, narcissistically cathected objects) and, via the working-through process, the projected or otherwise mobilized structures are transformed and gradually reinternalized (transmuting internalization). Thus, in the last analysis, the qualitative difference between inspirational therapy and psychoanalysis can be understood as a quantitative one: the former works through the active establishment of object relations and massive identifications, the latter through the spontaneous establishment of transferences and minute processes of (transmuting) reinternalization.

The preceding statement, while correct in principle, must be modified to take account of two stages during which the internalization processes in the course of the analysis of narcissistic personalities are indeed temporarily not "minute" and not "transmuting" as predicated before, but gross, massive, and unassimilated. To be specific: gross identification processes can be observed either relatively early in the treatment (as precursors or harbingers of small-scale, structure-building, transmuting internalizations), or they may occur late, i.e., generally during the first part of the terminal phase, under the quasi-traumatic impact of the task of the ultimate relinquishment of the narcissistic transference object.

Gross identifications with the analyst—his behavior, mode of speaking, attitudes, tastes—are thus frequently observed in the early part of the analysis of narcissistic personalities. They are a favorable sign, in particular, if they do not occur immediately but after a period devoted to systematic work on broad resistances which oppose the establishment of the appropriate narcissistic transference, and they should be welcomed by the analyst as a first step toward the attainment of conditions which will permit the structure-building working-through processes to take place. It is especially instructive to study this change in the pattern of identification during analyses in which the profession of the analysand facilitates —and serves to rationalize!—his adoption of the professional behavior of the analyst as he observes it in his own analysis.

During certain training analyses of candidates with narcissistic personality organizations, for example, or in the therapeutic analyses of psychiatrists, the following specific sequence of events may at times take place. There is at first a phase in which there appears to be no evidence of transference reactivity. Treatment interruptions, for example, seem to call forth no noticeable reaction in the analysand. This stage is followed by a period in which the analysand responds to disturbances of the narcissistic transference—e.g., an interruption in the sessions—by gross, unassimilated identifications with single features of the analyst. (He will, for example, during the analyst's absence feel drawn to buy a particular piece of clothing which, as he discovers only later to his great surprise, is identical with one worn by the analyst.) Gradually, however, as these events are worked through repeatedly, the nature of the identificatory processes changes: they are not gross and indiscriminate anymore, but become selective —increasingly focusing on features and qualities which are indeed compatible with the analysand's personality and enhance (up to now dormant) talents of the patient himself. Thus, certain selectively compatible, favorable professional qualities and skills of the analyst become more and more assimilated by the patient in the identificatory process; they do not constitute identificatory foreign bodies anymore (such as the frequently occurring identifications with the aggressor formed in response to the activities of the analyst which the patient experiences as traumatic), to be discarded after they have served some emergency purpose. Ultimately the patient, paralleling the gradual achievement of an internal relinquishment of the (narcissistically cathected) analyst, may discover with calm but deep and genuine pleasure that he has acquired solid nuclei of autonomous function and initiative —in his everyday life and in the mode of his perception and understanding of his own patients, including his own, individually specific, mode of communicating with them.

Some evidence of a renewed propensity toward the establishment of gross identifications may also be encountered in the terminal phase (especially in the early part of this phase) of the analysis of narcissistic personality disturbances. This phenomenon should be viewed without undue alarm by the analyst and should be taken as grist for the analytic mill, just as are the previously described gross identifications which occur earlier during the treatment.

Mr. I., for example, portrayed the reconcretization of the

(formerly appropriately: small-scale) processes of transmuting internalization during the terminal phase of his analysis in dreams which occurred a few months before the expected end of his analysis. During this period the analysand alternated, on the one hand, between hypochondriacal worries about the stability and sufficient development of his own psychological equipment and, on the other hand, a confident mood in which he looked forward to the final separation from the analyst with an anticipatory enjoyment of his autonomous functioning. During the worried periods there was evidence of the regressive perception of his need to buttress his psychological structure through further internalizations in the form of (resexualized) oral and anal incorporative urges. He would overeat, and he had dreams of a passive-homosexual nature in which the analyst was to enter into him through the anus. During the further processes of mastering this resurgence of internalization needs he portrayed the grossness of this last-minute attempt to obtain still more from (or rather: of) the analyst in the following, almost humorous, dreams (the patient had indeed acquired a modicum of humor during the analysis—one of the very reliable signs of success in these cases). In one dream (early in the termination phase) the analyst is discovered by X-rays to be dwelling inside the patient's bowels. In another dream (later in the termination phase) the patient swallows a clarinet (the analyst's penis; or rather his voice, i.e., the instrument of his influence and efficacy in the analytic situation). After the musical instrument has been swallowed, however, it continues to play music from the patient's inside. (Compare this dream with the masturbation fantasies of case A. In this context see, in particular, Chapter 3, note 4.)

THE GOALS OF THE WORKING-THROUGH PROCESS
CONCERNING THE ACTIVATED GRANDIOSE SELF

The nature of the psychological transformations which are brought about by analytic therapy can frequently be understood best by focusing on intermediary, transitional stages of the relevant working-through process. In the analysis of narcissistic personalities, while the work is concerned with the gradual realistic integration of the grandiosity and exhibitionism of the grandiose self, we encounter, frequently and characteristically, a specific stage in which the psychologically impoverishing repression of the deeper-lying sources of self-confidence and of pleasure in the self seems to have been largely abolished and a victory of realism and ego dominance thus seems already to have been won. Closer scrutiny reveals, however, a partial persistence of superficial compliance rather than the achievement of a completed structural change. I shall illustrate this important transitional stage with the aid of two clinical vignettes.

Mr. J., a gifted creative writer in his early thirties, had been in analysis with me for some time and seemed to be achieving a degree of mastery over his unmodified grandiosity and exhibitionism which constituted a grave disturbance of his well-being and productivity. In many of his dreams during this early phase of his analysis his grandiosity was expressed in Superman terms: he was able to fly. Finally, rather suddenly after I had made a forceful statement concerning the persistence of certain aspects of the patient's grandiosity in his work, the flying disappeared from his dreams and the patient began indeed to walk in his dreams like an ordinary mortal. Despite this dramatic change of the manifest content of his dreams, however, the grandiosity of his methods and goals regarding his work persisted and I expressed doubts about the patient's pointedly walking in the dreams. It was then that the analysand was able to recognize and admit that, though he had seemed to walk in his dreams and was not flying anymore, his feet were still a tiny distance off the ground. To all onlookers he appeared to be walking normally —only *he* knew that his feet never actually touched the ground.

Another phenomenon which indicates the presence of an

analogous transitional stage during the working-through process concerning the grandiose self is the appearance of dreams in (techni)color. Mr. A., a professional man in his late twenties, with homosexual preoccupations and strong narcissistic fixations, had made steady progress in the course of his analysis and had, in consequence of the internal change, been able to improve his external life situation considerably. He had formed a meaningful attachment to a woman and had undertaken important steps toward the achievement of independence and success in his professional pursuits. Although the hub of his psychopathology was related to a fixation on an idealized father imago and although the major part of the working-through process dealt with his unceasing search for an idealized male figure and with his wish to attach himself to such a powerful, idealized protector, the episode to be described occurred during a late phase of the working-through process that was focused on a subsidiary area of psychopathology: the fixation on the grandiose self and the corresponding mirror transference. The analytic material of recent months had dealt with his attempt to face the realistic difficulties and setbacks of his professional life without succumbing to the regressive pull of the grandiose fantasies which related to periods in his childhood when he had replaced his father whose prolonged absences from home and realistic helplessness in the face of overwhelming external circumstances had led both to a demand for the revival of an all-powerful self-object and to the intensification of the cathexis of his grandiose self. Recently, however, the patient had indeed been able to function realistically and, while still often discouraged and overly sensitive concerning certain unavoidable setbacks, had resisted the tendency toward prolonged narcissistic retreat. Gradually the external situation changed for the better and he recognized that his realism was paying off.

One day, when he was obviously pleased about a series of favorable developments in his professional life, he reported a dream which alluded to various recent successes and to the fact that he was now a responsible and adult man, involved in the battles of life and accepting the reality of this role with its shortcomings and pleasures. To this portrayal of his realism and success the patient added two afterthoughts: his most recent sexual performance had not yet been as good as it should have been; i.e., his ejaculation had come too quickly, and—seemingly unrelated to the complaint about the sexual performance—he mentioned that the people in the dream had been somewhat like toy soldiers or puppets and that the whole dream had been in color.

I am omitting from the present account the intermediary links which permitted me to grasp the significance of the patient's current psychological condition and will report only my final conclusion. In essence, I explained to the patient that seeing himself as an adult in real life was still a new experience for him, that he felt it partly as if it were the fantasy of a small child who plays at being a grownup (a fantasy that is suddenly destroyed when the father comes home), and that he therefore reacted to his realistic achievements with some anxious excitement—hurriedly as if they were not solid and would disappear. And I pointed out to him that his ego was not yet completely done with the task of accepting this new image of himself, calmly and without hurry and apprehension. The hurried performance of the sexual act—always such a sensitive indicator of the equilibrium of the personality—was probably the expression of these inner conditions, and the unrealistic features in the dream, and especially the fact that the dream was in color, were similarly the expression of the incompleteness of the ego's ability to integrate the new self concept fully: some of the old grandiosity and exhibitionism were still, in their unchanged form, mixed in with the adult self-concept, without having undergone a complete transformation. After brief reflection, the patient replied quietly that I had understood him well and, he added, that the dream was not just in color, but had been in an exaggerated and not quite real color: in technicolor.

I should like to add here the general statement that dreams in color are frequently dreams in technicolor. They often appear to signify the intrusion of unmodified material into the ego in the guise of realism, and the ego's inability to integrate it completely. One might say that the technicolor expresses the ego's subliminally experienced anxious hypomanic excitement over certain intrusions of the grandiosity and the exhibitionism of the grandiose self.

Although the metapsychology of ejaculatio praecox does not, strictly speaking, belong in the present context, a few words about it may be in order since it is not an infrequent symptom in narcissistic personality disturbances. In general, it may be said that the inability to elaborate the sexual impulse during the sexual act through a variety of experiences and activities and thus to maintain the sexual tension without immediate discharge is due to a defect in the basic, drive-controlling structure of the psyche. This defect is the result of a chronic lack of structure-forming experiences of optimal frustration during the preoedipal period. It makes little difference whether this lack of basic structure is the result of the pathological personality of the parents (which is the usual cause) or of other circumstances (such as the absence of parental figures). What is decisive is the fact that there is a lack of opportunities for the gradual decathexis of the child's preoedipal objects, a dearth of structure-building internalizations in the psyche, and thus the child's capacity to desexualize and otherwise neutralize his impulses and wishes remains incomplete. Stated in different terms: the secondary process in such individuals occupies only a thin surface layer of the psyche, it does not provide the reliable psychological elaboration of drive-near psychic processes, and it is fragile and (as in the present example concerning Mr. A.) easily swept away under the impact of various stresses. Mr. A.'s tendency toward the (homo)sexual experience of his needs and wishes and his tendency toward ejaculatio praecox were, therefore, due to the same defect in the basic neutralizing structure of his psyche.

The working-through process in such personalities implements and completes the insufficient and insecure internalizations acquired in early life and thus brings about not only an increasing dominance of the secondary process but also *pari passu* a decrease of the tendency toward the sexual experience of nonsexual psychic material. The need for desexualizing (and de-aggressivizing) psychic structure is at times dreamed about by such patients (by Mr. E., for example) as a search for such symbols of the secondary process as books or libraries, especially during periods when there are separations from the analyst who is beginning to be experienced by the analysand as an external, auxiliary psychic structure which not only functions as a stimulus barrier vis-à-vis stresses that are imposed from the outside but also enables him to control and to modify his drives through their neutralization and psychic elaboration.

Adults who possess a reliably functioning drive-neutralizing and drive-elaborating psychic structure can temporarily relinquish their secondary processes, with pleasure and without anxiety, since they feel certain of their ability to regain them. Sleep and orgasm are, therefore, the foremost proving ground for a person's capacity to decathect the secondary processes. Persons, on the other hand, whose basic psychic structure is flimsy, brittle, or only insecurely established tend to be afraid of the decathexis of the secondary processes. They may thus experience difficulties in falling asleep, and their capacity to abandon themselves to the enjoyment of orgasm may be disturbed in a variety of ways.[5]

[5] An instructive illustration of the specific anxiety which the orgastic experience may produce in a person whose drive-controlling and drive-elaborating psychic structure is only precariously established is furnished by Paul Tolpin (1969). Tolpin's patient depicted the sleeping ego's experience of mounting sexual tension leading to a nocturnal emission in a dream in which he was riding on a fast-moving train. He got up from his seat and began to move forward, passing on from car to car. When he realized that he had left his books on his seat, he wanted to return to the car from which he had started out. But it was too late: he realized with horror that the part of the train

The foregoing clinical examples illustrate in some detail certain specific reactions that may occur during the working-through process of the mirror transference before a more secure integration of the archaic grandiose self with the structure of the ego has taken place. Whatever these intermediate stages may be, however, in the end the grandiose self will gradually become integrated with the structure of the ego if the working-through process is not interfered with. Concomitantly, the more archaic forms of the therapeutic mobilization of the grandiose self tend to become replaced by a mirror transference (in the narrower sense of the term) in which the analyst's separateness is more and more acknowledged by the analysand (see Chapter 5). Even at this stage, however, the analysand acknowledges the object only as a source of approval, praise, and empathic participation: the analyst is a need-satisfying object (cf. Hartmann, 1952; Anna Freud, 1952) in the area of the patient's narcissistic requirements.

Finally, in some instances, the mirror transference disappears altogether toward the end of the analysis and the analyst may then become either (a) a narcissistically idealized figure (idealizing transference) or (b) a love object toward whom the patient extends neutralized narcissistic cathexes in the form of that aim-inhibited exhibitionism, heightened self-esteem, and overestimation of the love object which are the normal narcissistic accompaniments of (infantile-incestuous and mature) love.

If a mirror transference becomes ultimately replaced by a stable idealizing transference (either as the third phase in instances of secondary mirror transference or at the end of a primary mirror transference), then we can assume that a part

---

on which he was now riding had become separated from the part where he had left his books. This dream portrays the experience of mounting sexual tension (walking from car to car) and the anxious recognition that the ego has now irreversibly been taken over by the sexual experience; i.e., that it has lost its access to the drive-controlling and drive-elaborating secondary processes (the books). The fact that this patient's major symptom was ejaculatio praecox is, of course, fully compatible with his deficiency of drive-neutralizing and drive-elaborating psychic structure.

of the narcissistic cathexes has been altogether deflected from the grandiose self and is now employed in the cathexis of the idealized parent imago. A part of the narcissistic cathexes thus becomes ultimately available for the reinforcement of the idealization of the superego.

These results of the working-through process of a mirror transference must, however, be considered as secondary. Just as the primary goal of the working-through processes in the idealizing transference is the strengthening of the basic neutralizing structure of the psyche and the acquisition and strengthening of ideals, so is the primary goal of the working-through processes in the mirror transference the transformation of the grandiose self which results in a firming of the ego's potential for action (through the increasing realism of the ambitions of the personality) and in a strengthening of realistic self-esteem.

THE FUNCTIONS OF THE ANALYST IN THE
ANALYSIS OF THE MIRROR TRANSFERENCE

As in the analysis of the transference neuroses, the analyst's essential activity lies in the main in the cognitive field: he listens, he tries to comprehend, and he interprets. His evenly hovering attention must move with the flow of the analytic material as he participates in the slow, painstaking, and for him emotionally usually less stimulating task of analyzing the manifestations of the activated grandiose self during the working-through phase of the mirror transference in which the analysand assigns to him the performance of only one function: to reflect and echo his grandiosity and exhibitionism; or in which (in the merger and the twinship) the analysand confines the analyst to the more or less anonymous existence either of being included in the system of his grandiose self or of being its faithful replica.[6]

    [6] See in this context Koff (1957; esp. p. 430f.). The analyst's becoming "a willing extension of the patient" is described as being in the service of the establishment of "rapport." (Cf. my discussion of the difference between "rapport" and "narcissistic transference" in Chapters 1 and 8.)

The analysand's demands for attention, admiration, and a variety of other forms of mirroring and echoing responses to the mobilized grandiose self, which fill the mirror transference in the narrow sense of the term, do not usually constitute great cognitive problems for the analyst, although much subtlety of understanding may have to be mobilized by the analyst to keep pace with the patient's defensive denials of his demands and with the general retreat from them when an immediate empathic response to them is not forthcoming. If the analyst, however, truly comprehends the phase-appropriateness of the demands of the grandiose self and if he grasps the fact that for a long time it is erroneous to emphasize to the patient that his demands are unrealistic but that, on the contrary, he must demonstrate to the patient that they are appropriate within the context of the total early phase that is being revived in the transference and that they have to be expressed, then the patient will gradually reveal the urges and fantasies of the grandiose self and the slow process is thus initiated which leads—by almost imperceptible steps, and often without any specific explanations from the side of the analyst—to the integration of the grandiose self into the structure of the reality ego and to an adaptively useful transformation of its energies.

The acceptance by the analyst of the phase-appropriateness of the analysand's narcissistic demands counteracts the chronic tendency of the reality ego to wall itself off from the unrealistic narcissistic structures by such mechanisms as repression, isolation, or disavowal.[7] Correlated to the last-named mechanism is a specific, chronic structural change to which I would like to refer, in a modification of Freud's terminology (1927, 1937b), as a *vertical split in the psyche*. The ideational

---

[7] For a comparison with similar conditions which prevail with regard to the idealized object, see Chapter 4, n. 1. Basch (1968), reviewing the relationship between external reality and disavowal, examined the significant position occupied by disavowal among defense mechanisms.

and emotional manifestations of a vertical split in the psyche —in contrast to such *horizontal splits* as those brought about on a deeper level by repression and on a higher level by negation (Freud, 1925)—are correlated to the side-by-side, conscious existence of otherwise incompatible psychological attitudes *in depth.*[8]

The nature of the analyst's interventions is decisively influenced by his grasp of the metapsychological basis of the psychopathology which he analyzes. With regard to the metapsychology of the psychopathology of those patients with narcissistic personality disorders in whom a faulty integration of the grandiose self forms the basis of the disturbance, two groups should be differentiated. To the first, less numerous, group belong those persons in whom the archaic grandiose self is present predominantly in a repressed and/or negated state. Since we are here dealing with a horizontal split in the psyche which deprives the reality ego of the narcissistic nutriment from the deep sources of narcissistic energy, the symptomatology is that of narcissistic deficiency (diminished self-confidence, vague depressions, absence of zest for work, lack of initiative, etc.).

The second group, more numerous than the first, comprises those cases in whom the more or less unmodified grandiose self is excluded from the domain of the realistic sector of the psyche by a vertical split. Since the grandiose self may, therefore, be said to be present in consciousness and, at any rate, influences many activities of these personalities, the sympto-

---

[8] The fetish of the fetishist, too, must be understood as the psychic content of a (vertically) split-off sector of the psyche *in depth.* The ego part of this split-off sector of the psyche of the fetishist is under the influence of the id part with which it is in unbroken contact. (In this context see Schafer [1968, p. 99] who speaks of "suborganizations [which] include elements of the id and superego systems as well as of the ego system.") The manifest result— in harmony with these structural relationships—is, therefore, not an openly held belief that women have penises. Instead, the fetishist experiences conscious desires which are in tune with the conviction of the existence of the female phallus which is held in the deeper (unconscious) layers of the split-off sector of the psyche.

matic effect is, in part, different from that seen in the first group of cases. The patients' overt attitudes are, however, inconsistent. On the one hand, they are vain, boastful, and intemperately assertive with regard to their grandiose claims. On the other hand, since they harbor (in addition to their conscious but split-off grandiosity) a silently repressed grandiose self which is inaccessibly buried in the depths of the personality (horizontal split), they manifest symptoms and attitudes which resemble those of the first group of patients, but which are strongly at variance with the openly displayed grandiosity of the split-off sector.[9] The conditions which prevail in this second group of patients will be illustrated shortly with the aid of a case vignette (case J.; see also case F. in Chapter 11).

The technically decisive maxim which determines the analyst's attitude, however, is the following. The analyst addresses himself neither to the part of the psyche where the grandiosity is repressed (i.e., the analyst does not speak to the id) nor to that part of the psyche (including its ego aspect) which is split off. He always addresses himself to the reality ego (or to the remnants of the reality ego). He should no more try to educate the conscious grandiose sector of the psyche than he would try to educate the id—he must concentrate his efforts on the task of explaining the (vertically and horizontally) split-off parts of the psyche to the reality ego (including the reality ego's defensive struggles against them) in order to open the road toward its ultimate dominance. Only through a grasp of these relationships is the seeming

---

[9] It goes without saying that there is a third mode of the distributions of narcissism, approximating the optimum conditions, in which grandiosity and exhibitionism are neither repressed nor split off and repressed to a psychoeconomically significant degree, but where the deep sources of grandiosity and exhibitionism—after being appropriately aim-inhibited, tamed, and neutralized—find access to and become alloyed with the reality-oriented surface aspects of the ego.

paradox resolved that even the overt, and sometimes noisily displayed narcissistic demands of the analysand are to be countered not by an educational attitude of prohibition and admonishing realism but, on the contrary, by an attitude of acceptance which stresses the phase-appropriateness of these demands within the context of the transference revival of an archaic state. The patient will then come face to face with formerly unrecognized defenses which had protected him against the discovery that, despite the seemingly self-assured assertion of narcissistic claims by one sector of his psyche, the most centrally significant sector of his personality is deprived of the influx of self-esteem-sustaining narcissistic libido.

The actual clinical circumstances are frequently very complex since ego distortions (which then temporarily require a bit of educational pressure [see Kernberg, 1969]) may during certain periods also occur in the central, most reality-near sector of the psyche. Finally, as indicated before, we are confronted not only with the reality ego's reluctance to face squarely the conscious but split-off aspects of the grandiosity and to accept their psychological relevance, but also with its (unconscious) fear of the demands of the repressed archaic grandiose self which bear little resemblance to the patient's consciously maintained claims of greatness or uniqueness. Here, indeed, lies an area in which the analyst's empathy and specific clinical experience must combine with much patience to allow him to identify those concrete, yet often very subtle, points of leverage that will enable him to mobilize and to remove the endopsychic obstacles which block the approach to the repressed or otherwise inaccessible aspects of the archaic grandiose self.

Case J., for example, whose grandiosity and exhibitionism were in some areas flagrantly displayed, seemed for a long time to offer no access to deeper-lying aspects of his grandiose self, and the temptation was great to counter his unrealistic demands with exhortations and other educational means.

One day (this episode took place *after* the one described above) the patient mentioned casually that, when he was done with shaving in the morning, he always carefully rinsed his shaving brush, cleaned and dried his safety razor, and even scrubbed the sink, before he washed and dried his face. The account seemed irrelevant; yet it was given in a slightly arrogant and tense fashion which caught the analyst's attention. The arrogance which was discernible in the patient as he told the analyst about his shaving habit contrasted strongly with the open arrogance with which he pursued many of his narcissistic claims. The current feeling tone was that of a *defensive* arrogance (a reaction, as will become intelligible shortly, that was motivated by the sudden awareness that the central narcissistic transference was becoming engaged in the psychoanalytic process). It appeared in the form of an embarrassed and tense haughtiness.

I shall not go into the clinical details of this episode and will in particular disregard the specific resistances which opposed the investigation of the patient's apparently trivial statement. In retrospect, however, it can be evaluated as the first hint at the presence of a path which led to the discovery of a significant aspect of the patient's personality and to the uncovering of a genetically important part of the patient's childhood history. We had up to this point been aware only of the patient's overt vanity and of that part of his childhood history which was correlated to his arrogance—namely that he had received his mother's (as it seemed: inordinate) acclaim for various performances in which he was shown off by her for the enhancement of her own self-esteem. This noisily displayed grandiose-exhibitionistic sector of his personality had occupied throughout his life the conscious center of the psychic stage. Yet it was not fully real to him, provided no lasting satisfaction, and remained split off from the coexisting, more centrally located sector of his psyche in which he experienced those vague depressions coupled with shame and hypochondria that had motivated him to seek psychoanalytic help.

At first it was tempting to explain the patient's depressions, shame propensity, and hypochondria by assuming the existence of a direct dynamic relationship between these symptoms and the patient's overt grandiosity. One might have thought, in other words, that his mother's ambitious expectations of him had become internalized in the superego and had there formed an unreachably high, unrealistic ego ideal (Saul, 1947, p. 92ff.; Piers and Singer, 1953) or ideal self (Sandler et al., 1963, p. 156f.), by comparison with which the patient felt himself to be a shameful failure.[10] The actual psycholog-

---

10 Small (subliminal) shame signals play a role in maintaining a homeostatic narcissistic equilibrium between superego and ego and the basic processes between id (the unconscious grandiose self) and ego which are responsible for the production of painful shame may secondarily be utilized by whole cultures (Benedict, 1934) and by individual (parental) educators (Sandler et al., 1963) in the service of values which become integrated into the superego. The notion that shame is in general a reaction of an ego that has failed to fulfill the (perhaps unrealistic) demands and expectations of a strong ego ideal (Saul, 1947) must be rejected, not only on theoretical grounds but especially on the basis of clinical observation. Many shame-prone individuals do not possess strong ideals, but most of them are exhibitionistic people who are driven by their ambitions; i.e., their characteristic psychic imbalance (experienced as shame) is due to a flooding of the ego with unneutralized exhibitionism and not to a relative ego weakness vis-à-vis an overly strong system of ideals. The intense reactions of such people to their setbacks and failures, too, are—with rare exceptions—not due to the activity of the superego. After suffering defeats in the pursuit of their ambitious and exhibitionistic aims, such individuals experience at first searing shame and then often, comparing themselves with a successful rival, intense envy. This state of shame and envy may ultimately be followed by self-destructive impulses. These, too, are to be understood not as attacks of the superego on the ego but as attempts of the suffering ego to do away with the self in order to wipe out the offending, disappointing reality of failure. In other words, the self-destructive impulses are to be understood here not as analogous to the suicidal impulses of the depressed patient but as the expression of narcissistic rage. Finally, it must be kept in mind that progress in the analysis of shame-prone people is usually not achieved on the basis of trying to diminish the power of overly strong ideals—a frequent technical error!—but often (in addition to the strengthening of the ego vis-à-vis the demands of the grandiose self and thus the achievement of increasing mastery of exhibitionism and grandiosity) on the basis of a shift of the narcissistic investments from the grandiose self to the superego, i.e., on the basis of a strengthening of the idealization of this structure.

ical situation, however, was quite different. The apparently trivial symptomatic bit of the patient's behavior, i.e., his specific shaving habit, was the first indication of the presence of a hitherto uninvestigated area of the patient's personality. It led the analysis into a new direction which permitted access to an unconscious (to be exact: insecurely repressed) archaic grandiose self. It was the repression of this psychological structure, however, and not the demands of an idealized superego, which was the cause of the patient's depressed moods and of his shame propensity and hypochondria.

The masochistically tinged shaving habit was the outgrowth of a specific rejection of his body-self; it was the endopsychic replica of the interplay between his need for a response to certain archaic—but now anxiously repressed—grandiose-exhibitionistic wishes concerning the acceptance of his body-self and his mother's inability to respond to them. Gradually, and against strong resistances (motivated by deep shame, fear of overstimulation, fear of traumatic disappointment), the narcissistic transference began to center around his need to have his body-mind-self confirmed by the analyst's admiring acceptance. And gradually we began to understand the pivotal dynamic position in the transference of the patient's apprehension that the analyst—like his self-centered mother who could love only what she totally possessed and controlled (her jewelry, furniture, china, silverware)—would prefer his material possessions to the patient and would value the patient only as a vehicle to his own aggrandizement; and that I would not accept him if he claimed his own initiative toward the display of his body and mind, and if he insisted on obtaining his own, independent narcissistic rewards. It was only after he had acquired increased insights into these aspects of his personality that the patient began to experience the deepest yearning for the acceptance of an archaic, unmodified grandiose-exhibitionistic body-self which had for so long been hidden by the open display of narcissistic demands via a split-off sector of the psyche, and that a working-through process was initiated which enabled him ultimately, as he put it jokingly, "to prefer my face to the razor."[11]

In general one can thus say that, as illustrated in the preceding case vignette, the time-consuming work which brings about the lowering of the defense barrier which opposes the integration of a "vertically" split-off sector with the central sector of the psyche leads to a new dynamic balance in the analysand.

What is the nature of the analytic work which is performed at such "vertical" barriers? What are the activities of the analyst that enhance the correlated endopsychic transformations? The substance of the psychological task is clearly not the classical one of "making conscious" with the aid of interpretations. It is akin to the abolishing of the defense mechanism of "isolation" as it occurs in the analysis of the obsessional patient. But, while the circumstances here bear a certain resemblance to those in obsessional neurosis, they are by no means identical. In the narcissistic personality disturbances (including, especially, certain perversions) we are not dealing with the isolation of circumscribed contents from one another, or with the isolation of ideation from affect, but with the side-by-side existence of disparate personality attitudes in depth; i.e., the side-by-side existence of cohesive personality attitudes with different goal structures, different pleasure aims, different moral and aesthetic values. It is the aim of the analytic work in such cases to bring the central sector of the personality to an acknowledgment of the psychic reality of the simultaneous existence (1) of unaltered conscious and preconscious narcissistic and/or perverse aims, and (2) of the realistic goal structures and the moral and aesthetic standards which reside in the central

11 The communicative power inherent in such remarks is matched by their ability to serve as retrospective foci of hard-earned, valid insights. Despite their repetitive use, they do not have the empty and defensive quality of a cliché, but they radiate the warmth and deep meaning of a "family joke" (E. Kris, as reported by Stein [1958] in his valuable essay on the cliché in analysis). See also Kris (1956b).

sector. The innumerable ways by which the increasing inte-gration of the split-off sector is brought about defy descrip-tion. But as a concrete and frequently occurring example I mention the overcoming of the often severe resistances —mainly motivated by shame—which oppose the patient's "mere" description of his overt narcissistic behavior, of his conscious perverse fantasies or activities, and the like. To say "mere" description is, of course, based on a profound misunderstanding of the dynamic relationships which prevail in such individuals. The informed analyst will understand how difficult it is for the patient to accept the split-off sector as truly contiguous with the central one, and he will realize the extent of the endopsychic changes which have been achieved when the patient has become able to drop the for-mer veil of ambiguity and indirectness and to describe his perverse fantasies or conscious grandiose claims and behavior without distortion. Seemingly paradoxically, the true accept-ance of the reality of the split-off sector is often accompanied by a feeling of astonished estrangement. "Is this really me?" the patient asks; "how did this get into me?" Or, for exam-ple, while still engaged in the enactment of perverse activi-ties: "What am I doing here?" This feeling of astonishment and estrangement must, of course, not be confused with the manifestations of the former split-off state. On the contrary, it is due to the fact that for the first time the central sector, with its own goals and its own aesthetic and moral values, is now truly in contact with the other self and is able to behold it in its totality.

Whatever the substance of the cooperative work of analy-sand and analyst during this period of the analysis might be, however, the analytically decisive result is the increased en-gagement of the central sector of the psyche in the transfer-ence, and thus the activation of the patient's *un*conscious narcissistic demands and their becoming available for a sys-tematic working-through process. It is only this latter work, however—and not any educational efforts with regard to the patient's split-off, overt grandiosity—which can lead to the ultimate integration of the analysand's narcissistic demands within the web of his realistic potentialities. Hand in hand with the increasing acceptance of his archaic narcissism, and with the increasing dominance of his ego over it, the patient will also grasp the inefficacy of the former narcissistic display in the split-off sector. Just as a hysterical patient may throughout his lifetime re-enact a traumatic infantile scene in innumerable hysterical attacks without achieving an iota

DIAGRAM 3

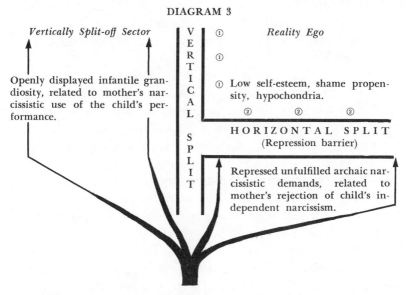

Vertically Split-off Sector

Openly displayed infantile grandiosity, related to mother's narcissistic use of the child's performance.

VERTICAL SPLIT

①   *Reality Ego*

①

① Low self-esteem, shame propensity, hypochondria.

②   ②   ②

HORIZONTAL SPLIT
(Repression barrier)

Repressed unfulfilled archaic narcissistic demands, related to mother's rejection of child's independent narcissism.

The arrows in the diagram represent the flow of narcissistic energies (exhibitionism and grandiosity). In the first part of the analysis the major therapeutic effort is directed (at the points marked ①) toward taking down the vertical barrier (maintained by disavowal), so that the reality ego is enabled to control the formerly uncurbed infantile narcissism in the split-off sector of the psyche. The narcissistic energies which are thus prevented from finding expression in the vertically split-off sector (left side of diagram) now reinforce the narcissistic pressure against the repression barrier (right side of diagram). The major effort in the second part of the analysis is directed (at the points marked ②) toward taking down the horizontal barrier (maintained by repression), so that the (self representation in the) reality ego is now provided with narcissistic energies, thus doing away with the low self-esteem, shame-propensity, and hypochondria which had prevailed in this structure so long as it was deprived of narcissistic energies.

of wholesome structural change, so also with the expression of a person's narcissistic claims via the (vertically) split-off sector of his personality. The gradual acceptance of the deep narcissistic demands by the reality ego, however, will lead to those wholesome transformations in the narcissistic realm which are the goal of the working-through process in the analysis of patients with narcissistic personality disorders.

Although the diagrammatic rendition of psychological relationships can be rightfully criticized as being of necessity an oversimplification, the preceding sketch should be excused since it is designed to serve the reader as an aid toward the comprehension of the structuro-dynamic complexities of the clinical illustration presented above.

The building up of psychological structure which is achieved via the liberation of the instinctual energies that had been bound to the archaic narcissistic configurations was discussed in connection with the relinquishment of the pre-structural, archaic self-object: the idealized parent imago. The hypothesis offered in that context also comprehends the principles of structure formation involved in the structure-building transformations of the grandiose self.

I shall now add a general remark about structure formation with regard to the archaic narcissistic configurations as well as some specific remarks about differences that exist between the role played by the idealized parent imago and the role played by the grandiose self in this context.

With the exception of the idealization of the superego which is the result of the oedipal internalization of the idealized parent imago, the new structures belong in general to the *area of progressive neutralization,* a sector of the mental apparatus in which the depth of the psyche is in unbroken contact with the surface (see the diagram on p. 136 in Kohut and Seitz, 1963).

Those of the structures laid down in this realm that are derived from the preoedipal internalizations of the idealized parent imago serve in general a drive-curbing function. Specifically, in our context, they constitute a modifying influence —in the nature of a sieve-in-depth—to the expression of archaic narcissistic demands and they form the elements which account for the ability of the psychic structure to neutralize them. As stated in Chapter 2, however, I believe that these narcissistic structural elements also play a (secondary) role in the neutralization of the object-directed sexual and aggressive drives. Analogous to their role in the superego, the narcissistic cathexes are, here too, amalgamated to drive-opposing sexual and aggressive cathexes (see Hartmann, 1950b, p. 132), providing them with that modicum of absolutarian authority which—as is the case with the superego—accounts for their power and effectiveness.

The structures which are acquired preoedipally in response to the gradual integration of the archaic grandiose self also are laid down in the area of progressive neutralization, i.e., in the sector of the personality where the depth and the surface form an uninterrupted continuum and where the reality-oriented layers of the psyche are thus able to use the deeper sources of energy for their purposes. (In contrast to the condition of *ego autonomy* [Hartmann, 1939], I would refer to this condition as *ego dominance*. In Freud's analogy [1923] one might think of the first as of the rider *off* the horse; of the second as of the rider *on* the horse.) Different from the structuralizations, however, that are laid down in consequence of the gradual decathexis of the idealized parent imago, the structures built up in response to the claims of the grandiose self appear in general to deal less with the curbing of the narcissistic demands but with the channeling and modification of their expression. The preoedipally laid down structures lead here specifically to a variety of phase-appropriate basic elaborations of the narcissistic urges, all of which leave their imprint on the adult personality. No hard and fast rule, however, can be set up here since a great deal depends on the specific interaction between child and parents. All one can say is perhaps that the drive-curbing aspects of the preoedipally acquired basic fabric of the psyche (including their narcissistic components) are more strongly influenced by the frustrations of the environment, while the drive-channeling structures (again, including their narcissistic components) are more strongly influenced by the child's innate drive equipment, by the innate resources of his ego, and by the substitution-offering guidance of the parents. The question how strongly the specific cultural milieu and congenital factors in the child's psychic makeup influence these conditions cannot, however, be answered within the context of a study (such as the present one) which is in the main based on the observation of material obtained in the psychoanalytic situation.

During the oedipal period, finally, simultaneous with and parallel to the decathexis of the glorified self-object, the child also relinquishes his unrealistic, grandiose self-image under the impact of the phase-appropriate recognition of the illusory nature of the unmodified oedipal fantasies of victorious phallic narcissism. It is this final massive (but phase-appropriate) decathexis of unmodified infantile grandiosity, however, which now supplies the narcissistic energies for the cohesive cathexis of a realistic self, for realistic self-esteem, and for the capacity to enjoy one's realistic functions and activities.

Although the foregoing considerations were presented in developmental terms, they apply *mutatis mutandis* with equal relevance to the analytic situation which, indeed, is in essence designed to bring about a process in which the original developmental conditions are reactivated and old developmental opportunities are again brought into play. The empathic comprehension of the manifestations of the *earlier* developmental stages of the grandiose self in the transference is, however, not achieved easily. It is, for example, usually difficult for the analyst to hold fast to the realization that the relative contentlessness of the analysis during prolonged periods—i.e., the meagerness of object-related imagery both in general as regards the current and past figures in the patient's life as well as in a narrower transference sense as regards the figure of the analyst himself—is the appropriate manifestation of an archaic narcissistic relationship. If a merger with the analyst has been established through the extension of an archaic grandiose self, the associative material may contain no recognizable references to the analyst; and in a twinship[12] psychological references to the analyst arise systematically and cohesively only with regard to the analysand's archaic experience of his own grandiose self as it gradually emerges from repression (② in Diagram 3) or is acknowledged as relevant by the reality ego after the barrier of disavowal (① in Diagram 3), which separated a split-off grandiosity from the reality ego, has been sufficiently removed.

A frequent misunderstanding of the mirror transference in general and of the therapeutic activation of the most archaic stages of the grandiose self in particular thus consists in its being mistaken for the outgrowth of a widespread resistance against the establishment of an object-instinctual transference. And many analyses of narcissistic personality disorders are either short-circuited at this point (leading to a comparatively brief, premature analysis of subsidiary sectors of the personality in which ordinary transferences do occur while the principal disturbance, which is narcissistic, remains untouched) or are forced into a mistaken and unprofitable direction against diffuse, nonspecific, and chronic ego resistances of the analysand.

Circumscribed resistances do, of course, exist and they may at times be intense and hard to overcome. In essence, however, they are motivated by specific fears aroused by the task of revealing the fantasies and urges of the grandiose self but not primarily by conflicts about the expression of object-directed libidinal or aggressive impulses. At any rate the absence of object-related references to the analyst is not a manifestation of resistance but is an expression of the fact

[12] See, for example, the description of the alter-ego transference of patient C. further on in this chapter.

that the pathognomonic regression led to the revival of a stage in which the object relationship is a narcissistic one. It is, therefore, just as erroneous (a) to explain the references to the analyst which do occur (e.g., demands that he serve as a reflecting, approving, and admiring mirror) as manifestations of currently active object demands (to be responded to as justified requests; or to be interpreted as the transference revival of object-instinctual strivings from childhood) as it is (b) to explain their absence as due to the patient's reluctance to establish a present-day therapeutic rapport, or to interpret it as a resistance against the development of an (object-instinctual) transference. In the narcissistic personality disorders, as I tried to express it on a previous occasion (1959), "the analyst is not the screen for the projection of internal structure . . . but the direct continuation of an early reality . . . [that could not be] transformed into solid psychological structures" (p. 470f.). This "early reality," however, is still experienced as co-substantial with the self.

THE SIGNIFICANCE OF THE MIRROR TRANSFERENCE AS THE
INSTRUMENTALITY OF THE WORKING-THROUGH PROCESS

The therapeutic regression (to the pathognomonic fixation point, i.e., the therapeutic activation of the unmodified grandiose self), which leads to the establishment of the mirror transference, is at times accompanied by anxiety, at times in the form of dreams of falling which occur during the early weeks of analysis. Once the pathognomonic regressive level has established itself, however, the major resistances against the gradual therapeutic disclosure of the grandiose self are motivated (1) by the patient's fear that his grandiosity will isolate him and lead to permanent object loss, and (2) by his desire to escape from the discomfort caused by the intrusion of the narcissistic-exhibitionistic libido into the ego where faulty discharge patterns tend initially to produce a mood of uneasy elation alternating with periods of painful self-consciousness, shame tension, and hypochondria. The ego tries to deny these painful emotions by a noisy counterphobic assertion of fearlessness and unconcern; to avoid them by renewed repression and/or by a reintensification of the vertical split in the psyche; or to bind and discharge the intruding narcissistic structures through the formation of emergency symptoms, especially in the form of asocial action.

The transference, however, functions here as a specific therapeutic buffer. In the mirror transference in the narrower sense the patient is able to mobilize his grandiose fantasies and exhibitionism on the basis of the hope that the therapist's empathic participation and emotional response will not allow the narcissistic tensions to reach excessively painful or dangerous levels. The patient hopes that his remobilized grandiose fantasies and exhibitionistic demands will not encounter the traumatic lack of approval, echo, or reflection to which they were exposed in childhood since the analyst will communicate to the patient his accepting empathic understanding for the role which they played in the patient's psychological development and will acknowledge the patient's present need to express them. In the twinship or the merger the analogous protection is provided by the long-term deployment of the narcissistic cathexes upon the therapist who now is the carrier of the patient's infantile greatness and exhibitionism. In these forms of the mirror transference the mobilized narcissistic cathexes attach themselves to the therapist who—without being idealized, admired, or loved—becomes a part of the patient's expanded self. The mirror transference in all its forms thus creates for the patient a position of relative security which enables him to persevere with the painful task of exposing the grandiose self to a confrontation with reality.

Developmentally, the position of the analyst in some forms of the transferencelike conditions that are established through the reactivation of the grandiose self (in particular those referred to as twinship or alter-ego transference) may be akin to that taken by certain types of imaginary playmates of narcissistic children (Editha Sterba, 1960). Whatever the variant of the mirror transference that has established itself may be, however, i.e., whether the mobilization of the narcissistic cathexes refers to earlier or to later stages in the development of the grandiose self, therapeutically most important is the fact that a workable object constancy in the narcissistic realm can be attained. The crucial function of the mirror transference is, in other words, that it brings about a condition which maintains the momentum of the therapeutic process.

We must not disregard, of course, the influence of the patient's conscious motivation: the wish to be relieved of his deficiencies and his suffering. And although unable to formulate the deeper purposes of the analysis, the analysand may sense that the therapeutic process will lead him from an insecure existence dominated by rapid emotional oscillations— between unbridled ambitions and a sense of failure, and between grandiose vanity and searing shame—to that increased equanimity, inner peace, and security which result from the transformation of archaic narcissism into cherished ideals, realistic goals and ambitions, and restrained self-esteem. The rational aims of therapy, however, could not, by themselves, persuade the vulnerable ego of the narcissistically fixated analysand to forego repression, disavowal, and acting out, and to face the needs and desires of the archaic grandiose self. In order to actuate, and to maintain in motion, the painful process which leads to the confrontation of the grandiose fantasies with a realistic conception of the self, and to the realization that life offers only limited possibilities for the gratification of the narcissistic-exhibitionistic wishes, a mirror transference in one of its forms must be established. If it does not develop, however, or if its establishment is interfered with by the therapist's rejection, or by his premature or prematurely massive transference interpretations, then the patient's grandiosity remains concentrated upon the grandiose self, and the therapist is experienced as foreign and inimical and thus excluded from meaningful participation. Under these conditions, the ego's defensive position remains rigid, and ego expansion cannot take place.

I shall conclude the discussion of the significance of the mirror transference as the instrumentality of the working-through process by supplying a clinical vignette.[13] The re-mobilization of the grandiose self in the specific instance to be described occurred in the form of an alter-ego trans-ference.

Patient C. was in analysis with me for four years. He was a professional man in his mid-forties who, though married, with several children, and moderately successful in his academic career, had on numerous occasions throughout his adult life obtained psychotherapy of various sorts (including several attempts at psychoanalysis). Some of these therapeutic attempts had been short-lived, others had lasted as long as a year, but none, he said, had been successful and none had dealt with his essential psychic disturbance. By contrast, as he stated with more and more conviction as the treatment proceeded, the present analysis had indeed become focused on the central area of his psychopathology and was thus leading to slowly achieved but meaningful and solid results. Although his manifest complaint was of a mild ejaculatio praecox and of a lack of emotional involvement during intercourse, it could be recognized that (as is frequent in cases of this type) the symptomatology was vague, widespread, and hard to put into words. It consisted of a pervasive feeling that he was not fully alive (though he was not depressed); of painful tension states which lay on the borderline of physical and psychological experience; and of a tendency toward a brooding worrisomeness about his physical and mental functions.

Although in the later phases of the analysis he expressed

[13] A more extensive presentation of a case of mirror transference (corresponding to the case of Mr. A. [Chapter 3], who served as an example for the mobilization of the idealized parent imago in an idealizing transference) will be made in Chapter 9.

on several occasions his warm gratitude for the unusual help and understanding which he felt he had received, he did not idealize the therapist and kept his laudatory remarks within the limits of an (affectively positively toned) reasonable and realistic appraisal. The analysis, however, proceeded on the basis of a twinship (alter-ego) transference in the following characteristic way. Concerning each new theme in the patient's analysis, his associations would regularly, and for prolonged periods, refer at first not to himself but to the analyst; yet this working-through phase which manifestly dealt with the analyst always produced significant psychological changes in the patient. Only after this part of the work was done could the patient focus on himself, on his own relevant conflicts, and on the dynamic and genetic context of his own personality and his own developmental history. If, however, during the first part of the typical cycle, I stated or implied that the patient was "projecting," the patient responded with emotional retreat and with the unambiguous feeling that he had been misunderstood. Even in the later phases of his analysis when he already anticipated that he would end up talking about his own psyche, he continued to proceed in the characteristic sequence: he would first, and for prolonged periods, see in me the (usually anxiety-provoking) affect, wish, ambition, or fantasy with which he was dealing, and even then it was only after he had worked through the currently activated complex in this way that he would turn to it with reference to himself.

Let me now illustrate the process of working through in this specific instance of a twinship transference by reference to specific episodes which occurred during various phases of the middle period of the analysis. The patient would, for example, begin to see me as a person devoid of ambitions, as emotionally shallow, pathologically even-tempered, withdrawn, and inactive, and—although this image was at variance with some of my actual personality features and activities that were known to the patient—his sense of conviction

about these fantasies was not disturbed by the coexisting contradictory information. A prolonged working-through process
then ensued in which my personality was scrutinized and experienced as being torn by conflict. What was the analyst
afraid of? Did he really have no ambitions? Was he really
never envious? Or did he have to flee from his ambitions and
from his envious feelings for fear that they might destroy
him? After long periods of such doubts and worries the patient's perception of me would gradually change, and he
would now remember attitudes—things that he had always
known about me—which made me appear in quite a different
light. (The direct experience of the analyst by the patient in
the analytic session itself would also change in harmony with
the new image that had been attained by the patient.) Only
following these experiences concerning the analyst would the
patient begin to refer to himself.

This turning point was usually preceded by the patient's
reporting external occurrences which demonstrated that he
had already made significant progress in the specific area with
which he had been dealing via the analyst. He would, for
example, report the experience of envying a professional
colleague, accompanied by the wish to outshine him and to
get a share of the credit for some achievement that up to now
he had silently given over to the other. Then, for a comparatively brief span of time, which, however, was filled with intense feelings, the patient not only experienced the conflict
fully in himself but was often able to connect it with poig-
nantly remembered childhood events and childhood emotions. Although these events were not genetically determin-
ing factors in the same sense as are those that can be remembered or reconstructed in the transference neuroses, they
were, nevertheless, important as early precursors of the adult
personality disturbance. He thus remembered his childhood
loneliness, the bizarre fantasies of greatness and power in
which he had indulged for prolonged periods, and the apprehension that he might not be able to return from them to

the world of reality. How even as a child he had become afraid of emotionally cathected competitiveness for fear of the underlying (near-delusional) fantasies of exerting absolute, sadistic power; and how he had saved a modicum of human participation and realism (a) by developing fantasies concerning an imaginary playmate, especially during the time when his chronically depressed mother was pregnant and after his only sibling, a brother, was born when the patient was six (similar to the fantasies of patient K. [Chapter 9], the still unborn sibling became a central focus of these preoccupations); (b) by turning from emotionally meaningful wishes to dry and detached intellectual pursuits; and (c) through the device of submitting the initiation and guidance of all his purposes and goals to a conscientiously exerted rationality, thus excluding emotions and imaginativeness, and foregoing all spontaneous joy.

GENERAL REMARKS ABOUT THE MECHANISMS WHICH BRING ABOUT THERAPEUTIC PROGRESS IN PSYCHOANALYSIS

The experiential content and the nature of the object of the central transference differ widely in the working-through processes which bring about the therapeutic progress in the classical transference neuroses, on the one hand, and in the narcissistic personality disturbances, on the other. As seen from a broad psychoeconomic and dynamic vantage point, however, the predominant mechanisms which underlie the move toward psychological health are the same in these two classes of analyzable psychopathology. The essential constellation of factors which accounts for the therapeutic effect of analysis in the transference neuroses and in the narcissistic personality disturbances is the following. (1) The analytic process mobilizes the instinctual energies which are bound to those childhood wishes which have not become integrated (e.g., through repression) with the rest of the psyche and which have therefore not participated in the maturation and development of the rest of the personality. (2) The analytic process (a) prevents the satisfaction of the childhood wish on the infantile level (optimal frustration; analytic abstinence); it consistently counteracts (through interpretations) the regressive evasion of the infantile wish or need (including attempts toward its re-repression or toward other forms of its re-exclusion from the analytically established contact with the centrally located (pre)conscious areas of the psyche). (3) Being thus, on the one hand, continuously reactivated without being gratified and, on the other, prevented from regressive escape, only one way remains open to the infantile drive, wish, or need: its increasing integration into the mature and reality-adapted sectors and segments of the psyche through the accretion of specific, new psychological structures which master the drive, lead to its controlled use, or transform it into a variety of mature and realistic thought and action patterns. In other words, the analytic process attempts to keep the infantile need activated while simultaneously cutting off all roads except the one toward maturation and realistic employment.

It will be helpful to illustrate the foregoing dynamic formulation of the therapeutic action of the working-through process in concrete terms. Although it could easily be demonstrated within the context of a case of classical transference neurosis, the example used, within the framework of the present examination, will be not the child's oedipal desires but the infantile wish for mirroring, confirmatory praise or approval as specifically encountered in the narcissistic personality disturbances. Genetically, we must realize that the traumatic frustration of the phase-appropriate wish or need for parental acceptance leads immediately to its strong intensification, as is the case with any other frustrated phase-specific need or wish. The intensified wish, in combination with the persisting or even increasing external frustration (or threat of punishment), creates a severe psychic imbalance which leads to the exclusion of the wish or need from further authentic and consistent participation in the rest of the psychic activities. A wall of defenses is subsequently built up which protects the psyche against the reactivation of the infantile wish—in the present example of the genesis of one specific class of narcissistic personality disturbance: against the reactivation of the wish for parental approval—because of the fear of renewed traumatic rejection. Depending on the psychic location of the defenses, the resulting cleavage in the personality is either (1) "vertical," i.e., a split which separates a whole segment of the psyche from the one that carries the central self, manifested by an alternation between (a) states of grandiosity which deny the frustrated need for approval and (b) states of overt feelings of emptiness and low self-esteem; and/or (2) "horizontal," i.e., a repression barrier, manifested by the patient's emotional coldness and by his insistence on keeping his distance from objects from whom he might want narcissistic sustenance.

The first task in the working-through process may be the overcoming of a resistance against the establishment of the narcissistic transference (the mirror transference in the present example), i.e., the remobilization in consciousness of the infantile wish or need for parental acceptance. In the next phase of the analysis it is the therapeutic task to keep the mirror transference active, despite the fact that the infantile need is again in essence frustrated. It is during this phase that the time-consuming, repetitive experiences of the working-through process are being confronted. Under the pressure of the renewed frustrations the patient tries to avoid the pain (a) by re-creating the pre-transference equilibrium through the establishment of a vertical split and/or of a repression barrier; or (b) through regressive evasion, i.e., by a retreat to levels of psychic functioning which are older than that of the pathogenic fixation (see Diagram 2 in Chapter 4 for a schematic summary of these regressive swings). Transference interpretations and genetic reconstructions, however, enable the cooperative sector of the analysand's psyche to block these two undesirable escape routes and to keep the infantile need activated despite the discomfort which is thereby created. (The skillful analyst will assist the patient by keeping this discomfort within tolerable limits; i.e., he will conduct the analysis according to the principle of optimal frustration.)

In view of the fact that all regressive roads are blocked while the infantile wish for mirroring is kept alive without being gratified in its infantile form, the psyche is forced to create new structures which transform and elaborate the infantile need along aim-inhibited and realistic lines. In behavioral and experiential terms: there is a gradual increase of realistic self-esteem, of realistic enjoyment of success; a moderate use of fantasies of achievement (merging into plans for possible realistic action); and the establishment of such complex developments within the realistic sector of the personality as humor, empathy, wisdom, and creativeness (see Chapter 12).

PART III

CLINICAL AND TECHNICAL PROBLEMS
IN THE NARCISSISTIC TRANSFERENCES

CHAPTER 8

GENERAL REMARKS ABOUT NARCISSISTIC TRANSFERENCES

THEORETICAL CONSIDERATIONS

One of the vexing questions which arises with regard to the cohesive therapeutic mobilization of the narcissistic structures is a theoretical and terminological one. Should the cohesive reactivations of the idealized parent imago and of the grandiose self be regarded as transferences, either in the metapsychological or in the clinical sense of the word, and should they be referred to by the term transference?

The question whether the analyst's comprehensive inclusion into the therapeutic activation of a narcissistically invested psychic structure should be referred to as transference is, in principle, of no greater relevance with regard to the various clinical forms in which the activation of the grandiose self becomes manifest than with regard to the activation of the idealized parent imago in the idealizing transference. Since the idealizing transference, however, has at times external features which may resemble the clinical manifestations of the classical transference neuroses, it is advisable to emphasize the intrinsic conditions which differentiate this clinical situation from the transference neuroses proper and to highlight the fact that the apparent transference manifestations in the idealizing transference are due to the mobilization of narcissistic cathexes and not of object libido. The mobilization of the developmentally comparatively late stages of the grandiose self (the mirror transference in the narrower sense of the term) leads also to a clinical picture which, externally, resembles the transference in the analysis of the transference neuroses and here, too, it is therefore necessary to emphasize that the analyst, though cognitively acknowledged as separate and autonomous, is nevertheless important only within the context of the analysand's narcissistic needs and is appealed to and otherwise reacted to only insofar as he is felt to fulfill or to frustrate the patient's demands for an echo, approval, and confirmation of his grandiosity and exhibitionism. The situation is reversed, however, with regard to the mobilization of the developmentally earlier stages of the grandiose self, i.e., in the twinship (alter-ego) transference and in the merger through the extension of the grandiose self. Here the internal conditions and, especially, the clinical picture created by the inclusion of the analyst in the therapeutic mobilization of the grandiose self seem so vastly different from the structure and the therapeutic manifestations of the transference neuroses, that it becomes necessary in a first presentation to compare the two conditions and to emphasize their similarities. Only by pointing up analogies can the fact be demonstrated that, despite the archaic nature of the interpersonal conditions which are re-created by the therapeutic activation of the early stages of the grandiose self, the analyst does indeed enter into a stable, structurally founded, clinical relationship with the analysand which decisively sustains the maintenance of the analytic process.

The question whether the idealizing transference and the mirror transference should be classified as transferences ought to be answered (a) by taking into account the metapsychological assessment of the clinical analytic situation, and (b) by making specific choices concerning the definition of the concept "transference."

Here I shall bypass taking sides concerning the decision whether the narcissistic transferences are transferences in the strict metapsychological sense of the word. Without denying the importance of a strict conceptual clarification, I shall in general continue to speak of the various manifestations of the therapeutic activation of the idealized parent imago and of the grandiose self as transferences. In view of the unquestionable fact that the image of the analyst has entered a long-term, relatively reliable relationship with the mobilized narcissistic structures which permits the maintenance of a specific, systematic process of working through, there is ample justification for the use of the term transference in the (by now traditional) broad clinical sense, independent of the niceties of a metapsychological assessment.[1]

The two narcissistic transferences will now be examined against the background of conceptual trends which already exist in this theoretical area, and the concepts advanced in this monograph will be compared with older ones in order to delimit them more sharply. Specifically, I shall examine (1) the relationship of the idealizing transference and the mirror transference to the condition to which Freud referred frequently as that spontaneously arising "positive transference" which forms the motor of the analytic treatment and the emotional basis for the efficacy of the analyst's therapeutic interventions (see, for example, 1912, p. 105f.); and (2) the relationship of the idealizing transference and the mirror transference to the projective-introjective activities to which some analysts assign a conspicuous place of dominant influence in the clinical transference of all analysands, in con-

[1] Anna Freud, commenting on the present study in a personal communication, expressed this line of thought in the following way: "In these cases the patient uses the analyst not for the revival of object-directed strivings, but for inclusion in a libidinal (i.e., narcissistic) state to which he has regressed or at which he has become arrested. One may call that transference; or one may call it a subspecialty of transference. . . . This does not matter, really, so long as it is understood that the phenomenon is not produced by cathecting the analyst with object libido."

formance with the assumptions of M. Klein's "English school" of psychoanalysis—this imaginative and pioneering (but, unfortunately, theoretically not solidly based) attempt to plumb the most concealed depths of human experience— that there exist in infancy two ubiquitous primary positions, the "paranoid" and the "depressive" (see E. Bibring, 1947; Glover, 1945; Waelder, 1936).

As concerns the basic "positive transference" (Waelder, [1939], and especially E. Kris [1951], who refers to the fact that Freud "stresses an area of cooperation between analyst and patient"[2]), I should like to repeat the formulation that I suggested previously (1959); namely, that we should "differentiate between (1) nontransference object choices patterned after childhood models (. . . often erroneously called the positive 'transference') and (2) true transferences." The former are composed of "strivings toward objects which, although emerging from the depths, do not cross a repression barrier" and of "those strivings of the ego which, although originally transferences, have later severed the ties with the repressed and have thus become autonomous object choices of the ego." And I summarized this differentiation aphoristically by stating "while it is true that all transferences are repetitions, not all repetitions are transferences" (p. 472).

It is undoubtedly true that an "area of cooperation between analyst and patient" (Kris, 1951) must be preserved if the analytic work is to achieve lasting results. Without "allying ourselves with the ego of the person under treatment" (Freud, 1937) analysis would be a passive and fleeting

---

[2] "As is well known, the analytic situation consists in our allying ourselves with the ego of the person under treatment, in order to subdue portions of his id which are uncontrolled—that is to say to include them in the synthesis of his ego. . . . The ego, if we are to be able to make such a pact with it, must be a normal one. But a normal ego is . . . an ideal fiction. . . . Every normal person, in fact, is only normal on the average. His ego approximates to that of the psychotic in some part . . . ; and the degree of its remoteness from one end of the series and of its proximity to the other will furnish us with a provisional measure of . . . 'alteration of the ego' " (Freud, 1937, p. 235).

experience comparable to hypnosis. Furthermore, it is undoubtedly true that the therapeutic dichotomy of an observing and experiencing ego (R. Sterba, 1934) is best maintained when the observing ego cooperates with the analyst in the performance of the analytic task on the basis of a realistic bond which, in turn, rests on "nontransference object choices patterned after childhood models" and on "autonomous object choices of the ego" (Kohut, 1959), the latter, of course, meant in the sense of "secondary autonomy" (Hartmann, 1950, 1952). These conditions are as necessary in the psychoanalytic treatment of narcissistic personalities as they are in the analysis of the classical transference neuroses. The observing segment of the personality of the analysand which, in cooperation with the analyst, has actively shouldered the task of analyzing, is not, in essence, different in analyzable narcissistic disorders from that found in analyzable transference neuroses. In both types of cases an adequate area of realistic cooperation derived from positive experiences in childhood (in the object-cathected *and* narcissistic realm) is the precondition for the analysand's maintenance of the therapeutic split of the ego and for that fondness for the analyst which assures the maintenance of a sufficient trust in the processes and goals of analysis during stressful periods.

The idealizing transference, on the other hand, and the mirror transference are the *objects* of the analysis; i.e., the observing and analyzing part of the ego of the analysand, in cooperation with the analyst, is confronting them and, by gradually comprehending them in dynamic, economic, structural, and genetic dimensions, attempts to achieve a gradual mastery over them and to relinquish the demands that are correlated with them. The achievement of such mastery is the essential and specific therapeutic goal of the analysis of narcissistic disorders.

The "positive transference" (Freud), on the basis of "nontransference object choice" (Kohut), in the "area of cooperation between analyst and patient" (Kris) is only a tool used in the performance of this task; and it is the working through and the ultimate relinquishment of the mirror transference or of the idealization of the archaic self-object which lead to the specific therapeutic results that characterize the successful outcome of the psychoanalytic treatment of these cases.

The clear distinction between the narcissistic transferences and the realistic bond that establishes itself between analysand and analyst is important not only from a theoretical point of view but even more so because of practical, clinical considerations. From a theoretical point of view, as was indicated in the preceding paragraphs, the realistic bond between analyst and analysand (positive transference, rapport, working alliance, therapeutic alliance, etc.) is not a transference in the metapsychological sense, but a relationship which is based on early, wholesome interpersonal experiences, which, though gradually neutralized and thus aim-inhibited, have continued to influence all of the patient's adult object investments, including his relationship with the analyst. In the terms of the elaboration of the structural model of the mind (Kohut, 1961; Kohut and Seitz, 1963), these object attachments belong not in the *area of transference* but in the *area of progressive neutralization.*

From the point of view of technique, however, especially with regard to certain aspects of the narcissistic personality disorders, the analyst's ability to remain noninterfering while a narcissistic transference establishes itself and not to make any active moves designed to foster the development of a realistic therapeutic bond may at times be the decisive factor on the road to therapeutic success. A hypercathexis of the archaic grandiose self, for example, deprives the realistic self experience of libidinal nutriment (Rapaport, 1950). Vague feelings of not being real, of fraudulence, of not being quite alive, etc., are preconsciously present, but the analysand seems either completely unaware of the presence of this disturbance, or is vaguely and dimly conscious of it, or has learned to cover it up—not only to the world but also to himself. The manifestations of the inability of such patients to form a *realistic* bond with the analyst must not be treated by the analyst through active interventions designed to establish an "alliance." They must be examined dispassionately as hints of, and allusions to, a disturbance in the realm of the cathexis of the self and of the correlated disturbance of the patient's ability to feel alive and to experience the world as real.

Certain symptomatic acts in the beginning of the analysis which may impress the analyst as due to superego defects may in reality constitute manifestations of a narcissistic personality disorder. Unable to perceive clearly the underlying disturbance of the self image, and therefore unable to communicate it to the analyst, the patient may begin the analysis with a lie, or with some financial duplicity, or with some other bit of what seems to be fraudulent behavior. The analyst must neither make light of this initial acted-out communication nor must he respond to it by condemnation or active interference. All that the analyst needs to do in most instances is to point out the occurrence—but not to "confront" the patient with it in a condemnatory tone—discuss its realistic aspects if necessary, and stress that he cannot yet be sure whether it has any hidden significance; and if it does, what its significance might be. Any active interference which takes the symptomatic act as being entirely a realistic action may remove the very center of the patient's disturbance from the focus of the analytic work, since the patient will respond to the analyst's censure first with anger and rebellion and later with compliance—in short, there will be a change in the analysand's ego without a mobilization of the underlying pathogenic narcissistic configurations. Temporary mistakes which the analyst may make in responding to these initial symptomatic acts because he was unprepared, and because the activity with which the analysand confronted him had taken him by surprise, will do no permanent harm if the analyst can later return to the initial occurrence and reassess it in retrospect. If the analyst's all-too-realistic or moralistic response, however, is buttressed by a system of theoretical convictions that it is appropriate to set aside the analytic attitude vis-à-vis a patient's "real fraudulence," "real lack of integrity," or "real lack of commitment to the treatment," then the access to the analysis of the deeper narcissistic disturbance may indeed become blocked.

As stated before, the preconscious center from which these characterological disturbances emanate is the sense of an incomplete reality of the self and, secondarily, of the external world. It is important to realize not only that the psychoanalytic situation itself is specifically adapted to bring a hidden pathology of the self experience (and thus of the sense of the reality of the self and of the surroundings) into the open, but also that in analysis the gradual emergence of this condition allows the analysand to become aware of its dynamic source and structural roots (i.e., of the fixation on an archaic self image and of the dysfunction and insufficient cathexis of the [pre]conscious self), and thus a road to the general amelioration of the disturbance is opened.

The specific attribute of the analytic situation which allows, and encourages, the emergence of the pathological self is the following. In its central aspects the analytic situation is not real, in the usual sense of the word. It has a specific reality which resembles to a certain extent the reality of the artistic experience, such as that of the theater. A person must possess a modicum of stable self cathexis in order to be able to give himself over to the artistic reality of the make-believe. If we are sure of the reality of ourselves, we can temporarily turn away from ourselves and can suffer with the tragic hero on the stage, without being in danger of confusing the reality of our participating emotions with the reality of our everyday lives. People whose reality sense is insecure, however, may not be able to abandon themselves easily to the artistic experience; they must protect themselves, e.g., by telling themselves that what they are watching is "only" theater, "only" a play, "not real," etc. The analytic situation presents analogous problems. Analysands whose sense of their own reality is comparatively intact will, with the appropriate transitional resistances, allow themselves the requisite regression in the service of the analysis. They will thus be able to experience the quasi-artistic, indirect reality of transference feelings which once related to a different (then current and direct) reality in their past.[3] This regression takes place spontaneously, as it does in the theater. And, as is true in the theater, the decathexis of current reality is supported by a diminution of stimuli from the immediate surroundings. The analysand, furthermore, hardly needs to be taught what analysis is all about; he knows how to relate to the analytic situation, just as people know how they must relate to the play which they see in the theater.

I am disregarding here the practical secondary maneuvers which are undertaken in implementation of the principle that the adaptation to an unfamiliar set of experiences will

[3] The changing ego state as one gives oneself over to the play in the theater which is about to begin, i.e., the decathexis of current reality and the turning toward a world of imagination and artistically worked over memories, is beautifully expressed in *Zueignung*, the poem with which Goethe introduces *Faust*, the greatest and the most personally significant of all of his creations. Disregarding some minor inconsistencies, this poem may be said to describe perfectly the mental state which the shifting cathexes evoke in the analysand and, through empathic resonance, in the analyst. The last two lines of the poem, in particular (I was led to see the pertinence of these lines by Dr. Richard Sterba who quoted them in a related context [1969]), apply not only to the mental state brought about by the experience of a work of art, especially the play on the stage, but also to the mental state that characterizes the engagement of the analytic process as the patient's past is revived and the present recedes:

> Was ich besitze seh' ich wie im weiten,
> Und was verschwand wird mir zu Wirklichkeiten.

> What I possess, seems far away,
> And what is gone becomes reality.

[Goethe's *Faust*. Translated by Walter Kaufmann. Garden City, New York: Doubleday, 1961, p. 67.]

be eased by appropriate explanations. Thus, if a person has never been in a theater, a general explanation about this art form will make it easier for him to respond to the play. The essential psychological process, however, which is activated in the audience does not ned to be taught—indeed, it cannot be taught. Despite the numerous profound differences between the artistic and the analytic experience, considerations analogous to the foregoing also apply to the analytic situation. The establishment of the requisite psychological attitude toward analysis can be assisted through appropriate measures; but the essential psychological processes which permit the experience of the specific reality of transference feelings cannot be taught.

If there is a disturbance of those central functions which should enable the patient to experience the analytic reality, then neither educational measures (explanations) nor persuasion (moral pressure) should be employed, but the defect should be permitted to unfold freely so that its analysis can be undertaken. If, in other words, the patient's (preconscious) self was poorly cathected, then his difficulties with regard to the more or less spontaneous establishment of the analytic situation may themselves become the very center of the analytic work. But this important and central aspect of the patient's psychopathology would be removed from the focus of the analysis if the patient's inability to tolerate the decathexis of current reality and to accept the ambiguity of the analytic situation is seen within a moral framework and is responded to by persuasion and exhortation, or by an affirmation of reality or morality from the side of the analyst.

I now turn to the delimitation of the concepts of idealizing transference and mirror transference with their specifically appropriate working-through processes from the concepts of projective and introjective identification (Klein, 1946) and their therapeutic confrontation by the "English school" of psychoanalysis. The mirror transference may deal with an area which at least partly overlaps the area called "introjective identification" by the Kleinian school, and similarly the idealizing transference may cover some of the territory of so-called "projective identification." The characteristic theoretical viewpoint which distinguishes the approach taken in the present work from that of the English school—it leads also to a vastly different therapeutic attitude—needs no summarizing presentation at this point. Suffice it to say that, according to the view presented here, the mirror transference and the idealizing transference are the therapeutically activated forms of the two basic positions of the narcissistic libido which establish themselves subsequent to the stage of primary narcissism. Since these positions constitute healthy and necessary maturational steps, even fixations on them or regressions to them must in therapy be first understood as in essence neither ill nor evil. The patient learns first to recognize these forms of narcissism in their therapeutic activation —and he must first be able to accept them as maturationally healthy and necessary!—before he can undertake the task of gradually transforming them and of building them into the higher organization of the adult personality and of harnessing them to his mature goals and purposes. The analysand's ego is thus not set up against his archaic narcissism as if it were an enemy and a stranger, no ideational processes belonging to higher stages of object differentiation (such as specific fantasies regarding a wish to devour a frustrating object or the fear of being devoured by it) are imputed to the therapeutically mobilized areas, and no guilt tensions are created. There exist, of course, tensions which arise spontaneously in the course of the analysis. They are due to the influx of unmodified narcissistic libido into the ego, and they are experienced as hypochondria, self-consciousness, and shame. (They do not arise from a conflict with an idealized superego, a structure which does not exist at the developmental level with which we are dealing in these instances.) If the analyst bases his attitude on the foregoing theoretic considerations, the difficult job of recognizing the flux of regression to and the re-emergence from stages of lesser object differentiation —and the concomitant oscillation between the experience of preverbal tension states and verbalizable fantasies—will proceed in a task-oriented purposive atmosphere which encourages the maintenance of the autonomy of the observing and integrating part of the analysand's ego.[4]

But I shall not further pursue the comparison between the Kleinian theoretical and clinical outlook on psychopathology and the specific theoretical and clinical formulations suggested with regard to the narcissistic personality disorders. To undertake the task of drawing such a comparison in depth lies beyond the limits of this investigation since it would require the differentiating presentation of the psychopathology of paranoia and manic-depressive psychosis, on the one hand, and of the narcissistic personality disorders, on the other.[5] Instead I shall round out the theoretical clarification of the concepts of the mirror transference and the idealizing transference against the background (1) of the progressive-regressive movements between (a) the stage of the body-self nuclei of the fragmented body self (autoerotism) and (b) the stage of the cohesive body self (narcissism),[6] and (2) the correlated differentiation between (a) isolated psychological mechanisms and (b) the cohesive and structured total mind self.

The terms mirror transference and idealizing transference refer to the therapeutic activation not of isolated psycho-

---

[4] The analysis of the aggressive component of the preobject-differentiation stage of psychological organization proceeds along similar lines; i.e., the phenomenon of "narcissistic rage," too, can be illuminated maturationally, developmentally, and in its later dynamic-economic significance if its maturationally appropriate, original purpose and significance are kept in mind.

[5] The immediately following discussion of the differentiation between the functioning of isolated psychological mechanisms and the activity of cohesive psychological configurations is, however, not without some relevance with regard to the Kleinian theoretical system, which, in my opinion, tends to blur this important distinction.

In the present context see also the outline of the differential diagnosis between the psychoses and the narcissistic personality disorders in Chapter 1.

[6] See in this context the illuminating contribution by Nagera (1964).

logical mechanisms (such as introjection and projection) but of more or less stable and solid total personality configurations, independent of the predominant psychological mechanism or mechanisms which are employed by them, or which may even be characteristic of them. The developmental step from autoerotism to narcissism (Freud, 1914) is a move toward increased synthesis of the personality due to a shift from the libidinal cathexis of individual body parts, or of isolated physical or mental functions, to a cathexis of an (albeit at first grandiose, exhibitionistic, and unrealistic) cohesive self. In other words, the nuclei of the body self and of the mental self coalesce and form a superordinated unit. The preoccupation with one's own body which occurs regularly in physical illness is a manifestation of increased narcissism even when a single organ is in the center of the preoccupation, since that organ is still seen in the context of a total, suffering body self. In psychotic or prepsychotic hypochondriasis, however, e.g., in the early stages of schizophrenia, individual body parts, or isolated physical or mental functions, become isolated and hypercathected. The imago of the cohesive self is breaking up and the residual cohesive, observing part of the personality of the patient can do no more than attempt to explain the products of a regression which it is unable to control (Glover, 1939, p. 183ff.).

The difference between the narcissistic regression which accompanies physical illness and the prenarcissistic fragmentation of the body self which occurs in the early stages of schizophrenia becomes somewhat blurred under the following specific conditions. If a person with strong prenarcissistic fixations becomes physically ill, then the increase in body narcissism which accompanies the physical illness may bring about a further regression toward a stage of beginning body-self fragmentation and, instead of experiencing wholesome self-concern, the person will react with hypochondriacal anxiety. Physical illnesses with diffuse symptomatology (such as the initial nonspecific syndrome which ushers in a variety of infectious diseases, including the common cold) are in particular prone to elicit such hypochondriacal responses. The development of clear-cut symptoms, on the other hand, with the strong narcissistic cathexis of a specific organ (e.g., sore throat, runny nose, sneezing, etc.) which it brings about, tends to counteract the pull of the prenarcissistic fixation points. The appearance of such symptoms is for this reason in general welcomed by people with hypochondriacal propensities and is greeted with a sense of relief. Exquisitely painful illnesses of circumscribed body regions, even when they affect narcissistically highly cathected organs such as the genitals or the eyes, are therefore usually not prone to evoke hypochondriacal responses.

A regression analogous to that from (1) the stage of the cohesive body self (narcissism) to (2) the stage of the fragmented body self, i.e., the stage of psychologically isolated body parts and of their functions (autoerotism), can also be observed in the mental sphere. Stated differently, the cathexis of a person's total mental attitude (narcissism), even if it is present in a pathologically distorted or exaggerated form, must be differentiated from the hypercathexis of isolated mental functions and mechanisms (autoerotism) which occurs in consequence of the breakup of the narcissistically cathected, cohesive mind self. A task-oriented, adaptive, and in essence voluntary hypercathexis of the mind self takes place in psychoanalytic treatment; i.e., the psychoanalytic situation fosters a focusing of the analysand's attention on his own mental attitude and on the various functions of his mind. Yet here, too, as in the analogous circumstances in physical illness, a single symptom or a single psychological mechanism, however prominent and ego-alien it might be, is still seen and experienced within the context of the imago of a total (i.e., cohesive) suffering mind self. The hypercathexis of isolated mental functions and mechanisms, however, which occurs after fragmentation of the mental self, is a frequent complement to the physical hypochondriasis of early stages of psychotic regression and is thus experienced analogous to psychological hypochondriasis (i.e., for example, rationalized as worry over the loss of one's intellect, fear of insanity, and the like).

At times the analyst must pay detailed attention to individual psychological mechanisms. The mechanisms of introjection and projection, for example, will be employed—in defensive and in nondefensive (i.e., adaptive) modes—by analysands who suffer from narcissistic personality disorders as well as by analysands with ordinary transference neuroses. If these mechanisms have become isolated as part of a fragmenting, regressive breakup of the mind self, they are psychoanalytically unapproachable; i.e., only the surrounding aspects of the personality and the psychological events which precede the regressive fragmentation remain open to meaningful scrutiny. But so long as they remain the (albeit unconsciously executed) functions of a total, cohesive self, they constitute a legitimate target of the analyst's interpretations. To be specific: it is through interpretations that the analysand becomes increasingly aware of the connections which exist between his active and reactive self and the psychological mechanisms which had seemed to occur in an unpredictable and unmotivated fashion. Through analytic work these mechanisms are brought into increasing contact with the ego's initiative, and the realm of the ego's domination over them is expanded.

These differentiations (between isolated archaic mechanisms and mechanisms which are the meaningful constituents of a cohesive set of mental activities) become, unfortunately, even more complex because of the trend toward the personification of psychological mechanisms which is at times encountered in the psychoanalytic literature. Specifically, some writers appear, for example, to imbue the mechanisms of introjection and projection with personality qualities; i.e., the mechanism of introjection becomes an angry, devouring

child and projection a spitting or vomiting one. If such theoretic attitudes are brought to the clinical situation, they not
only induce guilt in the analysand but, what is even more important, they obliterate the crucial difference between (a)
cohesive narcissistic structures which are analyzable since
they are capable of forming a transference in the clinical
situation, and (b) autoerotic structures which are not analyzable because the cathexis is not on the cohesive narcissistic
configurations (the grandiose self; the idealized parent imago)
but on isolated physical or mental functions. During temporary
or chronic regressions the deployments of libido in the mirror transference may indeed become replaced by isolated
introjections, and the cohesive investments of an idealizing
transference may become dissolved and replaced by isolated
projections. In these latter instances the establishment of a
transference cannot be achieved and the pathogenic area itself is therefore (at least temporarily) not analyzable.

It is intriguing to compare the conceptualizations I have
employed (which were derived from the systematic psychoanalytic observation of adult patients with narcissistic personality disturbances) with those of Mahler and her coworkers[7]
which are derived from the systematic observation of severely
disturbed children. The present conceptualizations are in
conformance with the metapsychological viewpoints of psychoanalytic theory (in particular with the dynamic-economic
and the topographic-structural points of view), and the
broadly activated layers of archaic experience (the idealizing
transference, the mirror transference, the swings toward a
fleeting fragmentation of the self) require the empathic reconstruction of the corresponding childhood experiences.
Mahler's conceptualizations are derived from the psychoanalytically sophisticated observation of the behavior of small
children, and they are therefore—and appropriately—in harmony with a theoretical framework that is attuned to her

7 See, e.g., Mahler (1952, 1968), Mahler and Gosliner (1955), Mahler and
La Perriere (1965).

field of observation. Her formulations concerning the phases of autism-symbiosis and separation-individuation thus belong in the sociobiological framework of direct child observation.

The most concise summary of the difference in the theoretical standpoint from which the relevant empirical observations are made and then translated into general formulae is perhaps the following. In Mahler's conceptual framework the child is a psychobiological unit which interacts with the environment. And she conceptualizes a consistent psychobiological development of the child's relationship to the object: from (a) an absence of relatedness (autism), via (b) a union with it (symbiosis), toward (c) autonomy from it and mutuality with it (individuation). My metapsychological psychoanalytic viewpoint, which is in tune with my observational method, i.e., the transference revival of childhood experience, has led me to discern the side-by-side development not only of narcissism and object love (each moving from archaic to higher levels), but also of the two principal branches of narcissism itself (grandiose self, idealized parent imago). These differences in conceptualization are an outgrowth of two different basic observational attitudes: Mahler observes the behavior of small children; I reconstruct their inner life on the basis of transference reactivations.

A detailed comparison between the formulations of psychoanalytic metapsychology and the formulations of direct child observation in the area under discussion—in addition to the contributions of Mahler et al., the investigations of Benjamin (1950, 1961), Spitz (1949, 1950, 1957, 1961, 1965), and of many others who would have to be considered here[8]—is be-

---

[8] Therese Benedek's pioneering studies (1949, 1956, 1959), although not undertaken in a setting of methodical direct child observation, belong, like Mahler's, to the conceptual realm of a psychoanalytic interactionalism. This theoretical system is defined by the position of the observer who, equidistant from the interacting parties, occupies an imaginary point *outside* of the experiencing individual. The core area of psychoanalytic metapsychology, however (see Kohut, 1959), is defined by the position of the observer who occupies an imaginary point *inside* the psychic organization of the individual with whose introspection he empathically identifies (vicarious introspection).

yond the scope of this monograph. Especially in the last two decades the understanding of the early interplay between mother and infant or small child has been enriched through a significant number of important investigations by psychoanalysts. Mahler, however, who has made not only the most persistently systematic but also the most useful and influential relevant contributions, will in the following be regarded as the representative of this entire field.

Mahler's formulation of a progression from autism to symbiosis to individuation corresponds roughly to Freud's classical conception of libidinal development from autoerotism via narcissism to object love. The narcissistic transferences are therapeutic activations of developmental phases which probably correspond predominantly to the transitional period between a late part of the stage of symbiosis and an early part of the stages of individuation in Mahler's sense. I would, however, like to emphasize again that my own observations have led me to the conviction that it is fruitful, and consistent with the empirical data, to postulate two separate and largely independent developmental lines: one which leads from autoerotism via narcissism to object love; another which leads from autoerotism via narcissism to higher forms and transformations of narcissism. Concerning the first of these two lines of development it is, of course, not surprising that it will be claimed by some that rudimentary prestages of object love can already be discerned as early as during the autoerotic and narcissistic phases, i.e., that a separate line of development of object libido that begins with very archaic and rudimentary forms of object love should be assumed to exist. (See in this context M. Balint, 1937; and 1968, esp. p. 64ff.) My own inclination, however, leads me to remain faithful to the classical formulation—I am inclined to believe that the imputing to the very small child of the capacity for even rudimentary forms of object love (not to be confused, of course, with object relations) rests on retrospective falsifications and on adultomorphic errors in empathy.

CLINICAL CONSIDERATIONS

There are some patients in whom the differentiation between idealizing transference and mirror transference is not easily established since either the oscillations between the two positions occur very rapidly, or the narcissistic transference is itself a transitional or mixed one, with features of idealization of the analyst and the simultaneous presence of demands for mirroring, admiration or of an alter-ego or a merger relationship to him. Instances of this type, however, are not as frequent as those in which, at least for long periods during the analysis, a clear differentiation can indeed be made. In the transitional cases—particularly in those instances where rapid oscillations between the activation of the grandiose self and the idealized parent imago do not allow a sharp focusing of interpretations—it is advisable for the analyst to dwell neither on the fleetingly cathected grandiose self nor on the idealized parent imago but to focus his attention on the shifts which occurred between these positions and on the events which precipitated them. In certain cases at least, the rapidity of the oscillations seems to be in the service of a defensive denial of vulnerability. Whenever the patient extends a vulnerable tendril of idealization toward the analyst, or whenever he shyly attempts to exhibit his own beloved self and invites the analyst's admiring participation, he quickly veers back to the opposite position and—like the turtle in the fable—has been there all along and the analyst cannot catch up with him.

Another practical matter is the form of the interpretations which focus on the narcissistic transferences, especially in the mirror transference. Two antithetical pitfalls may become impediments in the course of the analysis of narcissistic personalities. The one concerns the analyst's readiness to take on an ethical, or ethically tinged, realistic stance vis-à-vis the patient's narcissism; the other concerns his tendency toward abstractness of the relevant interpretations.

In general it can be said that the triad of value judgment, reality ethics (cf. Hartmann's concept of health ethics [1960, p. 64]), and therapeutic activism (educational measures, exhortation, etc.) in which the analyst feels that he must step beyond the basic (i.e., interpreting) attitude and become the patient's leader, teacher, and guide is most likely to occur when the psychopathology under scrutiny is not understood metapsychologically. Since under these circumstances the analyst has to tolerate his therapeutic impotence and lack of success, he can hardly be blamed when he abandons the ineffective analytic armamentarium and turns to suggestion (offering himself to the patient as a model or an object to identify with, for example) in order to achieve therapeutic changes. If repeated lack of success in areas that are not yet understood metapsychologically is tolerated, however, without the abandonment of analytic means and without a turning to therapeutic activism, then the occurrence of new analytic insights is not prevented and scientific progress can be made.

Another related phenomenon can be observed in areas where metapsychological understanding is not lacking altogether but is incomplete. Here analysts tend to supplement their interpretations and reconstructions with suggestive pressure, and the weight of the personality of the therapist becomes of much greater importance than with cases that are metapsychologically well understood. There are certain analysts who are said to be exceptionally gifted in the analysis of narcissistic personality disturbances, and anecdotes about their therapeutic activities become widely known in analytic circles.[9] But just as the surgeon in the heroic era of

---

[9] The assessment of the influence of the therapist's personality is of particular importance in the evaluation of treatment results in the psychotherapy of the psychoses and of the so-called "borderline" states (A. Stern, 1938). There can be little doubt that a therapist's quasi-religious fervor or his deep feeling of inner saintliness (see, for example, Gertrude Schwing, 1940, p. 16) provides a strong therapeutic leverage in the treatment of very disturbed adults and children which accounts for some striking therapeutic successes.

surgery was a charismatically gifted man who performed great feats of individual courage and heroic skill while the modern surgeon tends to be a calm, well-trained craftsman, so also with the analyst. As our knowledge about the narcissistic disorders increases, the formerly so personally demanding treatment procedures will gradually become the skilled work of insightful and understanding analysts who do not employ any special charisma of their personalities but restrict themselves to the use of the only tools that provide rational success: interpretations and reconstructions.

The countertransference implications of the analyst's proclivity to respond to his analysands' narcissistic fixations with

---

The relevant influence may emanate from the charismatic therapist directly, or it may be transmitted via the therapeutic team of which he is the leader. (In this context one is reminded of C. G. Jung's commanding personality which undoubtedly exerted a deep influence on his coworkers and thus, indirectly, on the severely disturbed patients in the therapeutic community.) In the last analysis we are here dealing with a cure through love—albeit a largely narcissistic love!—related to the approach to which Freud took exception when he was confronted with Ferenzci's final therapeutic experiments. (See Freud's letter to Ferenzci of 13 December, 1931 as quoted by Jones [1957, p. 113].) Not only the messianic or saintly personality of the therapist, however, but also his life history seems to play an active role in the therapeutic successes, and a myth of having—like Christ—risen from death in an ascendancy of self-generated, life-giving love appears at times to form a particular part of the effective charisma (see in this context Victor Frankl [1946, 1958], whose surviving the concentration camp—the "death"(!) camp—became a central aspect of his therapeutic personality endowment and of his therapeutic stance). No one should, of course, object to therapeutic successes with otherwise nearly untreatable disorders on the ground that these successes were achieved via the direct or indirect influence of the therapist's personality. What *is* objectionable, however, are secondary rationalizations that attempt to give scientific respectability to the procedures that were employed. The decision whether a specific form of therapeutic management is in essence scientific or whether it is inspirational (i.e., the question whether the irrational forces involved had been under the rational control of the therapist) must be approached by answering these questions: (1) Do we have a systematical theoretical grasp of the processes involved in therapy? (2) Can the treatment method be communicated to others, i.e., can it be learned (and ultimately practiced) without the presence of its originator? And (3), most importantly: Does the treatment method remain successful after the death of its creator? It is specifically the last event which, alas, seems all too often to reveal that the therapeutic methodology was not a scientific one but that the success depended on the actual presence of a single, specifically endowed person.

annoyed impatience—be it ever so subtle—will be discussed in Chapter 11. Here I only repeat what I stated previously (1966a), namely, that it is the improper intrusion of the altruistic value system of Western civilization, and not objective considerations of developmental maturity or adaptive usefulness, which tends to lead to a wish from the side of the therapist to replace the patient's narcissistic position with object love. Stated conversely, in many instances, the reshaping of the narcissistic structures and their integration into the personality must be rated as a more genuine and valid result of therapy than the patient's precarious compliance with demands for a change of his narcissism into object love. There are, of course, moments in the analysis of some narcissistic personalities when a forceful statement will not come amiss as a final move in persuading the patient that the gratifications obtained from the unmodified narcissistic fantasies are spurious. A skillful analyst of an older generation, for example, as asserted by local psychoanalytic lore, would make his point at a strategic juncture by silently handing over a crown and scepter to his unsuspecting analysand instead of confronting him with yet another verbal interpretation.

In general, however, the psychoanalytic process is most enhanced when we demonstrate to the patient, in truthful and objectively accepting terms, the role which his narcissism plays in the archaic universe to which he has, despite reluctance and difficulty, admitted the analyst. And it is better for us to trust the spontaneous synthetic functions of the patient's ego to achieve gradual dominance over the narcissistic portions of the personality in an atmosphere of analytic-empathic acceptance, rather than to drive the analysand toward wholesale imitation of the analyst's scornful rejection of the analysand's lack of realism. The analyst is particularly effective in this respect if he is capable of broadly reconstructing archaic ego states and the specific role which the narcissistic positions played in them, and if he can establish the connections between the relevant transference experiences and corresponding childhood traumata.

Freud's brief allusion, in the last of his papers on technique (1937b), to the style and form of such reconstructions, although not specifically aimed at illustrating their role in the realm of the analysis of narcissistic disturbances, is an especially apt example in the present context of the tone of accepting explanatory objectivity that should be employed with these interventions. " 'Up to your *n*th year [Freud tells his imaginary patient] you regarded yourself as the sole and unlimited possessor of your mother; then came another baby and brought you grave disillusionment. Your mother left you for some time, and even after her reappearance she was never again devoted to you exclusively. Your feelings towards your mother became ambivalent, your father gained a new importance for you,' . . . and so on" (p. 261).

The relative appropriateness or inappropriateness of the analyst's exerting educational pressure on the patient—whether through coolly objective statements or in the form of moral admonishments—should be evaluated against the background of the metapsychological grasp of the unrealistic structures which occupy the therapeutic limelight. Apart from the patient's unrealistic idealizations, it is, of course, in particular his unrealistic grandiosity (especially as it expresses itself seemingly undisguised through attitudes of arrogant superiority or haughtiness, and through boundless demands for attention asserted apparently without any regard for either the rights or the limitations of others, e.g., of the analyst) to which the analyst will tend to respond automatically by educational means (confrontation with reality), i.e., to paraphrase Hartmann (1960), by an attitude of reality or maturity morality.

The ability to choose the appropriate response to the analysand's manifest grandiosity has, however, as its prerequisite a grasp of the specific structure and thus of the specific psychological significance of his demands. To be precise: overt narcissistic claims occur in narcissistic personality disorders in the following three forms which can be distinguished in structural and dynamic terms. Each of these forms should elicit therapeutic responses from the side of the analyst which are in tune with the specific structural and dynamic determinants of the patient's behavior.

1. Grandiose behavior may be a manifestation of the vertically split-off sector of the psyche (see the discussion of case J. and Diagram 3 in Chapter 7). I have come to see that it is not conducive to psychoanalytic progress, i.e., to the achievement of health through structural change, to confront the undisguised narcissistic manifestations of the split-off sector with reality in the form of educational persuasion, admonitions, and the like. The essential analytic work should be done on the border between the noisy split-off sector and the quiet centrally located reality ego through which the basic narcissistic transference is mediated. The resistance at this border, however, is not overcome by fighting the split-off arrogance but by explaining it (through dynamic-genetic reconstructions) to the centrally located sector of the personality in order to persuade the latter to accept the former into its realm. Increasing success in this endeavor leads to two results: (a) the moral, aesthetic, and the realistic adaptational forces of the central ego will by themselves begin to transform the archaic narcissistic claims and to make them more socially acceptable and psychoeconomically useful. And, even more importantly, (b) a shift of the archaic narcissistic cathexes from the vertically split-off sector to the central sector takes place which increases the propensity toward the establishment of a (narcissistic) transference. The emphasis is on bringing about a shift from a vertically split-off part of the psyche (which has no transference potential) to a horizontally split sector of the psyche (which is indeed able to form a [narcissistic] transference). I might add here that the same conditions prevail in the case of those perversions (they constitute the large majority) which are built on a narcissis-

tic foundation. The perverse behavior resides in the vertically split-off sector of the psyche and must first become integrated with the central sector of the psyche before the underlying instinctual forces become channeled into a narcissistic transference and thus become available for a systematic process of working through.

2. The second form in which narcissistic claims appear openly can also be defined in structuro-dynamic terms. In these instances we are dealing with an insecurely walled-off (horizontally split) grandiose structure in the central sector of the personality, whose spasmodic breakthroughs interrupt, for more or less brief periods, the prevailing chronic symptomatology of narcissistic depletion. Since these breakthroughs result in general in a psychoeconomic imbalance (e.g., overstimulation), they should be considered traumatic states.

3. Manifest narcissistic attitudes may finally occur in the form of a *defensive narcissism*, often buttressing (chronically, or as a temporary emergency measure) the defenses against the claims of much deeper lying archaic narcissistic configurations. Mr. J.'s temporary haughtiness when the claims of his archaic grandiose-exhibitionistic self were mobilized in the transference as he talked about his shaving habit belongs in this context. Here the analyst's appropriate response is again that of dynamic interpretation and genetic reconstruction. When, however, a chronic defensive grandiosity has secondarily become surrounded by a system of rationalizations (analogous to the disguise of a phobia by a rationalizing system of idiosyncratic tastes and preferences, and by prejudices, etc.), then a degree of educational pressure might indeed have to be exerted to undo the modification of the ego in this realm.

Having discussed the analyst's inappropriately ethical or prematurely realistic (in the sense of the advocacy of successful adaptation) responses to the analysand's narcissism, especially when transmitted in the form of openly or covertly moralizing or condemnatory statements, I now turn to the second pitfall of analytic technique in the analysis of these disorders, namely, that the analyst's interpretations regarding the narcissistic transference might become too abstract. This danger can be much diminished if we avoid falling victim to the widespread confusion between object relations and object love. As I stated previously (1966a), "The antithesis to narcissism is not the object relation but object love. An individual's profusion of object relations, in the sense of the observer of the social field, may conceal his narcissistic experience of the object world; and a person's seeming isolation and loneliness may be the setting for a wealth of current object investments" (p. 245). We must, therefore, bear in mind (a) that our interpretations about the idealizing transference and the mirror transference are statements about an intense object relationship, despite the fact that the object is invested with narcissistic cathexes; and (b) that we are explaining to the analysand how his very narcissism leads him to a heightened sensitivity about certain specific aspects and actions of the object, the analyst, whom he experiences in a narcissistic mode. If the analyst keeps in mind that, in the manifestations of the unfolding psychoanalytic process, the transference mobilization of the narcissistic psychic structures occurs in the form of a narcissistic object relationship, then he will be able to demonstrate to the patient in concrete terms not only how he reacts but also that the reactions are, in the present, specifically focused on the analyst whose attitudes and actions he experiences as the revival of significant narcissistically experienced situations, functions, and objects from the past. Since, furthermore, thought and action are still incompletely separated at the pathognomonic levels of regression which are mobilized in the analysis of the narcissistic disorders, the analyst must also learn to accept with equanimity what appears to be repeated "acting out" and to respond to it as an archaic means of communication.

If the analyst's interpretations are consistently noncondemnatory; if he can clarify to the patient in concrete terms

the significance and the meaning of his (often acted-out) messages, of his seemingly irrational hypersensitivity, and of the
back-and-forth flow of the cathexis of the narcissistic positions; and, especially, if he can demonstrate to the observing
and self-analyzing segment of the patient's ego that these
archaic attitudes are comprehensible, adaptive, and valuable
within the context of the total stage of personality development of which they form a part—then the mature segment of
the ego will not turn away from the grandiosity of the narcissistic self or from the awesome features of the overestimated, narcissistically experienced object. Over and over
again, in small, psychologically manageable portions, the ego
will deal with the disappointment at having to recognize that
the claims of the grandiose self are unrealistic. In response to
this experience, the ego will either mournfully withdraw a
part of the narcissistic investment from the archaic image of
the self, or it will, with the aid of newly acquired structure,
neutralize the associated narcissistic energies or channel them
into aim-inhibited pursuits. And over and over again, in
small, psychologically manageable portions, the ego will deal
with the disappointment of having to recognize that the
idealized self-object is unavailable or imperfect. In response
to this experience, it will withdraw a part of the idealizing
investment from the self-object and strengthen the corresponding internal structures. In short, if the ego learns first to
accept the presence of the mobilized narcissistic configurations, it will gradually integrate them into its own realm, and
the analyst will witness the establishment of ego dominance
and ego autonomy in the narcissistic sector of the personality.

Traumatic States

In view of the fact that the basic neutralizing structure of the
psyche is insufficiently developed in the great majority of patients with narcissistic personality disorders, these patients
not only are inclined to sexualize their needs and conflicts
but they manifest a number of other functional deficiencies.

They are easily hurt and offended, they become quickly over-stimulated, and their fears and worries tend to spread and to become boundless. It is, therefore, not surprising that in the course of analysis (as is indeed also the case in their everyday lives) these patients are subject to recurrent traumatic states, especially during the early phases of treatment. At such times the focus of the analysis shifts temporarily to a near-exclusive consideration of the overburdenedness of the psyche, i.e., to a consideration of the existing psychoeconomic imbalance.

Some of these traumatic states are, of course, due to ex-ternal events. Since these precipitating factors concern every-thing which arouses anxiety, apprehension, worry, and the like in every person, there is no point in discussing them specifically, except for stressing again that it is the immoder-ateness of the reaction, the intensity of the upset, and the temporary paralysis of psychic functions which is remarkable about this psychic state, but not the content of the precipi-tating occurrence itself. There is only one specific precipitat-ing event which I shall mention briefly because it illustrates well the excessiveness of the disturbance and the psycho-logical flavor of the experience: the *faux pas*. Many times (especially in the early phases of the analysis of narcissistic personalities) the patient arrives at his session flooded with shame and anxiety because of a *faux pas* that he felt he had committed.[10] He had told a joke which turned out to be out of place, he had talked too much about himself in company, he had been inappropriately dressed, etc. When examined in detail, the painfulness of many of these situations can be understood by recognizing that a rejection occurred, suddenly and unexpectedly, just at the moment when the patient was most vulnerable to it, i.e., at the very moment when he had expected to shine and was anticipating acclaim in his fan-

10 A complementary trend to be hypersensitive to and hypercritical of other people's real or imaginary inappropriateness (such as of attention-demanding behavior or flashy attire) is usually found in people in whom the integration of their own grandiosity and exhibitionism has remained imperfect.

tasies. (The shame which one experiences when one makes a slip of the tongue or other parapraxes is similar to that after a *faux pas*. It is partly caused by the sudden, narcissistically painful recognition that one had not been in control in the very realm in which one believes oneself to be undisputed master—one's own psyche [see Freud, 1917b].) The narcissistic patient tends to react to the memory of a *faux pas* with excessive shame and self-rejection. His mind returns again and again to the painful moment, in the attempt to eradicate the reality of the incident by magical means, i.e., to undo it. Simultaneously the patient may angrily wish to do away with himself in order to wipe out the tormenting memory in this fashion.

These can be very important moments in the analysis of narcissistic persons. They require the analyst's tolerance for the patient's repeated recounting of the painful scene, and for the anguish which the often seemingly trivial event causes him. For long periods the analyst must participate empathically in the psychic imbalance from which the patient suffers; he must show understanding for the patient's painful embarrassment and for his anger that the act that has been committed cannot be undone. Then, gradually, the dynamics of the situation can be approached and, again in accepting terms, the patient's wish for acclaim and the disturbing role of his childhood grandiosity and exhibitionism can be identified. Childhood grandiosity and exhibitionism, too, must, however, not be condemned. On the one hand, the analyst must show to the patient how the intrusion of unmodified childhood demands in this realm cause him realistic embarrassment; yet, on the other hand, there must also be sympathetic acceptance of the legitimate position of these strivings as seen in an empathically reconstructed genetic context. On the basis of such preliminary insights further progress toward the genetic understanding of the patient's intense rage and self-rejection can then be made. Relevant memories may emerge which tend to round out and correct the preliminary reconstructions. They often refer to situations in which the child's legitimate claim for the approving attention of the grownups had not been responded to, but in which the child had been belittled and ridiculed at the very moment when he most proudly had wanted to display himself.

The full span of analytic work in such a sector of the personality can, of course, not be completed in response to a single specific external event, such as a specific *faux pas* (or in response to a single similar incident within the context of the clinical transference). It is only via the slow, systematic analysis of repeated traumatic states of this type that, against strong resistances, the old grandiosity and exhibitionism which lay in the center of these reactions become intelligible and can now be tolerated by the ego without undue shame and fear of rebuff or ridicule. Only by their gaining access into the ego, however, is the ego capable of building up those specifically appropriate structures which transform the archaic narcissistic drives and ideations into acceptable ambitions, self-esteem, and pleasure in one's functioning.

There are certain other traumatic states which occur typically in the middle and even in the later stages of the analysis of narcissistic personalities, paradoxically often in response to correct and empathically given interpretations which should (and in the long run do) facilitate analytic progress. On first sight one is inclined to explain these reactions as a manifestation of the influence of unconscious guilt; i.e., one tends to surmise that they are a negative therapeutic reaction (Freud, 1923). For a number of reasons, however, this explanation is usually not the correct one. Narcissistic personalities are in general not predominantly swayed by guilt feelings (they are not inclined to react unduly to the pressure exerted by their idealized superego). Their predominant tendency is to be overwhelmed by shame, i.e., they react to the breakthrough of the archaic aspects of the grandiose self, especially to its unneutralized exhibitionism.

The following is an example of a traumatic state of the

second type (the kind that generally occurs *after* the beginning phases of the analysis) from the analytic treatment of
Mr. B. As mentioned before, these states of (often severe)
psychoeconomic imbalance and their psychic elaborations
are (a) triggered by correct interpretations, and are (b) maintained and prolonged by the analyst's temporary failure to
understand the nature of the patient's reaction.

The relevant session of Mr. B.'s analysis took place after a
weekend toward the end of the first year of his analysis. He
spoke rather calmly about his greater ability to tolerate separations. He had, for example, been able to go to sleep
without calming himself by masturbation even during the
weekend separation from the analysis and despite the absence
of his understanding and soothing girlfriend who had recently moved to another part of the country. The patient
then began to speculate about the specific "little boy needs"
which seemed to be at the core of his restless loneliness. He
spoke about the fact that his mother seemed to have disliked
her own body and had recoiled from physical closeness. At
this point the analyst said to the patient that his restlessness
and his tensions were related to the fact that, in consequence
of his mother's attitude, he had never learned to experience
himself as "lovable, loving, and touchable." After a moment's silence the patient responded to the analyst's statement with the words: "Crash! Bang! You hit it!" This ex-
clamation was followed by a brief elaboration concerning
some details of his love life. Then he referred again to his
mother (and his former wife) who had made him feel "like
vermin or filth." Finally he became silent; said that all this
moved him terribly; tears began to fill his eyes and he cried
wordlessly to the end of the session.

On the following day he arrived in a disheveled and deeply
troubled condition; and he remained excited and profoundly
disturbed for the ensuing week. He complained that the
analytic sessions were too short; reported that he couldn't go
to sleep at night and that, when he finally fell asleep ex-

haustedly, his sleep was not restful and that he had numerous anxious and exciting dreams. His associations led him to angry thoughts about unempathic women; he had overt, grossly sexual fantasies about the analyst; dreamed of eating, of breasts, of threatening oral-sadistic symbols (buzzing bees); said that he was not feeling alive, and described himself as being like a radio that is not working because the wires have all become tangled. And, most alarmingly, he began to spin out bizarre fantasies (of a kind that had previously occurred only at the beginning of the treatment) such as about "breasts in light sockets" and the like. The analyst who felt herself at sea about the patient's traumatic state tried to help him by referring to his unempathic mother—but to no avail. It was only after some time had elapsed, in retrospect (but subsequently confirmed during similar episodes), that the analyst came to understand the significance of this event (and could thus help the patient to get over his excitement quickly when he entered a similar state).

In essence the patient's traumatic state was due to the fact that he had reacted with overstimulation and excitement to the analyst's correct interpretation. His vulnerable psyche could not handle the satisfaction of a need (or the fulfillment of a wish) that had existed since childhood: the correct empathic response of an all-important figure in his environment. The childhood wish (or rather need) for his mother's empathic physical response had suddenly become intensely stimulated when the analyst put it into words. Her use of the terms "lovable and touchable" in particular broke through his chronic defenses. His psyche thus became flooded with excitement, and the suddenly intensely stimulated narcissistic libidinal tensions led to a frantic acceleration of psychic activity and to a gross sexualization of the narcissistic transference. In the last analysis, however, it was the patient's basic psychological defect which accounted for the excitement: his psyche lacked the capacity to neutralize the oral (and oral-sadistic) narcissistic tensions which were triggered by the analyst's interpretation, and he lacked those ego structures which would have enabled him to transform these tensions into more or less aim-inhibited fantasies and wishes about caresses, romantic idealizations, or even creativity and work.

The content of these often intensely upsetting reactions varies widely and is, of course, determined not only by the total personality makeup of the patient but also by the specific event which triggered the psychoeconomic imbalance and the helplessness of the ego (which in turn is due to the relative insufficiency of its regulatory functions). Some patients begin to act under such circumstances as if they were "crazy"—in the sense in which a hysteric may appear to act as if he were suffering from a bizarrely conceived neurological illness. The observer of such temporary states of mental imbalance obtains the puzzling impression that the patient behaves as if he were insane but that, in reality, he is neither insane nor malingering. The patient's grossly abnormal behavior may include dangerous activities which are undertaken outside of the analytic situation. In general, however, this acute form of psychopathology tends to manifest itself almost exclusively in the verbal sphere within the psychoanalytic situation itself; i.e., the patient usually has sufficient reality sense to prevent a socially dangerous acting out. But the behavior in the analytic situation is grossly and seemingly intentionally bizarre, with a regressive use of language, a characteristic regression of humor toward primary process-near punning, and a strong anal-sadistic or oral-sadistic flavor of the disjointed communications.

In a literary analogy certain aspects of Hamlet's behavior may be mentioned in this context. Hamlet's behavior, too, confronts the empathic observer with the seemingly unanswerable question whether he is truly suffering from a mental illness or whether he is—more or less consciously—only pretending to be insane. The puzzle resolves itself, I believe, as it does during the analogous traumatic episodes of our patients, as soon as one begins to understand the relative, temporary imbalance of Hamlet's ego which is overwhelmed by an enormous task of internal adaptation and change. To be specific, we may assume on the basis of many indications (including perhaps the nation's loving response to the prince) that Hamlet had been a highly idealistic young man, that he had seen the world, and especially his immediate human surroundings, as being essentially good and noble. When the event which is the prime mover of the tragedy (the murder of his father by his uncle and his mother's complicity in the misdeed) intrudes on him, a total reshuffling of his world view is now demanded of him, i.e., basically a devaluation of all his central values, and the creation of a new world view which acknowledges the reality of the role of evil in the world. The fact that this wholesale change in the (narcissistic) realm of values and ideals has to be accomplished while there is a simultaneous demand on the ego from the side of strongly mobilized oedipal tensions[11] contributes, of course, greatly to the overburdenedness of the psychic apparatus. The oedipal conflicts by themselves, however, cannot explain the extent and the nature of the traumatic state from which Hamlet suffers; Hamlet's psyche is "out of joint" because it has to confront the fact that the world in which he had believed has become "out of joint." At first he responds with denial toward the new reality which shatters his former idealistic outlook. The denial is followed by a partial breakthrough of the deeply upsetting, unwelcome reality into Hamlet's awareness in a quasi-delusional form (the appearance of the father's ghost). During this phase of partial acceptance of the new outlook on reality, a partial denial of the significance of his discovery is still maintained side by side with the recognition of the truth. Psychologically the truth is acknowledged by one part of Hamlet's personality but kept isolated from another part (a vertical split in the ego). Then follows a phase in which the traumatic state presents its most

11 See Freud's interpretation (1900, p. 264ff.); see also Jones (1910).

typical manifestations; it is characterized (a) by discharge phenomena, ranging from sarcastic punning to reckless, aggressive, outbursts (the killing of Polonius); and (b) by retreat phenomena, ranging from philosophical brooding to deeply melancholiac preoccupations.

Our patients do not face objectively ascertainable tasks of the magnitude of that which Hamlet's shattered image of his total world imposes on him. Yet, the relative imbalance which is set up in the fragile or incompletely structured ego of a narcissistically vulnerable person may produce a temporary clinical picture which resembles closely the one presented by Shakespeare's great prince.

The presence of the analyst, however, and the analyst's response to his patient's traumatic state are of great significance —not only because they may bring about quick relief for the flooded mental apparatus of the analysand, but especially because they contribute to the understanding which the patient gains about the causes of his states of mental imbalance and about the nature of his recurrent traumatic states.

If, in other words, the analyst has learned to recognize these traumatic states, if he understands that they are due to a flooding with unneutralized (often oral-sadistic) narcissistic libido, and if he communicates his understanding in appropriately presented interpretations, then the patient's excitement will usually subside. The analyst must, for example, tell the patient that the understanding and the insight which he had obtained in the previous session had shaken him considerably and that it was now difficult for him to regain his balance. Without referring again to the content of the previous interpretation (i.e., in Mr. B.'s case, for example, to the archaic need to be held and touched)—or referring to it either without emphasis or only tangentially— the analyst should tell the patient that it is sometimes very hard to become aware of the intensity of old wishes and needs, that the possibilty of their fulfillment may be more than the patient was able to handle all at once, and that the present state was an understandable attempt to rid himself of his excitement. Such dynamically significant details as Mr. B.'s impression that the sessions are now too short can be explained in terms of his inner psychic disequilibrium, as an expression of the awareness that there is a discrepancy between his tension and his ability to handle it. A reconstruction of the child's psyche vis-à-vis tensions may also be made; and it can be made clear not only that under such circumstances a child is in need of a tension-dispelling adult, but also that the patient is temporarily re-experiencing this old state since the personality of his mother had not permitted such optimal experiences in childhood.

All these foregoing statements must be taken only as examples, meant to describe the general attitude of the analyst in such moments of his patient's psychic imbalance. In my experience it is usually not difficult to come to terms with the excitement, and the patient in general not only soon calms down but he also learns a great deal about himself during the process. Last but not least, a development toward the building up of psychological structures is initiated. The insights obtained enable the patient to remain aware of the narcissistic tensions and thus to channel them into a variety of ideational contexts. In addition, he gradually learns to initiate the handling of these increasingly familiar tension states without the aid of the analyst. (Transitionally, patients will sometimes imagine the analyst's presence when they become flooded with excitement, for example, during the weekend. Or they will repeat the analyst's words to themselves— but these gross identifications are sooner or later dropped, and they are replaced by truly internalized attitudes and even by specific independently emerging personal acquisitions, i.e., by the flowering of capacities [such as humor] which had been present in a rudimentary and latent form but which had had no prior chance to develop.)

CHAPTER 9

CLINICAL ILLUSTRATION OF THE NARCISSISTIC TRANSFERENCES

It is difficult in an exposition such as the present one not only to demonstrate the reasonableness of the theoretical propositions and their consistency within the framework of psychoanalytic metapsychology (including developmental considerations) but also to show their empirical basis and their clinical relevance. No single expository device is likely to succeed, but we must alternate repeatedly between theoretical points and clinical vignettes, and between broader theoretical statements and case reports. Only by pursuing a multiple approach will it be possible to produce the desired result, namely, the cohesive theoretical and clinical-empirical understanding of the phenomena with which we are dealing.

In addition to serving as another implementation of the general maxim that the partnership between clinical observation and theoretical formulation must retain its place at the very center of scientific progress in psychoanalysis, the presentation of the following case study has two specific aims, which, however, are not related to each other.

1. The subsequent clinical report is offered as an example of the type of case in which it is specifically the therapeutic mobilization of the grandiose self which is correlated to the patient's predominant psychopathology. In contrast to the several preceding instances in which clinical material was

adduced to illustrate this or that specific feature of the mirror transference and of the psychopathology of which it is the cohesive therapeutic manifestation, the following sketch of certain clinical details and the outline of a summary of the underlying psychopathology aim at a degree of comprehensiveness (both longitudinally and in depth) which should provide a glimpse at the total structure of a representative specimen of this subgroup of narcissistic personality disorders. Within the framework of the present study, therefore, the case should be considered as occupying a position with regard to the subject matter of the mirror transference which is analogous to the position occupied by case A. (Chapter 3) with regard to the subject matter of the idealizing transference.

2. In addition to serving as the foremost specimen of the therapeutic mobilization of the grandiose self, the clinical material will also serve as the point of departure for extending the theoretical exploration (started in Chapter 7) of certain basic dynamic-structural conditions which are present in the narcissistic personality disturbances. The earlier examination involved the relationship between (1) the vertical split in the psyche which is frequently seen in narcissistic personality disorders; and (2) a horizontal split in the psyche which I believe to be present in all cases of this disturbance, either (less commonly) alone, or in combination with a vertical split (which is the usual case). As pointed out earlier (especially in the case of Mr. J.), the presence of the horizontal split is often difficult to ascertain and can be easily overlooked. Although the effects exerted by the horizontally split-off narcissistic configurations are profound, they are in general much less conspicuous than the grandiosity which is openly displayed by the vertically split-off sector. In view of the comparatively inconspicuous quality of the manifestations of the horizontally split-off narcissistic configurations, it is important to emphasize that, on the one hand, a careful and systematic psychoanalytic investigation will always reveal the presence of

a horizontal split in the psyche, while, on the other hand, one encounters indeed patients suffering from narcissistic personality disturbances in whom no significant vertical split in the psyche appears to exist. In these latter instances the archaic narcissistic configuration (an archaic grandiose self, for example) is submerged and has not become integrated with the mature layers of the personality. The comparatively silent result of this developmental fault is the presence of a variety of personality defects in the narcissistic realm. Some of these defects (such as lack of self-esteem) are due to the insufficient availability of narcissistic nutriment to the mature, reality-near configurations—e.g., the conscious representation of the self—in consequence of the fact that a great deal of the narcissistic libido has remained concentrated upon the submerged archaic structure. Other disturbances (such as hypochondriacal preoccupations and shame propensity, but also the appearance of spasmodically erected brittle walls of defensive arrogance, at times accompanied by brief surges of anxious hypomanic excitement) are due to the uncontrolled, fitful intrusions of the insufficiently walled-off archaic structures into the reality-near layers of the psyche.

In the majority of cases of mirror transference, however, it is the vertically split-off grandiosity which occupies the center of the behavioral stage, and the unconscious, horizontally split-off grandiosity ultimately becomes drawn into the working-through process only after a significant degree of progress toward the integration of the vertically split-off sector with the reality sector has been made. (See the report of case J., and Diagram 3.) The motivation for the creation and the maintenance of the vertical split is on the whole intelligible: it is the specific anxiety vis-à-vis the threat of a specific psychoeconomic imbalance in the narcissistic realm. The nature of the barrier between the vertically split-off sector of the psyche and the reality ego, however, and the method by which it achieves its effect, are in need of much further study. What is the metapsychological essence of the opposition which the reality ego mobilizes when it is encouraged to confront the manifest arrogance and the open narcissistic claims of the split-off sector? Why is it that the psyche's right hand (the centrally located reality ego with its low self-esteem, lack of initiative, and its shame propensity and hypochondria) does not know what its left hand (the grandiose, split-off sector) is doing? Is the barrier, as I am inclined to believe, akin to the mechanism of disavowal which Freud (1927) described for the analogous conditions in the fetishist?

However important these questions might be, the following case report will not concern itself with the barrier between the vertically split-off sectors of the psyche but with the barrier which maintains the horizontal split. We will, in other words, be examining findings which are in many ways closer to the psychological conditions described by Freud (1915b) as forming the basis of the classical transference neuroses. One question, therefore, concerns the nature of the horizontal split in the psyche in narcissistic personality disorders—whether, as was the case with Mr. J., the horizontal split becomes apparent only after sufficient progress vis-à-vis the vertically split-off area has been made, or whether (as seemed to be the case with Mr. K., to be discussed in what follows) the pathogenic grandiose self is present mainly in an unconscious form, i.e., is buried in the depth of the personality.

The specific problem which I shall attempt to clarify concerns two correlated questions: (a) whether the narcissistic structures can be said to exist in repression (whatever other secondary defenses the ego might employ in order to buttress an underlying repression); and, if the first question is answered in the affirmative, (b) whether the metapsychological substance of the (pre)conscious and behavioral manifestations which are correlated to the repressed narcissistic configuration (in Mr. K., predominantly to the grandiose self) is the amalgamation of an activated unconscious structure with a suitable (pre)conscious mental content for which Freud (1900) used the term "transference." The meaning of the term transference has gradually shifted since Freud's structuro-dynamic definition of 1900 and now has a broad clinical acceptation. The concept to which it refers has thus tended to lose some of its early metapsychological precision. As asserted elsewhere (Kohut, 1959), however, Freud's early conceptualization of transference has by no means lost its basic, direction-setting significance.

Keeping the preceding introductory considerations in mind, we can now turn to the clinical illustration. Initially it concerns mainly some dream material, taken from the analysis of Mr. K., an industrial engineer in his early forties, who, after a brief period of idealization, had formed a relatively stable, comparatively silent narcissistic relationship to the analyst. This transference was at first on the borderline between merger and twinship, with little elaboration of object features; later there was an increasing appeal to the analyst for echo, approval, and confirmation; i.e., a mirror transference in the stricter sense of the term became gradually established.

The aspect of the clinical material on which I shall focus concerns certain reactions of the patient to the prospect of separations from me or to shifts in the appointment schedule. Under such circumstances he not only would tend to become generally withdrawn, emotionally shallow, and diffusely depressed, but he also manifested a striking change in his dream pattern. His usual dreams were filled with people; when faced with a separation from me, however, he dreamed regularly about complex machines, electrical wiring, and often of spinning wheels. At first he was not aware of the fact that his emotional reaction (a severe lowering of his self-esteem) was related to the separations; and interpretations on the level of object libido and object aggression produced no significant progress. The spinning wheels in his dreams, for example, expressed not, as I had first thought, his wish to keep me from leaving by interfering with my locomotion; they represented a regression to bodily tensions and to an intense concern about himself, experiences which were the analogue of early hypochondriacal preoccupations due to narcissistic tension states after certain significant childhood traumata. The wires, the wheels, and other aspects of the dream machinery could later in analysis be understood—at times in great detail—as referring to parts of his body about which he had worried and fantasied when he felt ignored and abandoned in childhood.

Stated in general terms we can say that, in instances like the present one, a current narcissistic injury may be followed by the emergence of specific unconscious narcissistic and autoerotic configurations—i.e., of early stages of the self, and of its fragmented precursors—the analysis of which leads to the recall of narcissistic and autoerotic responses in childhood. The observation of such sequences supplies the empirical basis for the assumption that a specific narcissistic or prenarcissistic focus existed in the psyche which remained unconscious until it became hypercathected by the influx of narcissistic libido which, in consequence of a recent narcissistic injury, had been withdrawn from aspects of the *present self* and had turned toward repressed *archaic self representations*.

The preceding clinical illustration demonstrates the existence of unconscious narcissistic structures, i.e., of specific repressed ideas and fantasies concerning the self which are cathected with narcissistic energies. The existence of unconscious structures alone, however, is not transference but only a precondition for it; we must, in addition, ascertain that the old self representation (in its activated state) exerts its influence on thought contents which relate to present-day reality and, conversely, that it, too, is responsive to current factors (i.e., that it is reactivated in response to current events which act as psychological triggers). In our clinical example we can indeed discern these two relationships between the therapeutically activated past and the present: (1) in the dream amalgamation of early body and self imagery with day residues in the form of preconscious ideation concerning machines and electrical systems (stimulated by the patient's current technological interests); and (2) in the equivalence of the events which set in motion the regression during the treatment (such as a canceled appointment) and those which had triggered analogous cathectic shifts in childhood (parental withdrawal).

We will first direct our attention to the dreams of machines, spinning wheels, and electrical wires. The metapsychological constructions of the machine dreams is that of a transference in the strict metapsychological sense of the term (Freud, 1900, p. 562; see also Kohut, 1959; Kohut and Seitz, 1963). It is not enough, however, to state that a preconscious day residue (current ideation concerning machinery) becomes the carrier for a repressed unconscious content (the archaic body self) since it could be asserted that I have demonstrated only the formal regression of representational symbolism. It could be maintained, in other words, that I have shown no more than that the patient dealt with an unconscious content not through verbal thought but with the aid of the pictorial language which becomes available during sleep, similar to the hypnagogic regressions described by Silberer (1909).

There can be no doubt, however, that the machines in the patient's dreams were more than generally available, universal body symbols since machines had constituted through the patient's entire life a significant conscious dimension of his expanded self experience. The mechanical toys and the sleds and tricycles of his childhood had been crucial means of overcoming specific archaic narcissistic and especially autoerotic tensions (hypochondriacal worries about his body); and various mechanical skills and in particular his outstanding ability to handle complex locomotive devices (e.g., he was an accomplished glider pilot) played a decisive role in the maintenance of his self-esteem in adult life and remained a significant constituent of his self image. Taking these factors into account we can say that the machines in his dreams occurred not only because of their suitability for pictorial representation but that, analogous to the dream transferences concerning object strivings in the transference neuroses, the appearance of the machines can be understood as the result of amalgamations and compromise formations between current and archaic aspects of the self representation. After a blow to the patient's self-esteem (the loss of the narcissistically experienced analyst), the (pre)conscious self representation became decathected, and unconscious archaic self images from childhood, at the borderline between the grandiose self and its autoerotic fragmentation, became hypercathected and strove toward expression, threatening painful narcissistic tensions in the body self. The outcome was a dream compromise in which the old and the new became intermingled and established a temporary equilibrium.

The preceding metapsychological analysis demonstrates several similarities between certain narcissistic formations and the analogous transference configurations in the transference neuroses. In both instances a repressed structure first becomes hypercathected with instinctual energies which have been withdrawn from a preconscious representation and have undergone regressive transformation; and the hypercathected structure then intrudes into the preconscious ego to merge, in amalgamations and compromise formations, with suitable contents of this psychological realm. Is the similarity sufficiently great to permit us to speak of such dreams as transference phenomena? On first sight one would have strong hesitations about doing so, since object-instinctual cathexis, one of the essential elements of the transference in the metapsychological sense, is lacking. Furthermore, apart from the decisive fact of the narcissistic quality of the instinctual forces which are being activated, no object is present even as defined in the cognitive ideational sense: neither the representation of the body self in the unconscious fantasies nor the representations of the machines in the preconscious imagery appear to have object qualities.

If we now turn from the metapsychological assessment of

the dreams to the psychological events which triggered the regression of the narcissistic libido, we obtain the immediate impression that we are on familiar ground, i.e., that we are dealing with a transference reaction—not perhaps in the strictest metapsychological meaning of the term, but at least in its broader clinical sense. And indeed most of the information obtained in the analysis seems to confirm this initial impression. After the removal of a number of surface resistances it became abundantly clear that the patient's emotional retreats took place in reaction to the analyst's having canceled or changed an appointment, to a forthcoming holiday or vacation, and the like. It could also be ascertained that similar reactions had happened before the analysis (especially in his relationship with his wife; they continued to occur side by side with the reactions to the analyst) and that they had taken place in childhood when his parents went away. Finally, ever-increasing evidence allowed the reconstruction, supported by many confirmatory memories, that the mother's pregnancy and the birth of a brother when the patient was three, and his mother's concomitant and subsequent withdrawal from him, had been a major focus of the narcissistic fixations which not only determined much of his later personality development but also undoubtedly became the nucleus of some of his later reactions to the analyst.

It must be emphasized that the birth of a brother cannot be considered the essential cause of the disturbances in the development of the child's narcissism. It was rather the narcissistic personality of the mother and the child's whole pathogenic relationship with her, preceding and subsequent to the brother's birth, which accounted for the traumatizing impact and the pathological consequences of this event. We might even hypothesize that narcissistic fixations would also have established themselves if there had not been another child, and we might, therefore, assume that the importance during the analysis of the memories surrounding the event of the brother's birth was due to the fact that they had become the focus of the tendency toward the telescoping of analogous (earlier and later) genetic experiences. As a matter of fact, the birth of the brother may in a certain sense also have contributed positively to the patient's psychic development, in particular in the realm of his narcissism. It interrupted the enmeshment with his ambivalent mother and motivated two specific attempts to escape from the developmental impasse, of which one, unfortunately, failed, while the other was only partially successful. The failure seems to have occurred in his relationship to his father to whom the child turned—a very typical move under such circumstances—in his search for an object for his narcissistic tensions. Although he should have been maturationally ready for such a step (he was three and one half years old), the attempt to attach himself to his father as to an admired, idealized parent imago (an image of masculine perfection) failed on three counts: (1) in consequence of his mother's subtle but very effective interference; (2) having been totally taken up with the intensely gratifying enmeshment with his mother, his previous development had left him unprepared for the shift that was now suddenly required; and, what seems even more important, (3) the depreciated father (who, for example, was secretive about his lower social stratum background by comparison with the aristocratic family of the mother) could not tolerate the son's idealization and withdrew from him.

The child was more successful in his attempt to discharge the narcissistic tensions through physical activities. Although they were always at the borderline of being grandiose and unrealistic (and therefore frequently endangered his life and health), they did contain a modicum of sublimatory possibilities and provided a stage on which some realistic gratifications of the underlying grandiose fantasies and of his exhibitionism could be obtained.

Are we justified to use the term transference for the narcissistic involvements which enabled Mr. K. to accomplish such wholesome therapeutic transformations? I believe that the answer to this question is not clear-cut and depends largely on the individual preference of the analytic theorist. Instead of pursuing these theoretical issues, I shall leave the question of terminology open and, returning to the clinical material, shall enumerate the most important factors concerning the concrete, experiential role which the analyst played for the patient during the course of the analysis.

1. During an early phase of the analysis the patient had given evidence of great admiration for the analyst and his professional ability. This attitude (an idealizing transference) established itself rapidly, lasted for several weeks, and was then gradually replaced by the more silent, yet strong bond, the disturbance of which formed the background to the changes in the patient's dream content which were discussed in the preceding pages. This transference bond contained few object elaborations. What little material emerged, however, pointed to the fact that the patient felt himself either as silently merged with the analyst or that he experienced the analyst as an alter-ego, i.e., someone like himself with whom he was able to share his thoughts and experiences. This narcissistic relationship enabled him gradually to reveal his intense narcissistic needs, in particular his exhibitionistic and grandiose aspirations in the area of physical prowess. This material related especially to the time when his mother, who had formerly given him intense, though pathologically prolonged, unconditional, nonselective narcissistic gratifications, had turned away from him. The child then attempted to channel his narcissistic libido into an idealizing relationship with his father; but, after this attempt failed, he seems to have retreated toward fantasies of a relationship with (alter-ego) playmates,[1] alternating with a depressively tinged brood-

1 Patient C., mentioned in a different context (see Chapter 7), recalled from a similar period of his childhood that he had fantasies that the new baby (in his anticipatory imagination: a twin) would be a playmate and would then fulfill some role in re-establishing his narcissistic balance which was severely disturbed by the pregnancy of his formerly narcissistically enmeshing mother who had now withdrawn from him.

ing loneliness (in which he must have reactivated some of the older feelings of merger with his mother). These stages of the grandiose self were revived in the analysis after the initial idealizing phase had passed and constituted the bulk of the secondary twinship-merger transference which dominated the analysis. As the analysis proceeded, however, the merger-twinship was gradually replaced by a mirror transference in the narrower sense; i.e., the patient became more aware of his demands for approval, echoing, and confirmation from the side of the analyst. Even now, however, the emphasis was clearly not yet on the analyst but on himself and on his narcissistic demands. Only during the last year of the patient's long analysis did a more cohesive idealizing transference seem to establish itself once more. It appeared to lead toward a final period of working through that specifically concerned his idealizing attempts (related to the time when he had turned to his father after being rejected by his mother). An external event unfortunately made it advisable to stop the analysis at that time and a reliable assessment of this last period could therefore not be achieved in this instance. Brief spurts of renewed idealization were, however, also occasionally encountered during the middle phases of the analysis while the merger-twinship transference held sway. These short periods of idealization could easily be identified as the manifestation of certain fleeting transitional stages in the movement of the narcissistic libido, in particular during times when the patient was on the way to re-establishing the basic mobilization of his grandiose self in the merger-twinship relationship to the analyst after it had been temporarily interrupted. The significance of an early brief period of the reactivation of the idealized parent imago as a fleeting precursor of the long-term remobilization of the grandiose self during the main part of the analysis has been discussed in the context of the secondary mirror transference (Chapter 6). Here I am mainly interested in the comparatively stable transference which formed the basis for the essential working-through processes during the analysis. In the following I shall, therefore, turn to this long-term bond and, especially, to certain of its vicissitudes in the course of the treatment.

2. As stated, the basic relationship was that of a more or less silent merger-twinship with little or no evidence of overt or covert admiration for the analyst and no elaboration of object-related features. The analyst was accepted as a silent presence or, in the later mirror variant of the relationship, as an echo of what the patient had expressed. The analyst's successful interpretations concerned mainly the patient's self-esteem, present and past, and his present and past aspirations and ambitions. Although these interpretations aroused severe specific resistances at times,[2] the presence of the analyst, who was experienced either as merged with the grandiose self or as a twinlike replica of it, served an important buffering function and the patient's self-assessment proceeded within manageable swings of tension (the extremes were anxious optimistic excitement, followed by a retreat from the over-stimulation by calming himself through various modes of self-indulgence). On the whole, however, the analytic process led the patient in a predictable forward direction toward greater realism, expanding working capacity, and increasing ability to shoulder appropriate responsibilities.

3. The analytic work always came to a standstill whenever the prospect of a separation from the analyst (or analogous occurrences) threatened the maintenance of the homeostatic buffering function that was provided by the presence of the alter-ego analyst or of the merger with him. During such periods the patient felt withdrawn, shallow, and dejected, and with the exception of reporting the machine dreams which occurred regularly at such times, he had no associations other than those that referred to his mood and to his physical and mental condition. Specifically there were no references whatever to the analyst at such times, except in somewhat

2 See the discussion of the resistances encountered during the working-through process in these cases in Chapter 7.

later phases as an expression of the increasing (pre)conscious knowledge that his tensions were due to being separated from him.

4. Interpretations formulated in terms of feelings about the analyst produced little effect and fell flat, whether they dealt with the possibility of affectionate longing or angry resentment and destructiveness. Genetic interpretations, too, produced little progress as long as the reconstructions were expressed in terms of object-libidinal and object-aggressive strivings toward the childhood imagoes, especially toward his mother.

5. Significant progress, however, began to be made (in his dreams the wheels ceased to spin and there was traction) as soon as his reactions (present and past) were approached on the narcissistic level. Specifically, we came to understand that, in the earlier phases of the analysis, he experienced the analyst not as a separate, distinct person whom he either loved or hated, but as a silent replica or extension of his own infantile narcissism; that the analyst's presence protected him from succumbing to his severe lack of self-esteem, and to the lethargy and lack of incentive which was associated with it, just as alter-ego playmates (either completely imaginary or, especially later, real playmates around whom he spun twinship fantasies) had partially protected him and had permitted him to maintain a modicum of self-esteem-supplying physical activities (a tricycle played a paramount role here) even though his mother had suddenly withdrawn her (formerly excessively intense and phase-inappropriately unqualified) involvement in his physical presence and exaggerated admiration for his achievements. In later phases of the analysis when, largely as the result of the working-through processes concerning the alter-ego status of the analyst, the merger-twinship had to some extent been replaced by a mirror transference in *sensu strictiori*, the content of the interpretations changed and the patient learned to recognize that he now felt drained of self-esteem, and that he suffered from his characteristic

painful lethargy, because he experienced the forthcoming absence of the analyst (or any number of other occurrences which, though outwardly quite dissimilar, had the same emotional connotations for the patient) as a withdrawal of narcissistic cathexes from a grandiose self that needed to perform continuously in front of an admiring mother. In either case, however, whether he was deprived of the analyst as an extension of himself, in his role as an alter-ego, or in his function as an echoing, admiring, and approving mirror, the narcissistic investment regressed from the level which it had maintained while the narcissistic transference was relatively undisturbed, and it reinforced the cathexis of the ideationally less differentiated precursor of the cohesive grandiose self: the archaic, fragmented body self. The hypercathexis of the archaic body self, however, led to a painful autoerotic tension state which the patient experienced in the form of hypochondriacal preoccupations concerning his physical and mental health. We may say that, within the realm of the grandiose self, a regression from narcissism to autoerotism, from the cohesiveness of the self to its fragmentation, had taken place.

The influence which the personality of the patient's mother exerted on the formation of the patient's rather severe narcissistic fixation cannot be examined in detail. As stated before, the clustering of relevant memories surrounding the birth of the patient's brother when the patient was three and one half years old indicates that this event had been a turning point in the patient's relationship to his mother. The principal causative external circumstance (as differentiated from the genetic data which relate to the child's endopsychic elaborations of, and reactions to, external influences) responsible for the child's narcissistic fixation was, however, a psychosocial one, namely, the fact that his narcissistic mother appeared to be able to maintain a relationship with only *one* child at a time.

This emotional restriction of the mother can frequently be ascertained in the childhood history of those patients suffering from narcissistic personality disorders whose emerging memories appear at first to point to the birth of a sibling as the primary cause of their disturbance. It is, however, not the birth of a sibling which is to blame—most children do indeed survive this event without disabling fixations in the narcissistic realm—but the complete and sudden shift from the mother's narcissistic enmeshment with the older child to an equally single-minded involvement with the new baby. To be exact, such mothers seem to be able to feel genuine emotions only for a small, preoedipal boy (the father is usually depreciated, and older children are usually dropped emotionally or ambivalently infantilized by her); but this relationship, while it lasts, is indeed a very intense one. The preoedipal boy is intensely cathected with narcissistic libido by the mother, and the glorification of the child is maintained beyond the time when such a maternal attitude is still phase-appropriately in tune with the boy's needs. As soon as another child is on the way, however, the mother invests the new baby with the narcissistic cathexes which she withdraws from the older child with traumatic abruptness.

It may be added here that the objective assessment of the pathogenic personality of patients' parents, though at times tactically useful in analysis since such an act of intellectual mastery may give support to the patient's ego, is not strictly speaking a psychoanalytic task, but belongs to that most important extension and application of psychoanalysis to social psychology: the psychoanalytically informed examination of the child's environment.[3] Here I must restrict myself to re-

[3] Since I am here expressing a preference for considering the investigation of objectively ascertainable factors in the child's environment as lying outside the domain of psychoanalysis in its strictest definition, I must make explicit that this preference is not arbitrary but that it is based on the, in my judgment, useful distinction between (a) the genetic point of view, one of the essential approaches of psychoanalytic metapsychology (see Hartmann and Kris, 1945), and (b) etiological investigations (which are carried out with conceptual and technical tools that belong to a number of neighboring disciplines such as biology, biological genetics, sociology and social psychology, to name only a few). The *genetic approach* in psychoanalysis relates to the investiga-

peating that in many cases the prolonged narcissistic experience of the parent by the child appears to occur in response to a similar attitude of a narcissistically fixated parent to the child. The spectrum of parental disturbance in this respect may extend from mild narcissistic fixation to latent or overt psychosis. It is my impression that a specific type of covert psychosis in a parent tends to produce broader and deeper fixations in the narcissistic and, especially, in the prenarcissistic (autoerotic) realm than does overt psychosis. In the latter instances (a parent's overt psychosis) the child is usually more removed from the deleterious influence of the parent and, even if the parent is not hospitalized, the fact that his behavior is grossly abnormal is acknowledged by the environment. The child is thus supported in his striving toward the development of autonomous nuclei of his body-mind-self.

The result of the influence of a severely pathological parent —who not only was able to disguise the manifestations of his psychosis through rationalizations but also managed to enlist the support of the environment by creating a large following for his ideas—may be gleaned from the evidence which Niederland (1959b, 1960) and Baumeyer (1955) have been collecting about Schreber's father. It may be deduced from the evidence which these authors present not only that the father's personality had a severe pathogenic influence on the child but that the mother was subordinated to, submerged by, and interwoven with the father's overwhelming personality and strivings, thus permitting the son no refuge from the impact of the father's pathology. What was father Schreber's pathology? We have no accepted diagnostic category, but I believe he represented not a severe kind of psychoneurosis but a special kind of psychotic character structure in which reality test-

---

tion of those subjective psychological experiences of the child which usher in a chronic change in the distribution and further development of the endopsychic forces and structures. The *etiological approach*, on the other hand, relates to the investigation of those objectively ascertainable factors which, in interaction with the child's psyche as it is constituted at a given moment, may—or may not—elicit the genetically decisive experience.

ing remains broadly intact even though it is in the service of the psychosis, of a central *idée fixe*. It is probably a kind of healed-over psychosis, similar perhaps to Hitler's (see Erikson, 1950; and, especially, Bullock, 1952), who emerged from a lonely hypochondriacal phase with the fixed idea that the Jews had invaded the body of Germany and had to be eradicated. The absolute conviction with which Schreber's father upheld his central ideas, the unquestioning fanaticism with which he pursued his messianic health goals, betrays, I believe, their profoundly narcissistic and prenarcissistic character; and I would assume that a fear of hypochondriacal tensions lay behind his rather overt fight against masturbation, carried out in the form of his well-known teachings in the area of physical culture. These fanatical activities, though presented to the public at large through the medium of his books (cf., e.g., *Das Buch der Erziehung an Leib und Seele,* 1865) and lived out on the body of his son, are the expression of a hidden psychotic system. The son, in other words, was experienced by the father as a part of his psychotic self-world and not as separate. I believe that here lies a major source of the son's deep prenarcissistic fixations. To be stimulated and oppressed while being included in the hidden prenarcissistic-delusional system of the stimulating and oppressing adult does not further the child's elaboration of object-libidinal sexual fantasies or of vengeful fantasies directed against the object, but it predisposes to a narcissistic and prenarcissistic (autoerotic) distribution of the sexual and aggressive drives.

The foregoing speculations concerning the roots of Schreber's paranoia do, of course, bear only indirectly on the question of the etiology of the narcissistic personality disturbances. In most instances of the latter, the parental pathology is not a psychosis but consists in a characterological deformity of a narcissistic kind which determines the parent's attitude toward the child and thus leads to narcissistic fixations. But I have also come across several cases of narcissistic personality disorder in which there was strong evidence that the crucial parental pathology was that of a covert psychosis (e.g., the mothers of patients C. and D. seemed to be latent schizophrenics; the mother of patient J. developed in her old age an open persecutory delusional system about her possessions—a significant specific symptom in view of Mr. J.'s specific psychopathology).

I shall, however, not dwell any longer on the problem of the role of psychosocial factors in the etiology of the narcissistic personality disorders, but conclude the foregoing considerations with a summary of the structure of the psychopathology—and of the correlated course of the analysis—of Mr. K., the specific case of narcissistic personality disturbance which serves here as an example of the therapeutic activation of the grandiose self. After the failure of his abortive attempt to regain his narcissistic balance through the idealization of his father, the child regressed to a reactivation of his grandiose self, i.e., in essence, to a pathological version of the narcissistic position which he had held before his mother had turned away from him. The concomitantly occurring processes of fixation on the unmodified demands of an early stage of the grandiose self and on the archaic exhibitionism of an old body self, and the repression of a part of these structures (another part was sublimated in the patient's athletic interests), created the permanent pathogenic nucleus of his psychic organization. During the establishment of his narcissistic transference in analysis the current was reversed. It began with a fleeting idealizing transference (reviving the attempt to idealize his father), which was soon followed by a long-term secondary activation of the grandiose self, i.e., by the narcissistic mother transference, at first in the form of a merger-twinship. The merger-twinship, finally, was gradually replaced by a mirror transference in the narrower sense, with intensely experienced demands for admiration, and wishes to exhibit himself and his prowess to the analyst, which reactivated certain prominent aspects of his early enmeshment with his mother. The idealizing transference re-established

itself again toward the end of his analysis (as a remobilization
of the pivotal narcissistic father transference) after the working-through process with regard to the secondary mirror
transference had been completed.

The essential pathogenic psychological structures of this
patient's psychopathology were thus narcissistic ones, and certain of the crucial dynamic movements during analysis (manifested, for example, in the machine dreams) were psychological
shifts not from object love to narcissism but from one narcissistic position (the merger-mirror transference) to another
one (at the borderline between an archaic stage of narcissism
and that of the autoerotic, fragmented body self). This patient's reactivation of the grandiose self in the mirror transference is, therefore, to be understood not as predominantly
the revival of a fixation point on the road to full object love
(as a matter of fact there were other sectors of the patient's
personality in which he had attained a considerable depth
and breadth of his object investments) but as the remobilization of a fixation point on the developmental road of one of
the major forms of narcissism. The pathological relationship
to his mother, her sudden loss of interest in him, and the
failure of his attempt to idealize his father had interfered not
so much with the development of object love as it had with
the acquisition of mature ambitions and ego goals. It is quite
in keeping with this fact that the patient's major external
psychopathology lay not in the area of his capacity for love
and in his interpersonal relationships but in his ability to
devote himself consistently to his work and to commit himself
to worthwhile and absorbing long-term goals. Instead of the
transformation of the grandiose self into realistic ambitions
and aims and the employment of its instinctual investment
for a healthy sense of self-esteem, the archaic grandiose self
remained unmodified, and a large portion of the narcissistic
libido continued to invest not only this structure but at
times even the autoerotic, fragmented body self. The outcome was a life from which meaningful work and achievement

in the sphere of adult reality were excluded; he could, how-ever, find relief, both from autoerotic body tensions and from dangerous grandiose fantasies, by participating—and with great success—in various athletic activities and sports, in particular those which involved speedy locomotion. The pre-cariousness of this adjustment led to continual involvements in social conflicts and could not prevent the occurrence of states of depression and inner depletion.

CHAPTER 10

SOME REACTIONS OF THE ANALYST
TO THE IDEALIZING TRANSFERENCE

As may be expected, the analyst's major reactions (including his countertransferences) in the analysis of narcissistic disorders are rooted in the analyst's own narcissism and, especially, in the area of his own, unresolved narcissistic disturbances. These phenomena do not, in essence, differ from those which occur in the analysand, and they will here be considered only insofar as they are mobilized in the analyst in response to the circumscribed transference constellations of the narcissistic patient. The examination of the various reactions manifested by the analyst when he is predominantly confronted by the mobilization of the patient's idealized parent imago in the idealizing transference will, therefore, be separated from the examination of those which occur when the patient's grandiose self has come into the focus of the analytic work in the mirror transference (see Chapter 11).

I shall introduce the discussion of the analyst's reactions to the analysand's idealizing transference with a concrete example.

Some time ago I was consulted by a colleague concerning a prolonged stalemate in the analysis of a young woman (Miss L.) which seemed to have been present from the beginning of the treatment and to have persisted through two years of work. Despite the fact that he gave me an informative review of the patient's history and of the analysis, I was at first unable to determine the cause of the stalemate; and since the patient, an emotionally shallow, shiftless, and promiscuous woman, showed a severe disturbance of her ability to establish meaningful object relationships, and presented a history of severe childhood traumas, I tended initially to agree with the analyst that the extent of the narcissistic fixations prevented the establishment of that minimum of transferences without which analysis cannot proceed. Evidence of some warmth toward the analyst and of interest in the treatment, however, spoke against the espousal of an altogether pessimistic outlook; yet, the stalemate seemed in essence to have been present from the beginning of therapy. I therefore asked the analyst to give me an account of the early hours of the analysis, with particular attention to possible activities on his part which the patient might have experienced as a rebuff.

Among the earliest transference manifestations several dreams of this Catholic patient had contained the figure of an inspired, idealistic priest. While these early dreams had remained uninterpreted, the analyst remembered—clearly against some resistance—that he had subsequently mentioned to the patient that *he* was *not* a Catholic. He had seemingly not given her this information in response to the dreams, but had justified the move by her supposed need to be acquainted with a minimum of the actual situation since in his view the patient's hold on reality was tenuous. This event must have been very significant for the patient. We later understood that, as an initial, tentative transference step, she had reinstated an attitude of idealizing religious devotion from the beginning of adolescence, an attitude which in turn appeared to have been the revival of vague awe and admiration which she had experienced in early childhood. Later material from the analysis of this patient led to the conclusion that these earliest idealizations had been an attempt to escape from the threat of bizarre tensions and fantasies caused by traumatic stimulations and frustrations from the side of her severely pathological parents. The analyst's misguided remark, however, that he was not a Catholic—i.e., not like the priest of her dreams, not an idealized good and healthy version of the patient—was taken as a rebuff by the patient and led to the analytic stalemate which the analyst, with the aid of a number of consultations concerning this patient and his response to her, was later largely able to break.

I am focusing neither on the specific significance of the incipient (idealizing) transference, nor on the specific effect of the analyst's mistake—in this instance, it may have been partly provoked by the patient—on the course of the analysis; I am interested in the elucidation of a countertransference symptom. A single observation would not allow a valid conclusion; but a combination of factors (among them the fact that I observed similar incidents; one, occurring in a student whom I supervised, was almost identical) allows me to offer the following explanation with a high degree of conviction. The analytically unwarranted rejection of the patient's idealizing attitudes is usually motivated by a defensive fending off of painful narcissistic tensions (experienced as embarrassment, self-consciousness, and shame, and leading even to hypochondriacal preoccupations) which are generated in the analyst when the repressed fantasies of his grandiose self become stimulated by the patient's idealization.

The analyst's uneasiness at being idealized by the patient is especially likely to occur when the idealization takes place early and at a rapid pace, i.e., when the analyst is caught by surprise and has no time to prepare himself emotionally for his own reactions to being suddenly invested by an onrush of the patient's narcissistic-idealizing libido. Some discomfort, of course, when one is exposed to open and intense adulation is ubiquitous (and proverbial: "Praise to the face is a disgrace!"), and thus even analysts whose personalities have no undue narcissistic vulnerability may have to resist the temptation to fend off their patients' admiration. Unless there are unusual vulnerabilities in this respect, however, these reactions will be controlled and will be replaced by responses and attitudes which are more in keeping with the proper unfolding of the idealizing transference (and with the patient's internal resistances against it) and with the development of the analytic process. If the analyst, however, is not sufficiently aware of his intolerance for narcissistic tensions and, especially, if he has (via identifications and imitations, or on his own) formed a stable countertransference attitude either of quasi-theoretical convictions or of specific character defenses or (as is frequently the case) of both, then his effectiveness with certain groups of narcissistic personality disturbances is impaired.

It makes little difference whether the rejection of the patient's idealization is blunt, which is rare; or subtle (as in the instance reported), which is common; or, which is most frequent, almost concealed by correct, but prematurely given, genetic or dynamic interpretations (such as the analyst's quickly calling the patient's attention to idealized figures in his past or pointing out hostile impulses and contemptuous thoughts which supposedly underlie the idealizing ones). The rejection may express itself through no more than a slight overobjectivity of the analyst's attitude or a coolness in the analyst's voice; or it may reveal itself in the tendency to be jocular with the admiring patient or to disparage the narcissistic idealization in a humorous and kindly way. (In this context, see Kubie, 1971.)

It may be added here that it is their narcissistic vulnerability which motivates many excessively jocular people to employ these specific characterological defenses; i.e., they are continuously driven to deal with their narcissistic tensions (including the pressure of narcissistic rage) by belittling and self-belittling jokes. (For the differentiation, within the framework of the metapsychology of narcissism, of jocularity and sarcasm, on the one hand, from a genuine sense of humor, on the other hand, see Kohut, 1966a.)

Finally, to round out the account of the various ways by which the analyst, when he feels oppressed by his own narcissistic tensions, may attempt to fend off the patient's overt idealization (or by which he is led to overlook the defenses by which the patient disguises the manifestations of the therapeutic reactivation of the idealized parent imago), it is even deleterious to emphasize the patient's assets at a time when he attempts the idealizing expansion of the ingrained narcissistic positions and fels humble and insignificant by comparison with the therapist—appealing though it may seem when the analyst expresses respect for his patient. In short, during those phases of the analysis of narcissistic character disturbance when an idealizing transference begins to germinate, there is only one correct analytic attitude: to accept the admiration.

Are these failings of the analyst vis-à-vis the manifestation of an idealizing transference due to endopsychic constellations in the psychic apparatus of the analyst to which we should refer as countertransferences? This question which, it may be added here, can also be raised with regard to the analogous phenomena which occur during the analysis of the remobilized grandiose self in the mirror transference, leads us to a complex but by now familiar set of problems. I shall not address myself again to those aspects of the problem which hinge on the meaning of the term transference, i.e., whether we accept it as referring to a clinical phenomenon which is understood in its dynamic and genetic dimensions or whether, in addition to the above, we insist on a more rigorous metapsychological definition from the topographic-structural and psychoeconomic points of view (Chapters 8 and 9). Here I shall consider only the limited question whether the analyst's reactions are in the main motivated by current stress, or whether his faulty responses are due to specific long-term vulnerabilities which are related to the dangerous mobilization of specific repressed unconscious constellations. Since I feel certain that either one of the aforementioned causative factors may be responsible, the answer to this question cannot be given in general terms but must be derived from the analytic investigation of individual instances.

Material obtained from the analysis of colleagues while they were engaged in the psychoanalytic treatment of narcissistic personalities as well as analogous self-analytic experiences have convinced me that these faulty reactions may relate to any point within a broad spectrum, i.e., from (a) simple defensive responses in a situation of momentary current stress to (b) responses which are part of ingrained countertransference attitudes. In the first case, the supervisor's or consultant's explanation, or the analyst's own rapid self-scrutiny, will usually remedy the situation if the significance of the idealizing transference is understood by the analyst and if he is willing to permit the spontaneous unfolding of the analytic situation. Brief interferences with the analyst's optimal functioning stem in these instances from the fact that, as stated before, a degree of narcissistic vulnerability is ubiquitous and that open praise and glorification (and, especially, the anticipatory tensions when narcissistic stimulation is expected) tend to make most civilized people uncomfortable and thus defensive. Specific ingrained resistances to allowing the unfolding of a cohesive idealizing attitude, however, can be recognized not only by the fact that simple explanations do not suffice in changing the analyst's deleterious attitude, but often also by a characteristic specificity and rigidity of the analyst's responses. He may be convinced, for example, that hostility always lies behind the patient's wish to admire the analyst; he is certain that the maintenance of a friendly rapport with the patient requires that the analyst respond with modest realism, etc. Since either one of these two assumptions may indeed be correct if the analyst is not dealing with an idealizing transference, his error cannot be demonstrated without reference to the fact that it has been committed on the basis of a blunting of his usual professional perceptivity and empathic sensitivity. These feelings usually become especially blatant when the analyst fails to grasp the unmistakable significance of the patient's expression of the fact that the analyst had misunderstood him. Clearly, there must be disturbing (unconscious) factors at work when an experienced analyst confuses the exaggerated praise of a patient which is accompanied by allusions to unconscious hostility with the shyly germinating tendrils of idealization which an analysand may extend (in his dreams, for example) while an idealizing transference begins to establish itself. And equally clearly, the automatic emphasis at the beginning of an analysis on the analyst's realism vis-à-vis a patient's idealization is no more justified than would be an analyst's protestation that he is not his patient's parent in response to the first hint of the patient's oedipal strivings.

In a letter to Binswanger (February 20, 1913) Freud expressed himself as follows about the problem of countertransference which he considered "one of the most difficult ones technically in psychoanalysis." "What is given to the patient," Freud said, must be "consciously allotted, and then more or less of it as the need may arise. Occasionally a great deal. . . ." And later Freud sets down the crucial maxim: "To give someone too little because one loves him too much is being unjust to the patient and a technical error" (Binswanger, 1956, p. 50).

The present considerations constitute the analogue in the realm of the analysis of narcissistic personality disturbances to Freud's preceding statement about the countertransferences in the analysis of the transference neuroses. If, in the analysis of a transference neurosis, the patient's remobilized incestuous object-libidinal demands elicit an intense unconscious response in the analyst which the analyst does not understand, he may become cold and overly technical vis-à-vis the patient's wishes, he may reject them in some other way, or will not even recognize them. At any rate, his ego will not have the freedom to choose the response that is in harmony with the requirement of the analysis and he will not be able, as Freud expressed it, to allot consciously what he gives to the patient "more or less . . . as the need may arise." A parallel situation may occur in the analysis of a narcissistic personality disturbance when the remobilization of the idealized parent imago prompts the analysand to see the analyst as the embodiment of idealized perfection. If the analyst has not come to terms with his own grandiose self, he may respond to the idealization with an intense stimulation of his unconscious grandiose fantasies. These pressures will call forth an intensification of defenses and may, in an elaboration and buttressing of the defenses, bring about the analyst's rejection of the patient's idealizing transference. If the analyst's defensive attitude becomes chronic, the establishment of a workable idealizing transference is interfered with and the gradual working-through processes and concomitant transmuting internalizations in the realm of the idealized parent imago are prevented. The curtailment of the freedom of the analyst's "work ego" (Fliess, 1942) is due to his intolerance for a specific narcissistic demand of the patient. Paraphrasing Freud, he was unable to allow himself to be idealized "more or less . . . as the need may arise."

The slow analytic dissolution of the idealizing transference which occurs during extended working-through periods, usually late in the analysis, exposes the analyst to another emotional test in this area. In the initial phase, as described before, the analyst may feel oppressed by the stimulation of his narcissistic fantasies; in the late stage, he may resent being belittled by the very patients who had formerly idealized him.

Exaggerated fault-finding and belittling commonly also occur as defenses against the *establishment* of a comparatively uncomplicated idealizing transference, early in some analyses. The perceptive analyst will usually have no trouble recognizing the thinly disguised admiration which hides behind the patient's critical attitudes in these instances. These defenses require, of course, a different technical approach, and they call forth different reactions in the analyst than the attacks on him that precede and accompany the *withdrawal* of the idealizing libido. The knowledge that he is dealing with the patient's defense against the establishment of an idealizing transference will, in general, protect the analyst against the development of untoward reactions that might disturb his analytic posture.

The patient's attacks on the analyst which occur during the working-through periods of the later stages of the analysis, however, may indeed impose an emotional hardship on the analyst since most patients (in the context of their angry disappointment during the work of reality testing which precedes the waves of withdrawal of idealizing libido from the analyst) are able to fasten on some of the analyst's actual emotional, intellectual, physical, and social shortcomings. Still, serious difficulties in this area (i.e., reactions of the analyst which imperil the success of the analysis) are, according to my experience, not frequent. There are a number of reasons for the relative harmlessness of the reactions which occur when the analyst is under attack as the patient is working through his idealizations. If the analyst's narcissistic vulnerability is great (and especially if, in addition, his skill and experience with the analytic treatment of narcissistic disorders are insufficient), his patients are not likely to reach a stage in which the idealizing transference will be worked through systematically, and thus a phase in which the narcissistic libido is gradually withdrawn from the analyst does not occur. If, however, a systematic working-through process in this area is established, two factors combine to mitigate the harmful effect of the analyst's impeditive reactions: (a) the patient's by now lessened propensity to respond to the analyst's errors with more than fleeting narcissistic and prenarcissistic withdrawal and retreat; and (b) the analyst's greater capacity to regain his balance after he has acted out through anger, emotional coolness, or misplaced interpretations. The patient's withdrawal, furthermore, of idealizing cathexes does not take place as rapidly as did the establishment of the initial temporary idealization, and the patient's fault-finding is usually intermingled with spontaneous swings back to his former attitude of idealization. The analyst thus becomes aware of these alternations between admiration and contempt and will be capable of viewing with optimal objectivity the attacks which are directed against him, because he can comprehend them within the context of the analysand's needs during the analytic process. He will grasp the dynamic interplay between the patient's attacks on him, the loosening of the idealizing cathexes, and the gradual strengthening of certain internalized narcissistic structures (e.g., of the patient's ideals). The enjoyment of the progress in a difficult therapeutic task and the intellectual pleasure of comprehending how it is being achieved are the emotional rewards which support the analyst when the analytic process proves to be especially stressful to him.

CHAPTER 11

SOME REACTIONS OF THE ANALYST TO THE MIRROR TRANSFERENCES

As was true for the analyst's experiences and his behavior during the remobilization of the idealized parent imago, so also for his emotional responses to the demands of the patient's therapeutically mobilized grandiose self: these reactions are determined not only by the analyst's level of professional experience with the analysis of narcissistic disorders but also, and often decisively, by his own personality and by his current state of mind. In addition, however, we must not disregard the fact that the therapeutic mobilization of the grandiose self occurs in different forms and that the corresponding transferencelike conditions present different clinical pictures which expose the analyst to different emotional tasks.

Thus in the mirror transference in the narrower sense of the term the analyst is the well-delimited target of the patient's demands that he reflect, echo, approve, and admire his exhibitionism and greatness. When the therapeutic remobilization of the patient's grandiose self, however, leads the analysand to perceive the analyst as an alter-ego or twin, and even more so when the analysand's expanded grandiose self begins to experience the representation of the analyst as a part of itself (merger), then the emotional demands on the analyst are of a different nature. In the mirror transference in the narrower sense of the word the patient does acknowledge the presence of the analyst to a limited extent: he is aware of the analyst insofar as the latter fulfills his functions with regard to the patient's narcissistic needs; the patient insists that the analyst's activities become focused entirely on these needs, and he responds with various emotions to the ebb and flow of the analyst's empathy with his demands. In the twinship (alter-ego) and merger varieties of the remobilization of the grandiose self, however, the analyst as an independent individual tends to be blotted out altogether from the patient's associations and he is then deprived of that very minimum of narcissistic gratification that is still offered to him in the mirror transference: the patient's acknowledgment of his separate existence.[1]

Even the patient's demands in the mirror transference in the narrower sense of the term, however, impose a number of emotional hardships on the analyst and may call forth reactions which may interfere with the development and maintenance of the transference and with the process of working through. For prolonged periods while the analysand begins to remobilize old narcissistic needs and, often struggling against strong inner resistances, begins to deploy his exhibitionism and grandiosity in the treatment situation, the patient assigns to the analyst the role of being the echo and mirror of his reluctantly disclosed infantile narcissism. Apart from his tactful acceptance of the patient's exhibitionistic grandiosity, the analyst's contributions to the establishment and unfolding of the mirror transference are restricted to two

[1] See in this context the remarks about the specific applicability of the analogy between the adult's experience of his own body and mind, and of their functions, and the experience of the narcissistic object in the merger variety of the mirror transference (Chapter 5). It might be added here that just as one is in general not specifically aware of one's body and mind, but takes their presence and functioning for granted, so also with the patient's perception of the analyst in the merger transference. It is in general only when a disturbance in one's bodily and mental functioning occurs (or, by analogy, when the analyst in the merger transference goes away or is unempathic) that one becomes angrily aware of the fact that something which should function without question is refusing to do so.

cautiously employed sets of activities: he interprets the patient's resistances against the revelation of his grandiosity;
and he demonstrates to the patient not only that his grandiosity and exhibitionism once played a phase-appropriate
role but that they must now be allowed access to consciousness. For a long period of the analysis, however, it is almost
always deleterious for the analyst to emphasize the irration-
ality of the patient's grandiose fantasies or to stress that it is
realistically necessary that he curb his exhibitionistic demands. The realistic integration of the patient's infantile
grandiosity and exhibitionism will in fact take place quietly
and spontaneously (though very slowly) if the patient is able,
with the aid of the analyst's empathic understanding for
the mirror transference, to maintain the mobilization of the
grandiose self and to expose his ego to its demands (see the
discussion of the working-through process in the mirror transference in Chapter 7).

The analyst's own narcissistic needs, however, may make it
difficult for him to tolerate a situation in which he is reduced
to the seemingly passive role of being the mirror of the patient's infantile narcissism, and he may, therefore, subtly or
openly, through gross parapraxes and symptomatic acts or
through rationalized and theoretically buttressed behavior,
interfere with the establishment or the maintenance of the
mirror transference.

Most of the considerations concerning the analyst's reactions and countertransferences presented earlier with regard
to the idealizing transference apply also with regard to the
mirror transference and many of the results of the earlier
reflections can be easily applied to the present situation. In
particular, we will again remember Freud's dictum that the
analyst aware of the patient's needs and of his own reactions,
must be able to control how much he gives to the patient,
even "occasionally a great deal."[2] On the road toward the

2 This statement was quoted above (p. 266).

integration of the patient's infantile grandiosity and exhibitionism it is not only necessary that the analyst demonstrate for a long time his sympathetic understanding for the patient's demands that he be the reflector of the patient's cautious attempts at remobilizing early forms of self love, but he must indeed serve as an amplifying mirror of these needs through his nonrejectingly expressed interpretations of the —frequently only subtly alluded to—manifestations of the patient's remobilized infantile narcissism. The analyst, however, will be able to perform this task only if he can without resentment tolerate the fact that the patient sees him in essence as occupying a quite humble position and that he demands of him the fulfillment of a rather modest set of functions.

The analyst's problems, and thus his potential interference with the analytic remobilization of the grandiose self, are different when he becomes involved in the twinship (alter-ego) and the merger varieties of the therapeutic remobilization of the grandiose self. Exposed to a mirror transference, the analyst may become incapable of comprehending the patient's narcissistic needs and of responding to them by appropriate interpretations. The most common dangers to which the analyst is exposed vis-à-vis the twinship and merger are boredom, lack of emotional involvement with the patient, and precarious maintenance of attention (including such secondary reactions as overt anger, exhortations, and forced interpretation of resistances, as well as other forms of the rationalized acting out of tensions and impatience).

A comparatively simple set of causal factors is responsible for most instances of the analyst's tendency toward boredom with, and withdrawal of attention from, his patients during the alter-ego (twinship) and merger varieties of the transference. A brief look at the metapsychology of attention will direct us toward the comprehension of the analyst's specific tendency to become inattentive when he is confronted with the merger transference or the twinship.

True alertness and concentration during prolonged periods of observation can be maintained only when the observer's psyche is engaged in depth. Manifestations of object-directed strivings always tend to evoke emotional responses in those toward whom they are directed. Thus, even while the analyst is still at sea about the specific meaning of his patient's communications, the observation of (object-instinctual) transference manifestations is not usually boring to him.

The situation is, of course, different in the case of the analyst's defensive boredom. Although in these instances the analyst understands the transference meaning of the patient's communications only too well, he does not want to understand it. He may, for example, be unconsciously stimulated by libidinal transference appeals and therefore defend himself, by an attitude of disinterest, against the patient's attempt to seduce him. In all these instances we are dealing not with genuine boredom but with the rejection of an emotional involvement (including preconscious attention) which is currently present below the surface layer of the analyst's personality.

In instances of defensive boredom the deeper layers of the analyst's psychic apparatus are thus walled off by the defensive activity of the surface layer. During periods of unopposed even-hovering attention, however, i.e., when the analyst's basic observational attitude is not disturbed, the deeper layers of the analyst's psyche are open to the stimuli which emanate from the patient's communications while the intellectual activities of the higher layers of cognition are temporarily largely—but selectively!—suspended. Unless the analyst's unresolved conflicts concerning his own unconscious libidinal and aggressive responses interfere with his receptiveness to the patient's (object-instinctual) transference messages, the analyst will be able to remain an attentive listener for prolonged periods and will escape neither through an attitude of disinterested emotional withdrawal nor through the premature formulation of (pre)conscious closures.

The verbal and nonverbal behavior of analysands who suffer from narcissistic personality disorders, however, does not engage the analyst's unconscious responsiveness and attention in the same way as the associative material of the transference neuroses, which consists of object-directed instinctual strivings. True, the idealizing transference may deal with the analyst as a transitional object of a somewhat higher order, and thus, as described earlier, the analyst's own narcissism is either stimulated or disappointed and his attention therefore becomes more easily engaged.

The same also holds true in the mirror transference in the narrower sense of the term, though for somewhat different reasons. Despite the fact that the analyst is here of importance to the patient only as a mirror for and echo of his remobilized grandiose self, he is still appealed to, defended against, or withdrawn from in the context of the patient's activated narcissistic demands. A variety of emotional responses to these appeals are thus stimulated in the analyst, and they arouse his attention and maintain it.

When the activation of the grandiose self, however, occurs in the form of its merger with the psychic representations of the analyst (or, to a lesser extent, in an alter-ego transference), then there is no object investment and the patient's attachment to the analyst is of a specific archaic type. Thus, while the analyst's attention is aroused by the cognitive task of comprehending the puzzling manifestations of the archaic narcissistic relationship—and while he may feel oppressed by the patient's unqualified yet silent demands which, from the point of view of the target of the merger transference, are tantamount to total enslavement—the absence of object-instinctual cathexes often makes it difficult for him to remain reliably attentive during prolonged periods.

Although the preceding considerations refer to a human reaction propensity which is probably ubiquitous, it may well be demanded of a trained psychoanalyst that he should be able to master the tendency to withdraw his attention from a patient who does not stimulate him through the extension of object cathexes. In other words, the analyst should be able to mobilize and maintain his empathy and his cognitive involvement with the therapeutically activated narcissistic configurations of his narcissistic analysands. Still, in view of the frequency with which failures of this kind occur, it is unlikely that they are due to specific unconscious conflicts and fixations of the analyst and they should, therefore, not be classified as countertransferences. This contention is supported by the fact, furthermore, that the analyst's difficulties in this respect tend to diminish considerably when he acquires a deeper and more comprehensive understanding of this area of psychopathology, and when he becomes more clearly aware of the nature of the specific psychological tasks which are imposed on him.

There are, however, some instances when explanations (e.g., as given by a teacher, supervisor, or consultant; or as acquired in other ways), and the resulting expansion of the analyst's (pre)conscious comprehension concerning the specific psychological hardships in the treatment of narcissistic personality disorders, do not suffice and when the analyst's tendency toward inattentiveness, boredom, and defensive activity remains resistant to the consultant's or supervisor's comments and even to the analyst's own conscientious and persistent efforts at self-scrutiny. In such instances in which the analyst's unconscious fixations (generally in the realm of his own narcissism) appear to be responsible for his chronic inability to mobilize and maintain his attention, empathy, and comprehension, the term countertransference may indeed be appropriately employed. Here the analyst's need to evade the stress imposed by the chronic involvement in a complex interpersonal relationship which is devoid of significant object-instinctual cathexes appears to be due to the specifically frightening implication of feeling drawn into an anonymous existence in the narcissistic web of another person's psychological organization.

It is difficult to estimate the frequency of these specific fixation points in the personality makeup of analysts, especially in view of the fact that even if they are present they might not interfere with the analyst's professional activities in areas other than the analysis of narcissistic personality disturbance. They may thus escape detection since the analyst will usually avoid the treatment of such cases. I believe, however, that a modicum of vulnerability in this area is rather frequent among analysts since the specific development of empathic sensitivity often contributes to the motivation to become an analyst and remains indeed a professional asset so long as it is kept under the domination of the ego. While it must be admitted that the conscious ego does not play an active role in the psychological performance that leads to empathic perception, it controls it in a variety of ways: it decides whether or not to initiate the empathic mode of perception; it controls the depth of the regression during the state of even-hovering attention; and it replaces the empathic attitude with appropriate secondary process activities in order to assess the empathically perceived psychological data which have to be fitted into a realistic and logical context, and to which an appropriate response has to be chosen, be that silence, interpretation, or broad analytic constructions.

The potential for the acquisition of a special talent for empathic perception, however, as well as the propensity for the enjoyment of exercising this psychological function, is largely acquired early in life. And both the potential talent and the pleasure in exercising the function arise in the very situations which also form the nucleus for the vulnerabilities vis-à-vis the fear of archaic enmeshment which we are discussing here. If, for example, a narcissistic parent—in most, but not in all, cases it is the mother's personality whose influence is predominant in this respect—considers the child as the extension of herself, beyond the period in which such an attitude is appropriate, or more intensively than is optimal, or with a distorted selectivity of her relevant responses, then the child's immature psychic organization will become excessively attuned to the mother's (or father's) psychological organization. The long-term results of the psychological influence of such an early environment may differ widely. It may lead to the development of a sensitive psychological superstructure with unusually great ability for the perception and elaboration of psychological processes in others. Or the early excessive exposure to psychological overcloseness may, on the contrary, lead to a defensive hardening or blunting of the perceptive surfaces in order to protect the psyche from being traumatized by a pathogenic parent's anxiety-provoking responses.

Under optimal circumstances the grownup who is empathically merged with a small child will perceive the child's anxiety and will respond appropriately to the child's tensions. A child's severe anxiety tension, for example, will elicit an immediate empathic signal anxiety in the adult. After an assessment of the reality situation, however, the adult may recognize that no danger is present and he will become anxiety-free. He will then include the child in his own calmness by phase-appropriate actions which emphasize the empathic merger-transmission of the emotional state, by picking the child up, for example, and holding him close and the like.[3] Such interactions encourage the development of a wholesome and balanced empathic capacity in the child. If, however, the mother, instead of serving as a buffer for the child's tension experiences, tends to respond to a child's beginning, mild anxiety diffusely or selectively with the hypochondriacal magnification and elaboration of the painful emotion and threatens to infect the child with her own panic, then the child will attempt to protect himself against the development of a traumatic state through distancing and premature au-

---

[3] Replicas of such beneficial merger situations occur, of course, also between adults. When a person puts his arm around the shoulders of a friend who is upset, he not only dramatizes protection but also allows him, in voluntary regression, to merge temporarily with his own calmness.

tonomy, or, what is most important in this context, through the phase-inappropriate (i.e., premature) replacement of empathic perception by other modes of reality assessment.

Under specific, selectively favorable circumstances, even such early traumatization may not exclude later talent in the psychological field and, although encountered rarely, there are indeed some prominent psychoanalysts whose mastery of and scientific contributions to the field of analysis appear to be the result of a stunted empathic capacity that was replaced by an early capacity for assessing psychological reality through the secondary process. While most analysts collect their data through the empathic perception of large units of complex configurations in others (analogous to the recognition of a face through a single cognitive act), this group of psychologists does not similarly recognize the complex psychological state in one cognitive stroke, but they collect and fit together simple psychological details until they are able, in this way, to arrive at the grasp of a complex psychological configuration in others. In the process they achieve conscious awareness of many details which escape the empathic observer; on the other hand, however, they often waste a great deal of time perceiving what is plainly open to view, they are occasionally victims of grotesque misunderstandings, and they are frequently boring in their communications since they tend to belabor the obvious.

The aforementioned classification of personality types of psychoanalysts on the basis of the scrutiny of their attitudes and developmental responses in the realm of empathic sensitivity is, of course, oversimplified. These pure forms are in reality encountered less frequently than mixed forms, and thus no simple typology of the personality makeup of depth psychologists can be established. Experience does teach us, however, that many of those who choose a career in which the empathic preoccupation with others forms the center of the professional activity are persons who have suffered traumas (of tolerable proportions) in early phases of empathy development and who have secondarily responded to the apprehensiveness concerning the danger of retraumatization with two complementary reactions: (a) they developed a hypersensitivity of the perceptive surfaces; and (b) they responded to the need to master the threatening influx of stimuli with an unusual growth of secondary processes aimed at understanding the psychological data and bringing order to the psychological material.

The investigation of the varieties of specific gifts and specific disturbances in the area of empathy is beyond the scope of the present work. Suffice it to repeat, in regard to specific countertransferences during the analysis of narcissistic personality disturbances, that analysts with a good and even outstanding capacity for the empathic perception of the structural conflicts of the transference neuroses may nevertheless be selectively and specifically incapacitated with regard to the empathic perception of the structural defects, the traumatic states, and the narcissistic fixations which are encountered during the analysis of narcissistic personality disturbances. The archaic fear of being defenselessly flooded by the mother's overwhelming anxiety responses (or by other irrational or exaggerated emotional reactions) may lead certain analysts to an inhibition of their empathy because they fear that they might not be able to resist the merging needs of their analysands and because they have to defend themselves against the image of the intrusion of an archaic mother who will overwhelm the child with her own anxiety. Analysts with such personality makeups will therefore be selectively unable to relate empathically to patients who threaten them with an archaic narcissistic enmeshment. Hiding their specific inability through rationalizing statements expressing general therapeutic pessimism concerning such cases, they will defensively withdraw from the specific task of comprehending the mobilization of the patient's grandiose self in the twinship or, especially, in the merger transference.

I do not know how frequently such deep fears of merger

interfere specifically with the work which the analyst has to carry out in the analytic treatment of narcissistic personalities, but I would estimate that the occurence of permanently and seriously crippling merger apprehensions is not common. But if the analyst's lack of comprehension, boredom, withdrawal, or his defensive therapeutic activism will not yield to his increasing conscious grasp of the nature of his task; if explanations and conscious reflection will not produce any change; and if the cause of the inhibition is connected with old fears of traumatic overstimulation through loss of boundaries and uncontrollable flooding emanating from the mother's excitement—then such reactions should be classified as countertransferences in the broader, clinical meaning of the term.

Schools of psychoanalysis which give a prominent or even exclusive place in neurosogenesis to the earliest developmental stages and to primitive mental organizations tend to see as ubiquitous occurrences the specific phenomena discussed in this monograph. Since the explanatory concepts employed by these schools of thought—e.g., the "interpersonal" school of H. S. Sullivan (1940)—stem from their characteristic single-axis approach, they understand, from their point of view, the various forms and varieties of psychopathology as degrees and nuances of psychosis or as defenses against it.

It is against this background that one must view some of the similarities and differences in the approaches of various schools of psychoanalytic thought to the narcissistic disorders. Leon Grinberg (1956), for example, describes technical difficulties which have certain similarities to those described in the present work. But Grinberg's theoretical framework—the theoretical system which is the prevalent one in South America; it is strongly influenced by the Kleinian outlook—does not appear to provide for the distinction between a narcissistically cathected object and an object invested with object-instinctual cathexes; and projection and introjection are regarded as the dominant psychic mechanisms which the analysand mobilizes vis-à-vis the object.[4] The result is the obliteration of the crucial difference between those forms of psychopathology which are based on the structural conflicts of the differentiated psychic apparatus (the transference neuroses) and those psychic disorders in which the merging with and the detaching from an archaic self-object play the central role (the narcissistic personality disorders). As a consequence of this theoretical stance the transference neuroses are explained on the basis of archaic conflicts between mother and infant, while to the narcissistic disorders are imputed mechanisms—*secondary* projection and introjection—which come into being only after full structuralization of the psychic apparatus has been established and after the differentiation between self and object (including the investment of the latter with object-instinctual cathexes) has been accomplished. It is in harmony with the preceding considerations concerning Grinberg's theoretical approach that he sees the countertransferences which are mobilized on the basis of merger fears as ubiquitous phenomena. In reality, however, these phenomena are not frequent. They appear in consequence of specific vulnerabilities of specific analysts vis-à-vis a specific psychological task. They appear, in other words, when the intensely mobilized, specifically narcissistic, demands of patients with narcissistic personality disorders impinge on the psyche of an analyst whose own tendency toward self-object dedifferentiation has not been fully or reliably transformed into the capacity toward the extension of trial-mergers in the form of a controlled empathy.

Complex as the subject matter of the analyst's reactions during the therapeutic mobilization of the analysand's grandiose self might be, at times it may prove easier to outline the various forms metapsychologically than to comprehend and classify an analyst's relevant failure in a concrete clinical

---

[4] See the discussion of the "English school" of psychoanalysis in Chapter 8.

instance. The following description of a temporary empathic failure of the analyst during the analysis of a specific case involving the mobilization of the analysand's infantile grandiose self may help to illuminate the subject matter from a clinical viewpoint.

Miss F., age twenty-five, had sought analysis because of a number of diffuse dissatisfactions. Despite the fact that she was active in her profession, and had numerous social contacts and a series of love relationships, she felt that she was different from other people and isolated from them. Although she had many friends, she thought that she was not intimate with anyone; and, despite the fact that she had had several love relationships and some serious suitors, she had rejected marriage because she knew that such a step would be a sham. In the course of the analysis it gradually became evident that she suffered from sudden changes in her mood which were associated with a pervasive uncertainty about the reality of her feelings and thoughts. In metapsychological terms, her disturbance was due to a faulty integration of the grandiose self into the total psychic apparatus, with the resulting tendency toward swings between (1) states of anxious excitement and elation over a secret "preciousness" which made her vastly better than anyone else (during times when the ego came close to giving way to the grandiose substructure, i.e., the strongly cathected grandiose self); and (2) states of emotional depletion, blandness, and immobility (which reflected the ego's periodic enfeeblement when it used all its strength to wall itself off from its unrealistic, grandiose substructure). The patient established object relations not primarily because she was attracted to people but rather as an attempt to escape from the painful narcissistic tensions. Yet, while in later childhood as well as in adult life her social relations were, on the surface, comparatively undisturbed, they did little to mitigate the pain caused by the underlying narcissistic disturbance.

Genetically, as we could reconstruct with great certainty,

the fact that the mother had been depressed during several periods early in the child's life had prevented the gradual integration of the narcissistic-exhibitionistic cathexes of the grandiose self. During decisive periods of her childhood, the girl's presence and activities had not called forth maternal pleasure and approval. On the contrary, whenever she tried to speak about herself, the mother deflected, imperceptibly, the focus of attention to her own depressive self-preoccupations, and thus the child was deprived of that optimal maternal acceptance which transforms crude exhibitionism and grandiosity into adaptably useful self-esteem and self-enjoyment. Although the traumatic fixation on the infantile form of the grandiose self was not complete since the mother's depressive state had not been unmitigated, the pathological condition had later become reinforced by Miss F.'s relationship with her only sibling, a brother three years older than she, who (himself lacking in reliable parental approval) treated the sister sadistically, pushed himself into the limelight on all possible occasions, and used his superior intelligence to deflect parental attention from what the sister proudly said or did, thus interfering again with the realistic gratification of her narcissistic needs.

In the following I shall focus on that part of the clinical material which illustrates the analyst's specific problems during the analysis of the therapeutically activated grandiose self. During extended phases of the analysis, beginning at a time when I did not yet understand the genetic background of the patient's personality disturbance and still had only an unclear notion of the essential nature of the patient's psychopathology, the following progression of events frequently occurred during analytic sessions. The patient would arrive in a friendly mood, would settle down quietly, and begin to communicate her thoughts and feelings about a variety of subjects: interactions at work, with her family, or with the man with whom she was currently on friendly terms; dreams and relevant associations, including tentative but genuine references to the transference; and a variety of insights (arrived at against what seemed like appropriate resistances) concerning the connection between present and past, and between transferences upon the analyst and analogous strivings channeled toward others. In brief, in the first part of the analytic sessions during this phase, the process of therapy had the appearance of a well-moving self-analysis.

Three features, however, differentiated this stage of the patient's analysis from phases of genuine self-analysis when the analyst is, indeed, little else than an interested observer who holds himself in readiness for the next wave of resistances. (1) The stage in question lasted much longer than the periods of self-analysis encountered in other analyses. (2) I noted, furthermore, that I was not able to maintain the attitude of interested attention which normally establishes itself effortlessly and spontaneously when one listens to an analysand's work of free associations during periods of relatively unimpeded self-analysis; my attention would often lag, my thoughts began to drift, and a deliberate effort was required to keep my attention focused on the patient's communications. This tendency toward inattention was puzzling since the patient dealt with object-directed preoccupations, inside and outside the analytic situation, and present as well as past. Yet, while she spoke about currently invested objects, including fantasies about me, I recognized gradually that my inattentiveness was due to the fact that the communications themselves did not seem to be directed toward me and that my object-libidinal attention responses were, therefore, not spontaneously mobilized. (3) After a prolonged period of ignorance and misunderstanding during which I was often not only struggling with boredom and inattentiveness but was also inclined to argue with the patient about the correctness of my interpretations and to suspect the presence of stubborn, hidden resistances, I came to the crucial recognition that the patient demanded a specific response to her communications, and that she completely rejected any other.

Unlike the analysand during periods of genuine self-analysis, Miss F. could not tolerate my silence, nor would she be satisfied with noncommittal remarks; but, at approximately the midpoint of the sessions, she would suddenly get violently angry at me for being silent and would reproach me for not giving her any support. (The archaic nature of her need, it may be added, was betrayed by the suddenness with which it appeared—like the sudden transition from satiation to hunger or from hunger to satiation in very young children.) I gradually learned, however, that she would become immediately calm and content when I, at these moments, simply summarized or repeated what she had in essence already said (such as, "You are again struggling to free yourself from becoming embroiled in your mother's suspiciousness against men." Or, "You have worked your way through to the understanding that the fantasies about the visiting Englishman are reflections of fantasies about me"). But if I went beyond what the patient herself had already said or discovered, even by a single step only (such as: "The fantasies about the visiting foreigner are reflections of fantasies about me and, in addition, I think that they are a revival of the dangerous stimulation to which you felt exposed by your father's fantasy stories about you"), she would again get violently angry (regardless of the fact that what I had added might be known to her, too), and would furiously accuse me, in a tense, high-pitched voice, of undermining her; that with my remark I had destroyed everything she had built up; and that I was wrecking the analysis.

Certain convictions can be achieved only firsthand and I am thus not able to demonstrate in detail the correctness of my conclusions about the meaning of the patient's behavior and about the significance of the typical impasse (including specific aspects of the countertransference) which developed during these sessions. During this phase of the analysis the patient attempted, with the aid of my confirming, approving, and echoing presence (mirror transference), to integrate an archaic, narcissistically hypercathected self into the rest of her personality. This process began with a cautious reinstatement of a sense of the reality of her thoughts and feelings, and then moved gradually toward the transformation of her intense exhibitionistic needs into an ego-syntonic sense of her own value and an enjoyment of her activities. As a significant transitional undertaking (which was, however, carried on only temporarily) she began to take dancing lessons. These lessons (and her participation in various public performances) provided an important buffer for that excess of her narcissistic exhibitionistic needs that could not find satisfaction in the analytic situation and that she could not sublimate through any of her customary activities.

As I gradually began to realize, the analysand assigned to me a specific role within the framework of the world view of a very young child. During this phase of the analysis the patient had begun to remobilize an archaic, intensely cathected image of the self which had heretofore been kept in insecure repression. Concomitant with the remobilization of the grandiose self, on which she had remained fixated, there also arose the renewed need for an archaic object (a precursor of psychological structure) that would be nothing more than the embodiment of a psychological function which the patient's psyche could not yet perform for itself: to respond empathically to her narcissistic display and to provide her with narcissistic sustenance through approval, mirroring, and echoing.

Due to the fact that I was at that time not sufficiently alert to the pitfalls of such transference demands, many of my interventions interfered with the work of structure formation. But I know that the obstacles that stood in the way of my understanding lay not only in the cognitive area; and I can affirm, without transgressing the rules of decorum and without indulging in the kind of immodest self-revelation which ultimately hides more than it admits, that there were specific hindrances in my own personality which stood in the way.

There was a residual insistence, related to deep and old fixation points, on seeing myself in the narcissistic center of the stage; and, although I had of course for a long time struggled with the relevant childhood delusions and thought that I had, on the whole, achieved dominance over them, I was temporarily unable to cope with the cognitive task posed by the confrontation with the reactivated grandiose self of my patient. Thus I refused to entertain the possibility that I was not an object for the patient, not an amalgam with the patient's childhood loves and hatreds, but only, as I reluctantly came to see, an impersonal function, without significance except insofar as it related to the kingdom of her own remobilized narcissistic grandeur and exhibitionism.

For a long time I insisted, therefore, that the patient's reproaches related to specific transference fantasies and wishes on the oedipal level—but I could make no headway in this direction. It was ultimately, I believe, the high-pitched tone of her voice which led me on the right track. I realized that it expressed an utter conviction of being right—the conviction of a very young child—which had heretofore never found expression. Whenever I did more (or less) than provide simple approval or confirmation in response to the patient's reports of her own discoveries, I became for her the depressive mother who (sadistically, as the patient experienced it) deflected the narcissistic cathexes from the child upon herself, or who did not provide the needed narcissistic echo. Or, I became the brother who, as she felt, twisted her thoughts and put himself into the limelight.

The answer to the question whether the mother (or the brother, who in this context was seen by the patient as in a team with the mother, i.e., as an extension of or a substitute for her) had actually been consciously, preconsciously, or unconsciously sadistic, as the patient insisted for long periods of her analysis, is of small importance at this point. The archaic object is experienced as all-powerful and all-knowing, and thus the consequences of its actions and omissions are always viewed by the child's psyche as having been brought about intentionally. The patient therefore assumed—correctly within the framework of her mental organization—that the initial lack of my understanding of her was not due to my intellectual and emotional limitations but that it was the result of sadistic intentions. I do not believe that this misperception should simply be ascribed to a transference confusion. It must rather be understood as being due to the therapeutic regression to the level of the essential pathogenic fixation, i.e., to a narcissistic conception of the object and thus to an animistic confusion between effect and cause on the one hand, and between deed and intention on the other.

Whatever the mother's (and brother's) own conscious or unconscious motivation may have been, however, from the point of view of the metapsychological assessment of the patient's psychological development, their behavior had contributed to driving an archaic, highly cathected grandiose self into repression where it was not accessible to modification by reality and could not become available to the ego as a source of acceptable narcissistic motivations. Her father, to whom, it may be added here, the patient had turned more in search of a substitute for the narcissistic approval which she had not obtained from her mother than as an oedipal love object, had further traumatized the child by vacillating between attitudes of fantastic love for the girl and emotional disinterest and withdrawal over long stretches. His behavior stimulated the child's old narcissistic preoccupations without helping her to integrate them with a realistic conception of the self by an *optimal selectivity of his responses in a setting of reliably maintained interest.* He thus interfered with the establishment of a solid repression barrier and, through his inconsistent and seductive behavior, he reinforced the trend toward the resexualization of her needs, somewhat similar to the circumstances that brought about the resexualization of the need for narcissistic homeostasis in the case of Mr. A.

The clinical situation described in the preceding pages

and, especially, the analyst's therapeutic responses to it require further elucidation, even though the following discussion of the analytic process does not directly belong to the present specific subject matter, the countertransference in the mirror transference.

At first hearing I might seem to be stating that, in instances of this type, the analyst must indulge a transference wish of the analysand; specifically, that the patient had not received the necessary emotional echo or approval from the depressive mother, and that the analyst must now give it to her in order to provide a "corrective emotional experience" (Alexander, French, et al., 1946).

There are indeed patients for whom this type of indulgence is not only a temporary tactical requirement during certain stressful phases of analysis but who cannot ever undertake the steps which lead to that increased ego dominance over the childhood wish which is the specific aim of psychoanalytic work. And there is, furthermore, no doubt that, occasionally, the indulgence of an important childhood wish—especially if it is provided with an air of conviction and in a therapeutic atmosphere that carries a quasi-religious, magical connotation of the efficacy of love—can have lasting beneficial effects with regard to the relief of symptoms and behavioral change in the patient. Having received the bishop's handshake like Jean Valjean of Hugo's *Les Miserables*, the patient walks away from the therapeutic session as a changed person. (For a striking incident of a sudden cure following a wholesome experience outside of planned psychotherapy see the vignette adduced by K. R. Eissler [1965, p. 357ff.] from Justin [1960].)

The analytic process in analyzable cases, however, as in the case of Miss F., develops in a different way. After overcoming certain cognitive and emotional obstacles I recognized that the essential transference manifestation lay not in the content of the material (which related to later developmental phases and referred to the patient's defensively used, emotionally shallow interpersonal relations) but in the interactions which were taking place during the analytic session itself. Specifically, I recognized that the patient had reinstated me as the depressive, hypochondriacal mother of her early childhood who had deprived her of the narcissistic nutriment which she had been in need of. Although, for tactical reasons (e.g., in order to insure the cooperation of a segment of the patient's ego), the analyst might in such instances transitorily have to provide what one might call a *reluctant compliance with the childhood wish,* the true analytic aim is not indulgence but mastery based on insight, achieved in a setting of (tolerable) analytic abstinence.

As is the case in the transference neuroses with regard to object-instinctual drives, so also with regard to the narcissistically invested object in the analysis of narcissistic personality disturbances: the analyst does not interfere (either by premature interpretations or by other means) with the spontaneous mobilization of the transference wishes. In general, he begins his interpretative work concerning the transference only at the point when, because of the nonfulfillment of the transference wishes, the patient's cooperation ceases, i.e., when the transference has become a resistance.[5] And again, as in the case of the transference neuroses, so also—and even more—with the narcissistic personality disturbances: once the interpretative work has begun, the analyst will not expect that ego mastery over intense childhood desires can be achieved at the very moment when the patient is making the first steps toward allowing them access into consciousness. On the contrary, the analyst knows that a prolonged period of working through lies ahead in which the patient will, initially at least, put up resistances not so much by insisting on

[5] Interpretative references to the transference, especially early in the course of the analysis, which are not aimed at remobilizing the lost momentum of an analytic process that has become obstructed by transference resistances, will be correctly understood by the patient as prohibitions. No matter how friendly and kindly the analyst expresses himself, the analysand will hear him say: "Don't be that way—it's unrealistic, childish!" or the like.

the fulfillment of the infantile wishes but rather by renewed attempts at retreating from them, usually by expressing noisy claims concerning the satisfaction of demands in a split-off sector of the psyche while the central needs and wishes are again going into hiding. Neither the analyst's noninterference with the establishment of the transference wish, however, nor his sober-minded acceptance of the gradualness and complexity of the working-through process must be confused with that abrogation of analytic work implied in the notion of a "corrective emotional experience" or with that replacement of it by educational measures (and by other activities from the side of the analyst) which might be advocated as justified in the service of a need for the establishment and maintenance of the therapeutic alliance.

In the case of Miss F., my recognition that a specific childhood demand was being re-enacted constituted only the beginning of the working-through process concerning the grandiose self. After I had gained mastery over my own countertransference resistance which for a while made me insist that the patient was struggling with object-instinctual transferences, I was finally able to tell her that her anger at me was based on narcissistic processes, specifically on a transference confusion with the depressed mother who had deflected the child's narcissistic needs onto herself. These interpretations were followed by the recall of clusters of analogous memories concerning her mother's entering a phase of depressive self-preoccupation during later periods of the patient's life. Finally, the patient vividly recalled a central set of poignant memories, upon which a series of earlier and later ones seemed to be telescoped. They referred specifically to episodes when she came home from kindergarten and early elementary school. At such times she would rush home as fast as she could, joyfully anticipating telling her mother about her successes in school. She recalled then how her mother opened the door, but, instead of the mother's face lighting up, her expression remained blank; and how, when the patient began to talk about school and play and about her achievements and successes during the preceding hours, the mother appeared to listen and participate, but imperceptibly the topic of the conversation shifted and the mother began to talk about herself, her headache and her tiredness and her other physical self-preoccupations. All that the patient could directly recall about her own reactions was that she felt suddenly drained of energy and empty; she was for a long time unable to remember feeling any rage at her mother on such occasions. It was only after a prolonged period of working through that she could gradually establish connections between the rage which she experienced against me when I did not understand her demands and the feelings she had experienced in reaction to the narcissistic frustration which she had suffered as a child.

My interpretations thus led the patient to a gradually increasing awareness of the intensity of her demands and of her need for their fulfillment, a recognition which she resisted vigorously because she now could no longer deny the presence of an extreme neediness in this area which had been covered for a long time by a display of independence and self-sufficiency. This phase—to outline the sequence in rough approximation—was then followed by a slow, shame-provoking, and anxious revelation of her persistent infantile grandiosity and exhibitionism. The working through which was accomplished during this period led ultimately to increased ego dominance over the old grandiosity and exhibitionism, and thus to greater self-confidence and to other favorable transformations of her narcissism in this segment of her personality.

Leaving the specific clinical illustration, however, I will now summarize the analyst's cognitive and emotional tasks during analyses in which the vicissitudes of early stages of the patient's grandiose self are therapeutically remobilized in the various forms of the mirror transference. In order to function properly during the analysis of such personality disorders the

analyst must be capable of remaining interested in and attentive to the remobilized psychological structures despite the
absence of significant object-instinctual cathexes. Furthermore, he must be capable of accepting the fact that his position (which is in harmony with the specific level of the major
fixation) within the patient's therapeutically reactivated narcissistic world view is that of an archaic prestructural object,
i.e., specifically, that of a function in the service of the maintenance of the patient's narcissistic equilibrium. Not only
must the analyst be capable of a passive tolerance of these
aforementioned psychological facts (i.e., he must neither become impatient; nor must he interfere with the establishment of the narcissistic transference through premature
interpretations; nor must he withdraw his attention and
empathy), but he must remain positively involved with the
patient's narcissistic world in creative perceptivity since many
of the patient's experiences, because of their preverbal nature, must be empathically grasped by the analyst and their
meaning must be reconstructed, at least in approximation,
before the patient is able to recall analogous later memories
(through "telescoping") and can connect the current experiences with those of the past.

In performing the tasks which are imposed on him during
the analysis of the remobilized grandiose self, the analyst is
greatly aided by the theoretical grasp of the conditions with
which he is dealing. He must, furthermore, be aware of the
potential interference of his own narcissistic demands which
rebel against a chronic situation in which he is neither experienced as himself by the patient nor even confused with
an object of the patient's past. And, finally, in specific instances, the analyst must be free of the active interference
by archaic fears of dissolution through merger. He must not
wall himself off against the merger needs of certain patients
but must tolerate their activation without undue anxiety and
must himself remain capable of trial-mergers and signal

penetrability in the form of the controlled empathic grasp of the patient's narcissistic demands and of the requisite responses to them, i.e., the interpretations and reconstructions which lead to the gradual integration of the patient's narcissistic structures into the mature, reality-oriented personality. It bears repeating, however, as we are here once more surveying the analytic process in the treatment of these disturbances, that the analysand tends initially and for an extended period to have insufficient tolerance for his own narcissistic demands, and that he must first learn to accept and to understand them before his ego will gradually attempt to achieve further dominance over them.

CHAPTER 12

SOME THERAPEUTIC TRANSFORMATIONS IN THE ANALYSIS OF NARCISSISTIC PERSONALITIES

The mobilization of the archaic narcissistic positions during analysis permits the working through of the narcissistic transferences and results in both nonspecific and specific beneficial changes. The most prominent nonspecific change is the increase and the expansion of the patient's capacity for object love; the specific changes take place in the realm of narcissism itself.

INCREASE AND EXPANSION OF OBJECT LOVE

1. The increase in the capacity for object love which is encountered regularly in the analysis of narcissistic personalities must be considered an important but nonspecific and secondary result of the treatment. In general the newly emerging object love becomes available to the patient in consequence of the remobilization of object-libidinal incestuous affective ties which had formerly been hidden behind a wall of regressive narcissism and had therefore been unavailable to the patient. Hence, the increasing availability of object-instinctual cathexes as the analysis proceeds usually

does not indicate that a change of the mobilized narcissism into object love has taken place; it is rather due to a freeing of formerly repressed object libido; i.e., it is the result of therapeutic success in sectors of secondary psychopathology (transference neurosis) in a patient who is primarily suffering from a narcissistic personality disorder.

2. Certain aspects of the narcissistic patient's expanded capacity for object love, however, are more directly related to the working-through process in the primary area of the psychopathology. They are characterized not by a simple increase of the patient's object cathexes but by a greater refinement and emotional deepening of the already present (or newly mobilized) object strivings in consequence of the greater availability of idealizing libido. Due to a systematic working through of an idealizing transference, a surplus of idealizing libido may become available to the patient which can be amalgamated to object-libidinal cathexes. The attachment of idealizing cathexes to object love results in a deepening and a refinement of the patient's love experience, whether in the state of being in love, in his long-term fondness of another human being, or in his devotion to cherished tasks and purposes. Under these circumstances, the narcissistic component of the total love experience is in essence a subsidiary one. The narcissistic cathexes make a contribution to the intensity and to the flavor of the patient's love experience; the central instinctual investments, however, are object-libidinal.

3. An important nonspecific result of the systematic analysis of the narcissistic positions is, finally, the increased capacity for object love that is due to the firming of the self experience and to the correlated stronger cohesion and sharper delimitation of the self. Just as the ego's ability to perform a variety of tasks (e.g., professional pursuits) increases hand in hand with the increase of the cohesiveness of the self, so also for the ego's functioning as the executory focus of object love. To state an obvious fact in behavioral, phe-

nomenological, and dynamic terms: the more secure a person is regarding his own acceptability, the more certain his sense of who he is, and the more safely internalized his system of values—the more self-confidently and effectively will he be able to offer his love (i.e., to extend his object-libidinal cathexes) without undue fear of rejection and humiliation.

PROGRESSIVE AND INTEGRATIVE DEVELOPMENTS WITHIN
THE NARCISSISTIC REALM

The primary and essential results of the psychoanalytic treatment of narcissistic personalities lie within the narcissistic realm, and the changes achieved constitute, in the majority of cases, the most significant and the therapeutically decisive results. Since the major part of this monograph dealt with these progressive and integrative therapeutic developments in the narcissistic realm, I can restrict myself for the most part to giving a brief summary, expanding only on a number of newly acquired complex psychological attributes which could not be sufficiently discussed before.

1. In the area of the *idealized parent imago* the following therapeutic results are achieved through the functional integration of this narcissistic configuration with the ego and superego.

a. As the *early preoedipal* (still archaic) aspects of the idealized parent imago are gradually relinquished, they are internalized in a neutralized form and become part of the basic, drive-controlling and drive-channeling structure of the ego. Stated differently, the patient's psyche gradually (and silently) takes over the neutralizing, drive-controlling, and drive-channeling functions which the patient at first is able to perform only so long as he feels merged with and attached to the idealized analyst.

b. As the *late preoedipal* and *oedipal* (now more highly differentiated) aspects of the idealized parent imago are relinquished, they are internalized and deposited within the superego, leading to the idealization of this psychic structure, and thus to the strengthening of the values and standards of which it is the carrier. In other words, the superego of the patient functions increasingly as a source of meaningful internal leadership, guidance, and exhilarating approval, providing benefits in the realm of ego integration and narcissistic homeostasis which had formerly been available to him only so long as he felt himself connected with the idealized analyst and felt responded to by him.

2. In the area of the *grandiose self* the following therapeutic results are achieved through the gradual functional integration of the two major aspects of this narcissistic configuration with the ego:

a. The infantile grandiosity becomes gradually built into the ambitions and purposes of the personality and lends not only vigor to a person's mature strivings but also a sustaining positive feeling of the right to success. Under optimal circumstances, this "feeling of a conqueror" (Freud, 1917c, p. 26; as translated by Jones, 1953, p. 5) is therefore a fully tamed, yet active derivative of the former solipsistic absolutarianism of the infantile psyche.

b. The archaic exhibitionistic libido, again in a gradually controlled (i.e., neutralized) form, is step by step withdrawn from the infantile aims of direct satisfaction through crude display, and infuses instead the reality-adapted and socially meaningful activities of the adult personality. The formerly shame-provoking exhibitionism thus becomes a major source of the patient's self-esteem and ego-syntonic pleasure in his actions and his successes.

3. Although the working through of the narcissistic transference must be regarded as an achievement of the total personality, it is still contingent on the therapeutic mobilization of the archaic narcissistic positions. It leads to the acquisition of a number of highly valued sociocultural attributes (such as empathy, creativity, humor, and wisdom) which have indeed become so far removed from their origins that they

appear to be fully autonomous qualities of the most mature layers of the psyche. In the remainder of this study I shall comment on these four attributes because the understanding of their role and functioning, of their stunting or disturbance, and of their emergence in the therapeutic process, is of crucial importance for the assessment of the therapeutic goals in the analysis of narcissistic personality disorders.

Empathy

Empathy is a mode of cognition which is specifically attuned to the perception of complex psychological configurations. Under optimal circumstances, the ego will employ empathic observation when it is confronted with the gathering of psychological data and will use nonempathic modes of perception when the data which it gathers do not concern the area of the inner life of man.[1] There are a great number of pathological disturbances in the use of empathy; the resulting misperceptions of reality, however, can be classified by distinguishing two groups.

1. To the first group belongs the inappropriate employment of empathy in the observation of areas *outside* the field of complex psychological states. This use of empathy in the observation of the *nonpsychological* field leads to a faulty, prerational, animistic perception of reality and is, in general, the manifestation of a perceptual and cognitive infantilism.

In scientific psychology, too, empathy is restricted to being a tool for the gathering of psychological data; it does not by itself bring about their explanation. In other words: it is a mode of observation. The gathering of data must be followed by their ordering, by a scrutiny of the (for example, causal) interconnections of the observed phenomena in terms that are removed from the observations themselves (Hartmann, 1927). Therefore, if empathy, instead of limiting its role to that of a data-collecting process, begins to replace the ex-

[1] For a discussion of the borders between the psychological and the non-psychological field, see Freud (1915c).

planatory phases of scientific psychology (which is then only *verstehend* [see Dilthey, 1924; Jaspers, 1920] without also being *erklärend*), then we are witnessing a deterioration of scientific standards and a sentimentalizing regression to subjectivity, i.e., a cognitive infantilism in the realm of man's scientific activities.

2. The second group of relevant perceptual defects rests on the failure to use empathy in the observation of the *psychological* field, in particular in the area of complex psychological configurations. The replacement of empathy in this area by other modes of observation leads to a mechanistic and lifeless conception of psychological reality.

The most serious defects in the use of empathy that belong to this group are of a *primary* type; i.e., they are due to narcissistic fixations and regressions, specifically in the realm of archaic stages of the development of the self. They can be ascribed to early disturbances in the mother-child relationship (due to emotional coldness of the mother, the absence of consistent contact with the mother, the baby's congenital emotional coldness, the mother's withdrawal from an unresponsive baby, etc.). These disturbances appear to lead simultaneously to a failure in the establishment of an idealized parent imago (with a concomitant stunting of the important first stages of the baby's empathic interplay with the mother) and to a hypercathexis of, and fixation on, the primitive stages of the (autoerotic) body self and on the archaic (pre) stages of the grandiose self. The further development of the latter is also stunted by the child's lack of the needed admiring responses from his mother.

The frequently encountered lesser disturbances of empathy—such as the failure of certain students at analytic training institutions to achieve the requisite empathic attitude vis-à-vis their analysands—appear to be of a *secondary* type; they are reaction formations against faulty empathy, usually inhibitions due to a defense against the tendency toward an animistic perception of the world. These interferences with the use of empathy must, in most instances, be understood as part of a general personality disturbance of the obsessive-compulsive type in which the inhibition is due to stable reaction formations which keep magical beliefs and animistic tendencies either repressed or (as is more frequently the case) isolated or split off.

Occasionally empathy is considered to be the equivalent of intuition, leading to the setting up of a spurious contrast between (a) sentimental and subjective (i.e., nonscientific) intuitive-empathic reactions to the feelings of others; and (b) the sober and objective (i.e., scientific) assessment of psychological data.

Intuition, however, is not in principle related to empathy. Reactions, judgments, recognitions, or perceptions, etc., which strike the observer as having been arrived at intuitively, are in all likelihood not different in essence from nonintuitive reactions, judgments, etc., except for the speed with which the mental operation was performed. Great medical-diagnostic skill in a gifted and experienced clinician, for example, may impress the observer as intuitive. In reality, however, the result is simply due to the fact that the trained mind of the gifted physician has, at great speed (and largely preconsciously), collected and sifted a large number of details and has, like a specialized computer, evaluated the various combinations. What we call intuition is, therefore, in principle, resolvable into speedily performed mental activities which, in and of themselves, are not different from those mental activities which do not strike us as unusual in this particular sense. It must, however, be added here that a belief in magic, both in the performer of intuitive mental acts (arising from his wish to maintain the unaltered omniscience of an archaic grandiose self) and in a beholder (arising from his need for an awe-inspiring idealized parent imago) may, of course, contribute to resistances which oppose the realistic dissolution of intuitive acts into their components.

Talent, training, and experience will at times combine to produce results, in a variety of areas, which strike us as intuitive; thus we might find intuition at work not only in the empathic observation of the field of complex psychological states (such as is employed by psychoanalysts) but also, for example, as stated before, in medical diagnosis, or in the strategic decisions of a champion chess player, or in the planning of a physicist's experiments. On the other hand, slow and painstaking nonintuitive mental processes are not restricted to the nonempathic scrutiny of the physical world, but they may also be used in empathic observation. As a matter of fact, it may be said that it is one of the specific contributions of psychoanalysis to have transformed the intuitive empathy of artists and poets into the observational tool of a trained scientific investigator, notwithstanding the fact that some judgments of experienced psychoanalytic clinicians may strike the observer as equally intuitive as the analogous diagnostic performance of, let us say, an internist.

The scientific psychologist, in general, and the psychoanalyst in particular, not only must have free access to empathic understanding; they must also be able to relinquish the empathic attitude. If they cannot be empathic, they cannot observe and collect the data which they need; if they cannot step beyond empathy, they cannot set up hypotheses and theories, and thus, ultimately, cannot achieve explanations.

Shifting for a moment to a broader context, I may add here that the contrast between data-collecting empathy and the mental processes employed in the search for explanations is related (but does not entirely correspond) to the commonly evoked antithesis between practice and theory. Even clinical work would lead only to ephemeral results if it did not include increasing comprehension (i.e., insight) which goes beyond empathy. And theoretical work which lacks continuous contact with the material that can be observed only with the aid of empathy would soon become sterile and empty, tend toward preoccupation with the niceties of psychological mechanisms and structures, and lose touch with the breadth and depth of human experience on which ultimately all of psychoanalysis must be based.

In view of these facts it is, therefore, a specific task of the training analysis to loosen the student-analysand's narcissistic positions in those sectors of his personality which are related to his empathic capacities. A successful outcome of the working-through process in this area is indicated when we see the evidence that ego dominance has been established, i.e., that the student has attained the free (autonomous) ability to use, or to relinquish, the empathic attitude, depending on the exigencies of the professional task at hand.

A number of specific disturbances of the empathic capacity of analysts and some genetic factors which are responsible for (a) the vigorous development of empathy (and thus, indirectly, for the choice of a career which requires the use of empathy), as well as for (b) its stunting or devious development, have already been discussed (Chapter 11) and will not be taken up again at this point. Concerning the increasing scope and the refinement and deepening of the empathic capacity, however, which are the outgrowths of the therapeutic mobilization of the analysand's frozen archaic narcissism, some remarks will now be made. In general, the successful analysis of a narcissistic personality (whether it is a training analysis or a purely therapeutic one) will increase the analysand's empathic ability, while it often, simultaneously, tends to decrease his former intuitiveness. Whether the decrease in intuitiveness is genuine or only subjective is hard to evaluate since the psychological change which underlies the lessening of the propensity to arrive at intuitive conclusions and decisions is the replacement of magical thinking, and of the wish for omniscience, by (inductive) logic, empiricism, and the acceptance of realistic limitations of knowledge and skill, whether in psychological or nonpsychological pursuits. The abandonment of intuitive mental activities is in many instances simply due to a lessened need for them and to the newly acquired capacity not to have to jump to conclusions but to tolerate the delays which are imposed by careful observation and by the thoughtful assessment of data.

There are, however, exceptions. Especially in persons who have formed strong reaction formations against magical thinking and a belief in their own omniscience—psychological tendencies which are associated with fixations on the two major archaic narcissistic configurations—the increase in rationality which the analysis of the mobilized narcissism provides, may result in a greater freedom not only to make observations and to assess their meaning and significance, but also, if the circumstances permit such cognitive processes, to make these observations and assessments preconsciously and speedily instead of, as was the case previously, ploddingly, laboriously, and without imagination.

Whatever the trend in intuitiveness, however, the expansion of empathy in successful analyses is always genuine. The mobilization of the archaic narcissistic structures and their working through in the realms of both the idealized object and the grandiose self lead to an increased empathic capacity —in the case of the idealized object, more in the area of empathy for others; in that of the grandiose self, predominantly in the area of empathy for oneself (empathy for the analysand's own past experiences, for example; or for his various present experiences; or the anticipatory empathy with what he might be like, or feel like, or how he might react in the future). Although patients always experience their expanding and deepening empathy as very enjoyable and often express deep gratitude for this result of the analysis, there are a number of resistances which may block analytic progress in this specific direction or reverse it temporarily after it had been achieved.

Since the genetic factors responsible for disturbances of empathy vary greatly (see Chapter 11), the correlated resistances to its acquisition in analysis are also of different kinds.

If, as is most frequently the case, the empathic disturbance is primarily related to the parents' lack of empathy (or to their faulty or unreliable empathy), the child has surrounded himself with distancing devices which protect him against the traumatic disappointment of not being understood and of not being correctly responded to. (Compare the present considerations with the discussion of the defenses of the schizoid personality in Chapter 1.) When in the course of the analysis of the remobilized narcissistic configurations the door toward empathic responses is opened again, the dangers to which the psyche feels exposed in this realm are of the following two kinds. (1) Despite the conscious wish to be in empathic contact with others and the immediate pleasure that the empathic grasp of another person's mental state arouses in the analysand, the pleasure is often followed by a sense of being painfully excited and stimulated, with anxiety about the danger of regressive merger experiences which occasionally appear in the form of temporary illusions of a corporeal identity with the other person, leading to the attempt to bind or to discharge the tensions through their gross sexualization (see the general discussion of traumatic states in Chapter 8). (2) Resistances that fit into a more advanced level of psychic functioning than those that are motivated by the aforementioned psychoeconomic imbalance relate to fears of passivity, often experienced by men as the danger of feminine submission. Fears of such dangers are most likely to occur in response to the newly achieved empathic understanding that the analyst, too, is a human being who is able to respond with emotions and empathy to the analysand.

The protection which the narcissistic isolation affords the personality, and the danger of giving up this security which is heightened when the analysis offers the possibility of empathic contact with another person and of participation in the world, were movingly portrayed by patient Q. in a dream. This man had lost his mother in very early childhood and had lost a number of other mother figures subsequent to the first loss. He dreamed that he was alone in his house, his fishing equipment by his side, looking out the window. Through the window he saw numbers of fishes swimming by, big and little, and attractive, and he was yearning to go fishing. He realized, however, that his house was at the bottom of the lake and that as soon as he opened the window to fish the whole lake would flood the house and drown him.

Milder forms of these resistances often take on the form of rejecting the analyst's supposedly patronizing understanding. And empathy, especially when it is surrounded by an attitude of wanting to cure *directly* through the giving of loving understanding, may indeed become basically overbearing and annoying; i.e., it may rest on the therapist's unresolved omnipotence fantasies. Provided, however, that the analyst has largely come to terms with his wish to cure directly through the magic of his loving understanding and is indeed not patronizing toward the patient (i.e., he recognizes empathy as a tool of observation and of appropriate communication), the mere fact that the patient dropped his defenses against the possibility of being empathically understood and responded to exposes him to the archaic fear of earliest disappointments. He may temporarily become suspicious, get the feeling that the analyst is manipulating his mind, that the analyst leads him on in order to disappoint him sadistically, etc. These temporary paranoid attitudes occur not infrequently, but, alarming though they might seem, they are usually ephemeral and can be resolved by the correct dynamic and genetic interpretation. Whatever the vicissitudes of the resistances, however, a gradual increase in the capacity to be empathic with others and a gradually increasing acceptance of the expectation that others will also be able to grasp the patient's feelings, wishes, and needs can indeed be observed with great regularity in the properly conducted analysis of narcissistic personalities.

Creativeness

Creativeness, too, ranging from a new-found ability to perform a restricted range of tasks with zestful initiative to the emergence of brilliantly inventive artistic schemes or of penetrating scientific undertakings, may appear, seemingly spontaneously, in the course of many analyses of narcissistic personalities. Its appearance is again specifically related to the mobilization of formerly frozen narcissistic cathexes, in the area of both the grandiose self and the idealized parent imago.

I shall first address myself to the rather subtle problem whether not only artistic but also scientific pursuits should be considered creative activities, independent of the question whether such activities are undertaken spontaneously or in consequence of the psychoeconomic, dynamic, and structural shifts that are brought about in the course of analysis. It is necessary to examine this theoretical question because scientific and artistic activities arise and subside in the course of the analysis of narcissistic personality disturbances in the same essential context; i.e., they constitute transformations of the analysand's formerly archaic narcissism.

Viewed objectively, a strict differentiation between science and art is warranted *prima facie*. The distinction rests on the claim that the aim of science is the discovery of *pre-existing* formations, while art introduces *new* configurations into the world (Eissler, 1961, p. 245f.). Even in the objective sense, however (i.e., disregarding the psychological processes involved in scientific discovery and artistic production), this basic differentiation is not as clear-cut as it seems on first sight. Great scientific discoveries do not simply describe pre-existing phenomena, but they give the world a novel mode either of seeing their significance or of seeing their relationship to each other; and a great scientist who makes a pioneering discovery may channel scientific development into a specific direction, just as an artistic genius who creates a new style may thus determine the direction in which his field of art will develop. It may be an overestimation of the actual state of our scientific world view to believe that science could only have gone in the direction in which its development happened to have led.[2] On the other hand, we also must not forget that some of the greatest works of art are not new creations but the reflection of something pre-existing, rendered immortal through the artist's (creatively selective) application of pigment on his canvas or as language on the printed page. Still, if we evaluate and compare scientific and artistic works within an objective nonpsychological framework, we will remain inclined to reserve the attribute of creativeness for the latter and will feel that we have spoken metaphorically when we also apply it to the former.

If we turn from the objective assessment to a comparison between the personality of the scientist and that of the artist and to an examination of the scientist's and artist's psychological relationship to their work (especially, within the framework of the specific concern of this study: the deployment of the narcissistic cathexes), then some new light is thrown on this problem area and further differentiations can be made.

Broadly speaking, the narcissistic cathexes of the artist tend to be less neutralized than those of the creative man of science, and his exhibitionistic libido in particular appears to shift frequently with greater fluidity between himself and his narcissistically invested product than is the case with the scientist. Stated in the obverse, and again in full awareness of the many exceptions to the overall trend, one might say that, on the one hand, too strict a rein on an artist's exhibitionism will tend to interfere with his productivity, while, on the other hand, the intrusions of the unmodified grandiose and

2 For a sophisticated discussion of the quasi-artistic processes employed in some of the great discoveries in physics see the writings of Alexandre Koyré, especially his *Metaphysics and Measurement: Essays in Scientific Revolution in 17th Century Science* (1968).

exhibitionistic claims of an archaic grandiose self will be an obstacle to valid scientific production.

A comparison between the delightful arrogance and exhibitionism of the young Freud of the Fluss letters[3] and Freud's increasingly severe control over any wish toward exhibitionistic indulgence (his watchful awareness of the hypocritical and magical admixture contained in congratulatory messages; his nonparticipation in events organized to celebrate him publicly) is a good illustration of a typical life curve in a scientist's personality development. The great scientist, in other words, as exemplified by Freud, becomes increasingly less tolerant of the direct stimulation of his person-bound exhibitionism and restricts himself to the deployment of aim-inhibited and neutralized narcissistic cathexes upon his work.

In general it can therefore be said that the scientist's work usually involves more highly neutralized narcissistic cathexes and a greater admixture of object cathexes than are employed in the production of a work of art. This difference becomes most plain when we take notice of the fact that an artistic product, once it has been finished by the artist (be he a composer, sculptor, painter; or a poet or novelist) has become sacrosanct and, in principle, cannot be changed by another, whatever its imperfections and whatever the potential improvement might be. The work of the artist is unconsciously recognized as unalterably bound up with the personality of its creator and it must not be tampered with through the intrusions of another. The difference with regard to scientific creations is evident. When a scientist has formulated a new theory and another scientist detects a flaw in it and alters the previous formulation, he does no violence to the previous work. As a matter of fact, he gratefully acknowledges that the new discovery or improvement would not have been possible without the previous work, partly faulty or incomplete

[3] Written during 1872-1874 (see Freud, 1969). See also the perceptive review of this correspondence by Gedo and Wolf (1970).

though it was. The work of the scientist, in other words, is farther set apart from the personality of the scientific worker, is regarded as more of an independent object, than the work of the artist.

Although some minor modifications to the preceding general statements might still be required, I believe that they are true if taken as giving expression to an overall trend. I disregard the exceptional instance in which the discovery of a scientist sees the light of the world in a form that resembles a work of art and is then reacted to as if it were an artistic production. It must be admitted, however, that in the realm of art there are indeed instances of great works executed by anonymous masters (or by groups or successions of artists) that appear to run counter to the tenet that the work of art is intimately and inextricably interwoven with its creator. Relevant examples are the anonymous sculptures and cathedrals of the Middle Ages, in particular those of the early Gothic period. With regard to the sculptures it is easily recognized that, while the creator is unknown, we still react to his creation as an unalterable expression of his artistic act: one would not consider, for example, replacing an imperfectly shaped ear or nose of a medieval madonna (made by an unknown master) with one of a more pleasing form. With regard to the succession of the builders of the great Gothic cathedrals, however, the situation is more complex. Are these indeed artistic creations in which the narcissistic cathexes of the creator are felt to be as neutralized, and the end product as independent from the creator, as is the case in scientific work? Or does the vastness of the task which *ab initio* relies on the devoted exertions of successive generations of builders create here exceptional conditions which preclude the meaningful comparison with the other artistic endeavors of man?

But these questions cannot be pursued here. Suffice it to have recognized that, by comparison with the scientist, the artist invests his work, in general, with less neutralized narcissistic libido and remains more closely identified with his product. It is, however, not advisable to overemphasize these differences. They are not based on qualitative criteria but on the assessment of the degree of the neutralization of the narcissistic energies and of the degree of the narcissistic investment of the work. There is no doubt, furthermore, as mentioned earlier, that the scientific and artistic activities which are encountered during certain stages of the analysis of narcissistic personality disorders are analogous phenomena and occupy an analogous position in the analytic process. As far as the following clinical discussion is concerned, therefore, the two activities will not be separated but examined together as constituting one important avenue that may be opened to the narcissistic cathexes through their transformation in the course of the therapeutic psychoanalysis of narcissistic personalities.

The upsurge of artistic or scientific activities which occurs not infrequently as an emergency measure during those phases of the working-through process in the analysis of narcissistic personalities when the relatively unprepared ego of the patient has to deal with a sudden influx of formerly repressed narcissistic libido is in general short-lived. If the working-through process is consistently pursued, the grandiose-exhibitionistic or the idealizing libido will usually be invested in a number of the new stable distributions (e.g., as strengthened self-esteem or in ideal formation) which were indicated earlier, and the conspicuous artistic or scientific activities that had been temporarily mobilized will again subside (see, for example, Miss F.'s brief career as a dancer).

The situation is different, of course, when the sublimatory activity is not instituted *de novo* during the analysis of a narcissistic personality disorder but when the liberated narcissistic libido can flow into already preformed scientific or artistic activity patterns. To a certain extent such preformed patterns probably exist in all patients who avail themselves of this outlet for the deployment of their narcissistic energies since during almost every adolescence some experimentation with creativeness does occur. But there is a decisive quantitative difference between those who abandon all interest in creative pursuits with the passing of adolescence and those who cling to it, whatever their emotional impoverishment and their inhibitions. In these cases one can often see with great clarity how, step by step, the therapeutically remobilized narcissistic cathexes will now enrich the formerly only precariously maintained sublimatory interest and how a seemingly insignificant hobby can become a deeply fulfilling activity that—an unexpected but not unwelcome bonus—may even call forth external support to the patient's self-esteem through public approval of his achievements. The obligation to protect the patient's identity makes it unfortunately often inadvisable to spell out in detail how the formerly asocial narcissistic configuration can ultimately be transformed into a significant artistic and scientific product.

Mr. E.'s artistic activities, for example, appeared at first to be undertaken only as an emergency measure which permitted him to maintain himself during a trying weekend separation from the analyst (see Chapter 5). As the analysis progressed, however, this patient turned with increasing devotion and success to certain creative artistic pursuits— they were related to the aforementioned artistic emergency measure, but they were not the same—which constituted unmistakably a redeployment of the very narcissistic cathexes that had formerly driven him to dangerous voyeuristic activities. This perversion had given expression to archaic merger needs which had made their first appearance in later childhood in a setting of frustrated exhibitionistic urges. The sublimatory activities, to which he increasingly devoted his energies, provided him with an acceptable (visual) outlet for his contact needs, the intensity of which is easily grasped by a glance at his early history. He had been a premature baby who had to be kept in an incubator; even after he was brought home he was hardly touched by his parents; during his later childhood his mother became progressively ill and unavailable to him; she finally died when he was sixteen. The artistic work in which he engaged during the later stages of his analysis not only allowed a sublimated discharge for his merger and contact needs but also became an important source of external approval and even of financial success.

It was very instructive—for analyst and patient—to watch and understand, generally against the background of the vicissitudes of the mirror transference, the back-and-forth movements between (a) the archaic expression of his merger needs by temporary regressions to the perverse impulses (and even to fleeting hallucinatory experiences of merger with his dead mother) and (b) the sophisticated artistic activities of which he had become capable. During earlier phases of the analysis he was unable to perform his artistic work whenever he was separated from the analyst by time, space or had the feeling that he was not (empathically) understood. Later he became more and more capable of tolerating distance and delay, and he could maintain his work even when the analyst had misunderstood him or when the patient felt the analyst was emotionally withdrawn from him, since he could now anticipate a later return to an empathic closeness.

Mr. E.'s capacity to build up a reliable artistic sublimation, while not exceptional, is not the rule. He was undoubtedly able to use the artistic work to such advantage because he had already had some experience with it before he entered analysis. Most of the sublimations of this kind (such as Miss F.'s dancing) appear only fleetingly and cease as soon as the newly liberated narcissistic libido has found other employment.

The vicissitudes of Mr. E.'s artistic activities during analysis, especially during the period of their transitional establishment, i.e., before they finally achieved a fairly reliable degree of autonomy, demonstrate the fact that a modicum of working through (maturationally and developmentally; or, belatedly, in analysis) of the more archaic stages of the narcissistic needs is necessary to allow their aim-inhibited satisfaction through sublimated artistic or scientific pursuits.

The voyeuristic symptom of Mr. E. had first appeared in his later childhood when his mother had not been able to respond appropriately to the boy's exhibitionistic wishes. When she had shown no interest in watching his display of prowess on a swing on the fairground, he had turned toward the men's room and to voyeurism. The same sequence occurred during long periods of the analysis. Whenever the patient's need for an echo or empathic approval was not understood by the analyst, or was frustrated by the analyst in other ways, the patient's sublimatory activities deteriorated and he tended to revert to his perversion.

The intimate connection between frustrated contact needs and a persistent wish for merger, which, however, gradually changes into a broad, sublimated empathic merger with the surroundings, and finally brings about the development of a keenly sensitive attitude toward the world, can be seen in certain artists, notably in some poets. John Keats's tendency, for example, to identify with the objects of his observation— even with inanimate objects such as billiard balls—would strike one as pathological had it not become increasingly combined with an outstanding ability to communicate his feelingful understanding which could be maintained so long as he felt supported by the attention and approval of his friends (see Gittings, 1968, p. 152f.; esp. n. 2).

When the poet claims that he identifies with a billiard ball, he gives testimony to the essentially narcissistic nature of the creative person's relationship with the relevant aspect of his surroundings. There is no need, however, to rely exclusively on such gross examples to serve as proof for the narcissistic nature of the creative act. A modicum of creative potential—however narrow its scope may be—lies within the realm of the experience of many people, and the narcissistic nature of the creative act (the fact that the object of the creative interest is invested with narcissistic libido) can be approached through ordinary self-observation and empathy. Unsolved intellectual and aesthetic problems, for example, create a narcissistic imbalance which in turn propels the individual toward a solution—be it now the completion of a crossword puzzle or the search for the perfect place for the new sofa in the living room (cf. Zeigarnik, 1927). The solving of the intellectual or aesthetic problem, however, especially when the correct answer becomes apparent within a relatively short time span, always leads to a feeling of narcissistic pleasure, which is the emotional accompaniment of the suddenly restored narcissistic balance.[4]

A phenomenon which is distantly related to the fact that a modicum of empathic contact with the analyst is necessary for the maintenance of a newly acquired capacity for artistic sublimation can also be observed—quite outside the realm of pathology—when certain creative personalities appear to require a specific relationship (as in a narcissistic transference) during periods of intense creativity. This need is especially strong when the discoveries lead the creative mind into lonely areas that had not previously been explored by others.[5] The sense of isolation of the creative mind is both exhilarating and frightening, the latter because the experience repeats traumatically an early childhood fear of being alone, abandoned, unsupported. In such a situation even the genius may choose a person in his environment whom he can see as all-powerful, as a figure with whom he can temporarily blend. Certain types of narcissistically fixated personalities (even bordering on the paranoid) with their apparently absolute self-confidence and certainty lend themselves specifically to this role.[6] Such transferences established by creative minds during periods of intense creativity are much more closely

---

[4] The closely related "Aha!-Erlebnis" of Gestalt psychology (see Bühler, 1908; Maier, 1931; and Duncker, 1945) may well be evaluated in the light of, and in harmony with, the foregoing considerations. See also the different approach taken by Hendrick (1942), who posits an "instinct to master" in explanation of some cognate experiences.

[5] See in this context Székely's perceptive contributions (1968, 1970) concerning the fear of the new and unknown in scientists.

[6] See in this context the remarks in Chapter 9 about the messianic charisma of Schreber's father and, by extension, of other messianic leaders such as Hitler.

related to the transferences which occur during the analysis of narcissistic personalities than to the transferences which occur in the analysis of the transference neuroses. In other words, we are dealing either with an expansion of an active, creative self (resembling one of the varieties of a mirror transference) or, which is more frequently the case, with the wish to obtain strength from an idealized object (idealizing transference), but not predominantly with the revival of a figure from the past which is cathected with object libido. Fliess may well have been the embodiment of such a narcissistic transference for Freud during Freud's most important creative spell; and Freud was able to dispense with the illusionary sense of Fliess's greatness and thus with the narcissistic relationship—in contradistinction to a resolution of transference by insight—after he had accomplished his great creative task.

A relationship such as the one just described may, of course, develop not only in a scientist at a crucial juncture of his path toward a pioneering discovery but also in an artist during an important period of creativity. A letter of Melville to Hawthorne,[7] for example, alludes by the choice of metaphor to the intensity of the underlying wish for the approval of an idealized figure and for a narcissistic merger with it: Hawthorne, he says, is drinking from the flagon of his life. "And when I put it to my lips," Melville continues, "lo, they are yours and not mine. I feel that the Godhead is broken up like the bread at supper, and that we are the pieces." And, after imagining his life and work as a continuous letter to the great friend (and alter-ego?), he ends by invoking the ultimate reassurance of a merger fantasy: "The divine magnet is on you and my magnet responds. Which is the bigger? A foolish question—they are *one*."

---

[7] I was led to this document by Dr. Charles Kligerman who, speaking of a "narcissistic merger transference," quoted it in his contribution to the panel on Narcissistic Resistance (1969, p. 943). For a broad discussion of the narcissistic relationship between Melville and Hawthorne, and its influence on the vicissitudes of Melville's creativity, see Kligerman (1953).

The foregoing discussion concerns instances of scientific and artistic creativeness which occur during the middle phases of analysis. In the following I shall examine the emergence of similar sublimatory activities during the end phases of the treatment. Here, too, the creative, artistic, and scientific activities tend, in general, to be ephemeral. Occasionally, however, these acquisitions appear to be lasting (cf., for example, patient H. described by me in 1957 [pp. 399-403], who, as I discovered by chance, is still actively engaged in his creative musical pursuits more than ten years after the termination of his analysis).

Creativeness in psychoanalysts is another problem area that deserves special attention. It is my impression that toward the end of a successful training analysis the transformation of the narcissistic positions may lead not only to increasing empathic ability and to a nondefensive shift of attention to psychological matters beyond the confines of the analysand's own psyche, but occasionally also to the stirrings of true creativity. It would be of great interest to investigate the relationship between the specific residuals of individual psychopathology and the specific areas of research interest of the creative psychoanalyst. Just as in other scientific pursuits, creativity in analysts is incited by many stimuli and fed from many sources, including the worker's potentially pathogenic conflicts. The relationship between an analyst's scientific creativity and his psychopathology is, however, at times more specific than is the case with analogous creative activities outside our field. I believe that true psychoanalytic creativity may be motivated by the urge to investigate certain psychological areas that have remained incompletely elucidated in the personal analysis. Where the incompleteness of the training analysis is due to inner resistances in the analysand which the analysis was unable to overcome, or where it is due to obstacles from the side of the training analyst (e.g., countertransferences), the result will be the attempt to resolve the impasse through re-analysis (see Freud, 1937a) or self-analysis (see again Freud, 1937a; also

M. Kramer, 1959). Where the incompleteness of the analytic work, however, is due to the fact that the science of psychoanalysis itself has not yet made the relevant discoveries (for a striking example, see Freud's statement in "Analysis Terminable and Interminable" concerning the period when he did not yet know of the existence of the negative transference), then it may become the impelling force toward the discovery of a suprapersonal, creative solution.

It must be added, however, that the potentially fertilizing power in creative psychological research which is exerted by residual psychological tension states after the termination of the training analysis may be blocked if the incompleteness of the training analysis is not confronted openly but is covered up. Paradoxically, a blatant error in this respect is not likely to stand in the way of future creative efforts toward expanded understanding but, here as elsewhere, it is the small truth or the half-truth which is the greatest enemy of the truth. Thus no active search for a scientific solution in a still uncharted psychological area will be initiated after the termination of the training analysis if, at the end of the analysis, the remaining psychopathology is concealed by the exertion of the analysand's ego—in conformity with the wish of the training analyst who, due to faulty perception or narcissistically motivated distortion, has communicated to the analysand his erroneous belief that a psychoanalytically valid ego mastery has been achieved when in fact it has not.[8]

Let me add here only the point that in some potentially creative analysts certain unresolved aspects of a narcissistic transference toward the training analyst may, in the late stages of the analysis and after its termination, become shifted toward the image of Freud, the originator of our science. Creative endeavors in such analysts may then become involved in a variety of conflicts focused on the father imago of Freud. Fears aroused by the loss of the narcissistic transfer-

[8] For a discussion of these points see Kohut, 1970b; and the Minutes of the Meeting of the Ad Hoc Committee on Scientific Activities of May 4, 1967.

ence may, for example, block the carrying to completion of truly original steps that would significantly transgress the scope of Freud's own discoveries. Or, what seems to occur even more often, fears of the loss of a narcissistic merger with the archaic father image (or of the loss of the approving echo from the insufficiently internalized archaic imago) will motivate counterphobic rebellious attitudes. These lead not to creativeness, however, which would expand the frontiers of knowledge beyond the scope of Freud's discoveries but to an (often intensely) critical attitude vis-à-vis Freud's work. The manifest result—relevant examples are not hard to identify in the psychiatric and psychoanalytic literature—can often be found in the form of repeated theoretical polemics which are, however, never followed by the only sign of true internal emancipation, namely, a positive contribution which would constitute an expansion of our psychological understanding of man in health or disease.

Analysts have, in general, during their hours of therapeutic activity, only scant occasion to observe the sublimatory activities of their patients in depth and in detail, and it is my impression that an intensive and prolonged focusing on such activities during the early and middle phases of therapeutic analysis is usually in the service of defense. From the patient's side, the preoccupation with scientific or artistic work early in analysis may form part of those defensive maneuvers that are commonly referred to as "flight into health." An analyst's undue emphasis on his analysand's creative activities, on the other hand, may betray a tendency toward a replacement of the endeavor to achieve ego expansion through interpretations by the attempt to produce ego changes through educational and suggestive means—achieved usually via the mechanism of the patient's massive identification with the analyst (see Chapter 7). During the terminal phases especially of the analyses of narcissistic personalities, however, when the patient is truly achieving the dissolution of his narcissistic transference enmeshment with the analyst, we often encounter various nondefensively employed, sublimatory creative activities. They frequently constitute a revival of similar endeavors during latency and adolescence.

Analysts usually learn very little about the deeper dynamics of these activities from the direct analytic observation of the material which surrounds their temporary emergence during the end phase of the analysis. Yet, occasionally, it is possible to discover retrospectively that the narcissistic forces which are now directed toward a new self-object, the creative work, had been active much earlier, but had then been bound up in the noncreative elaboration of narcissistic tension states within the framework of a narcissistic transference. It is in particular the dreams of narcissistic patients which can at times clearly be recognized as having been the precursors of later artistic productivity.

The following is an example of a dream that may be considered to be such a precursor of artistic production. It was told by patient P., a gifted, sensitive, somewhat paranoid man in his mid-thirties, who toward the end of his long treatment began to write a number of short stories, some of which impressed me as hauntingly beautiful. These stories (which I know only because the patient spoke of them during the sessions—some of them may have been published later) dealt with the experiences of a late adolescent or of a young man. They described his loneliness, his estrangement from the world, his sensitive self-preoccupation, the fear of the disturbance of his psychic equilibrium through gross sexual stimulation (such as the hero of his stories encounters in honky-tonks, striptease establishments, and the like), and his search for a friend who, in essence, is similar to the patient and could thus through his empathy protect him from the dangers of traumatic overstimulation. The specific transference meaning of these stories, written at a time when the patient was indeed dealing during his analysis with the impending loss of an alter-ego transference, does not concern us in the present context. Here we are focusing on the connection between these later artistic accomplishments and the earlier more autoplastic elaborations of similar problems in a dream. Although a dream which the patient had early in the course of the analysis was the direct expression of the reactivated fear of the dangerous disturbance of an existing psychic equilibrium (currently the danger which the beginning analysis posed to him in this respect), the dream to be reported emerged in association to the aforementioned one, which it illuminated by allusion and analogy. The old dream, however, had been dreamed more than twenty years earlier, accompanying the patient's first seminal emission: it was a "wet dream." The patient's memory of the dream was vivid and his account seemed like that concerning a recent intense experience.

In the dream the patient was gazing on a landscape of great beauty and peacefulness. There were rolling meadows of a warm and dark green, and winding brooks filled with gaily moving water which reflected the blue of the cloudless sky. Small clumps of trees surrounded human dwellings of rustic style and, while no people could be seen, there was life: cows were grazing and in particular there were white patches of grazing sheep clearly outlined against the green background of the meadows. Unexpectedly the peace was disturbed by a distant rumble. The patient looked up and discovered that the landscape which he had beheld was a valley at the foot of a high dam. The threatening rumble seemed to emanate from there and suddenly the patient noticed deep rents in the dam. All the colors of the landscape changed, slightly but significantly.[9] The blue of the sky and of the waters became a blackish-blue. The green of the grass changed into a sharp, unnatural green; and the trees appeared

---

[9] The fact that the dream was in color (especially in the unnatural technicolor of the later part of the dream) is an expression of the fact that the dreamer's ego was unable to achieve the complete integration of the new experiences; that it was able fully to absorb neither the intensity nor the content of the drive demands. (For a discussion of the significance of dreams in color, see Chapter 7.)

darker. The cracks in the dam widened and then all of a sudden a maelstrom of ugly, dirty, destructive floods poured forth, overrunning the countryside with all its beauty, sweeping away the trees, houses, and animals. The last unforgettable impression, before he woke up in horror, was the sight of the white sheep changing into the spinning whiteness of the whitecaps that enveloped everything.

To resolve the complexity of condensation contained in this beautiful dream goes beyond the bounds of the present discussion. Suffice it to say that it was a quasi-artistic rendition of the experience of the disturbance of a blissful, self-absorbed narcissistic state (the landscape symbolized the patient's own body) by the intrusion of sadistic sexual elements which accompanied the seminal emission. Thus, a number of references to narcissistic and autoerotic experiences of early childhood could be recognized and identified in the dream.

As I previously indicated, the poetic powers of an artistically endowed ego which achieved the transformation of this patient's (pre)narcissistic tensions into the beautiful, yet autoplastic, imagery of the dream were later loosened sufficiently to participate in the shaping of artistic productions (short stories); i.e., they now invested self-objects of a higher order. The shift of the patient's creativeness from the production of dreams (concerning his experiences of the vicissitudes of the autoerotic and narcissistic cathexis of his body self) to that of works of art (dealing with experiences concerning his adolescent loneliness, self-absorption, and search for an alterego friendship) testifies to a significant advance on the scale of progress in the development of his narcissism. Through the newly liberated creative capacity a fitting of his narcissism into a social context was achieved and—above all, as far as the measurement of therapeutic success is concerned—the shift permitted an important and reliable (sublimatory) release for the patient's narcissistic tensions which had formerly constituted a grave threat to his emotional health and had

led to a number of dangerous states of emotional disequilibrium.

Although exceptions must be granted, it is my opinion that
many creative activities in the terminal phases of the analyses
of narcissistic personalities (analogous to the flowering of the
empathic ability in the end phases of some training analyses)
constitute the favorable result of the preceding analytic work
and that they are true transformations of the former pathogenic narcissistic positions. For this reason they do not
constitute material that requires psychoanalytic interpretations in the usual sense. (For further remarks concerning the
technical problems posed by the emergence of sublimatory
and creative activities in the end phases of analysis, see Kohut, 1966b, p. 203f.)

Humor and Wisdom

To begin with, I wish to affirm my conviction that the emergence of the capacity for genuine humor constitutes yet another important—and welcome—sign that a transformation
of archaic pathogenic narcissistic cathexes has taken place in
the course of the analysis of narcissistic personalities. The
humor of which the narcissistic patient becomes capable is, I
believe, the complement to another favorable result in the
course of the analysis of these patients: the strengthening of
their values and ideals. Humor alone (especially when it contains an oral-sadistic ring of sarcasm) may still be defensive
and is then not indicative of a transformation of the narcissistic cathexes; and an isolated, solemn, intense cathexis of
newly found ideals (akin to the "causes" of the paranoid) may
not yet signify a successful working through of the narcissistic
positions but simply their appearance in a new disguise. In
evaluating the patient's progress, it is of decisive significance
for the analyst to ascertain that the patient's devotion to his
values and ideals is not that of a fanatic but is accompanied
by a sense of proportion which can be expressed through
humor. The coexistence of idealism and humor demonstrates

not only that the content and psychological locus of the narcissistic positions have changed but also that the narcissistic energies are now tamed and neutralized and that they are following an aim-inhibited course. If, on the one hand, the patient's values now occupy a position of greater psychological importance, have become integrated with his ego's realistic goal structure, and quietly give new meaning to his life, while, on the other hand, he is now also able to contemplate with humor the very area of the formerly rigidly held narcissistic positions, then the analyst may indeed feel that the working-through processes have been successful and that the gains which have been made are solid.

Only detailed clinical descriptions could demonstrate the gradual transformation of the patient's grandiose fantasies or his exhibitionistic strivings and the relinquishment of his belief in the magical perfection of the narcissistically experienced object; and the appearance, in their stead, of a balanced mixture of ideals and humor.

In many, perhaps in most, instances the appearance of humor is sudden and constitutes the belated overt manifestation of the silently increasing dominance which the patient's ego has achieved vis-à-vis the previously so formidable power of the grandiose self and of the idealized object. All of a sudden, as if the sun were unexpectedly breaking through the clouds, the analyst will witness, to his great pleasure, how a genuine sense of humor expressed by the patient testifies to the fact that the ego can now see in realistic proportions the greatness aspirations of the infantile grandiose self or the former demands for the unlimited perfection and power of the idealized parent imago, and that the ego can now contemplate these old configurations with the amusement that is an expression of its freedom.

There are instructive instances, however, in which during transitional periods the patient's ego seems to linger at the borderline between its persistent fear of the not yet fully conquered narcissistic structures and its newly acquired courage that allows it to undertake tentative moves toward a humorous attitude with regard to them. I have learned that it is best under such circumstances not to laugh prematurely with the patient but rather to assist him by further interpretations concerning the emerging material and by an empathically transmitted explanation of the analysand's transitional ego state. (For a clinical illustration of a transitional state between tentative humor and still persisting apprehension see Mr. C.'s dream, reported in Chapter 7, which occurred at a time when an already strengthened ego was suddenly threatened by an upsurge of archaic grandiosity.)

I shall, however, not pursue the topic of the appearance of humor in its various forms during analysis any further, and will restrict myself to quoting the remark of Miss F., a childlike and self-absorbed personality who, toward the end of a long analysis, had acquired a sufficient sense of humor which enabled her to formulate, retrospectively, her transference problem by telling me: "I guess the crime that you have committed, and for which there can be no forgiveness, is that you are not I."

And now a brief remark about *wisdom*, a cognitive and emotional position the attainment of which might be considered one of the peaks of human development, not only, narrowly, in the analysis of the narcissistic personality disorders but in the growth and fulfillment of the human personality altogether.

While the increased realism of the narcissistic patient's ambitions, the strengthening of his ideals, his creativeness, and especially his growing sense of humor are often clearly in evidence at the end of a successful analysis, a claim of the therapeutic attainability of even a modicum of wisdom may seem exaggerated. And yet the progression from information through knowledge to wisdom, which characterizes the evolution of the cognitive sphere in a successfully lived, paradigmatic life, can also be observed in the successful analysis. As the treatment begins, analyst and analysand are gathering *information* about the patient and his history. Gradually, in the middle phases of the analysis, the data which have been collected become ordered and fitted together into a broader and deeper *knowledge* of the cohesive functioning of the patient's mind and of the continuity which exists between the present and the past. And, finally, in the termination phase of a good analysis, the analyst's knowledge and the patient's understanding of himself have taken on the quality of *wisdom*. In order to reach this experience the patient must first have come to terms with his unmodified infantile narcissism, whether his fixations were predominantly on the archaic grandiose self or on the archaic, narcissistically aggrandized, idealized self-object.

The establishment of ego dominance in the realm of the two great narcissistic configurations is, however, only the precondition for that total attitude that we call wisdom—it is not wisdom itself. The achievement of wisdom is a feat that we must not expect of our patients, nor, indeed, necessarily of ourselves. Since its full attainment includes the emotional acceptance of the transience of individual existence, we must admit that it can probably be reached by only a few and that its stable integration may well be beyond the compass of man's psychological capacity.

But a modicum of wisdom, specifically as it relates to the patient's attitude toward himself, toward his analyst, and toward the result of the analytic work, is indeed not a rarity. The analyst should not aim, nor indeed expect, to achieve it; and we should not, by any pressure, be it ever so subtle, induce the analysand to strive for it. As stated before, such pressures and expectations from the side of the analyst lead only to the establisment of insecure wholesale identifications, either with the analyst as he really is, or with the patient's fantasy of the analyst, or with the personality which the analyst may try to present to the patient.

The spontaneous emergence of an attitude of wisdom in the analysand, however, is often observed toward the end of a successful analysis—though, as stated above, in a modest and limited form. That modicum of wisdom which does indeed appear during the terminal phases of analysis (it may establish itself more broadly some time after the termination of the treatment) enables the patient to maintain his self-esteem despite the recognition of his limitations, and to feel friendly respect and gratitude toward the analyst despite the recognition of the analyst's conflicts and limitations. And, finally, patient and analyst may, upon the termination of the treatment, share in the acknowledgment of the fact that the analysis itself has of necessity remained incomplete. In a jointly held attitude of soberness and wisdom, yet without sarcasm or pessimism, analyst and patient will admit as they are parting that not all has been solved and that some conflicts, inhibitions, and symptoms, and some of the old tendencies toward self-aggrandizement and infantile idealization remain. These frailties, however, are now familiar and they can be contemplated with tolerance and composure.

Bibliography

Abraham, K. (1919), A Particular Form of Neurotic Resistance against the Psycho-Analytic Method. *Selected Papers of Karl Abraham.* London: Hogarth Press, 1927, pp. 303-311.

Adler, A. (1912), *The Neurotic Constitution.* New York: Moffat Yard, 1916; London: Kegan Paul, Trench & Trubner, 1918.

Aichhorn, A. (1936), The Narcissistic Transference of the "Juvenile Impostor." In: *Delinquency and Child Guidance: Selected Papers by August Aichhorn,* ed. O. Fleischmann, P. Kramer, & H. Ross. New York: International Universities Press, 1964, pp. 174-191.

Alexander, F., French, T. M., et al. (1946), *Psychoanalytic Therapy: Principles and Applications.* New York: Ronald Press.

Andreas-Salomé, L. (1962), The Dual Orientation of Narcissism. *Psychoanal. Quart.,* 31:1-30.

Argelander, H. (1968), Der psychoanalytische Dialog. *Psyche,* 22:325-339.

Arlow, J. A. (1966), Depersonalization and Derealization. In: *Psychoanalysis—A General Psychology,* ed. R. M. Loewenstein, L. M. Newman, M. Schur, & A. J. Solnit. New York: International Universities Press, pp. 456-478.

——— & Brenner, C. (1964), *Psychoanalytic Concepts and the Structural Theory.* New York: International Universities Press.

——— & ——— (1969), The Psychopathology of the Psychoses: A Proposed Revision. *Int. J. Psycho-Anal.,* 50:5-14.

Balint, M. (1937), Early Developmental Stages of the Ego: Primary Object-Love. *Primary Love and Psycho-Analytic Technique.* London: Hogarth Press, 1952, pp. 90-108.

——— (1968), *The Basic Fault: Therapeutic Aspects of Regression.* London: Tavistock Publications.

Barande, R. et al. (1965), Remarques sur le narcissisme dans le mouvement de la cure. *Rev. Franç. Psychoanal.,* 29:601-611.

Basch, M. F. (1968), External Reality and Disavowal (unpublished).

329

Baumeyer, F. (1955), Der Fall Schreber. *Psyche*, 9:513-536. English: The Schreber Case. *Int. J. Psycho-Anal.*, 37:61-74, 1956.

Bender, L. & Vogel, B. F. (1941), Imaginary Companions of Children. *Amer. J. Orthopsychiat.*, 11:56-66.

Benedek, T. F. (1949), The Psychosomatic Implications of the Primary Unit: Mother-Child. *Amer. J. Orthopsychiat.*, 19:642-654.

—— (1956), Toward the Biology of the Depressive Constellation. *J. Amer. Psychoanal. Assn.*, 4:389-427.

—— (1959), Parenthood as a Developmental Phase. *J. Amer. Psychoanal. Assn.*, 7:389-417.

Benedict, R. (1934), *Patterns of Culture*. New York: Penguin, 1946.

Benjamin, J. D. (1950), Methodological Considerations in the Validation and Elaboration of Psychoanalytic Personality Theory. *Amer. J. Orthopsychiat.*, 20:139-156.

—— (1961), Some Developmental Observations Relating to the Theory of Anxiety. *J. Amer. Psychoanal. Assn.*, 9:652-668.

Beres, D. (1956), Ego Deviation and the Concept of Schizophrenia. *The Psychoanalytic Study of the Child*, 11:164-233.

—— (1962), The Unconscious Fantasy. *Psychoanal. Quart.*, 31:309-328.

Bernstein, H. (1963), Identity and Sense of Identity. Paper read to the Chicago Psychoanalytic Society.

Bibring, E. (1947), The So-Called English School of Psychoanalysis. *Psychoanal. Quart.*, 16:69-93.

Bibring, G. L. (1964), Some Considerations Regarding the Ego Ideal in the Psychoanalytic Process. *J. Amer. Psychoanal. Assn.*, 12:517-521.

Bing, J., McLaughlin, F., & Marburg, R. (1959), The Metapsychology of Narcissism. *The Psychoanalytic Study of the Child*, 14:9-28.

—— & Marburg, R. O. (1962). Panel Report: Narcissism. *J. Amer. Psychoanal. Assn.*, 10:593-605.

Binswanger, L. (1956), *Sigmund Freud: Reminiscences of a Friendship*, tr. N. Guterman. New York: Grune & Stratton, 1957.

Bond, D. D. (1952), *The Love and the Fear of Flying*. New York: International Universities Press.

Boyer, L. B. (1956), On Maternal Overstimulation and Ego Defects. *The Psychoanalytic Study of the Child*, 11:236-256.

Braunschweig, D. R. (1965), Le narcissisme: aspects cliniques. *Rev. Franç. Psychanal.*, 29:589-600.

Brenner, C. (1968), Archaic Features of Ego Functioning. *Int. J. Psycho-Anal.*, 49:426-429.

Bressler, B. (1965), The Concept of the Self. *Psychoanal. Rev.*, 52:425-445.

Brodey, W. M. (1965), On the Dynamics of Narcissism. *The Psychoanalytic Study of the Child*, 20:165-193.

Bühler, K. (1908), Tatsachen und Probleme zu einer Psychologie der Denkvorgänge. Translated as: On Thought Connections. In: *Or-*

ganization and Pathology of Thought, tr. & ed. D. Rapaport. New
York: Columbia University Press, 1951, pp. 39-57.
———— (1930), *The Mental Development of the Child: A Summary of
Modern Psychological Theory.* New York: Harcourt, Brace.
Bullock, A. (1952), *Hitler: A Study in Tyranny.* New York & Evanston,
Ill.: Harper & Row, rev. ed., 1962.
Burlingham, D. & Robertson, J. (1966), *Nursery School for the Blind.*
Film produced by the Hampstead Child-Therapy Clinic, London.
[Distributor in the U.S.: New York University Film Library, 26
Washington Place, New York, N.Y. 10003.]
Bychowski, G. (1947), The Preschizophrenic Ego. *Psychoanal. Quart.,*
16:225-233.
Deutsch, H. (1942), Some Forms of Emotional Disturbance and Their
Relation to Schizophrenia. *Neurosis and Character Types.* New
York: International Universities Press, 1965, pp. 262-286.
———— (1964), Some Clinical Considerations of the Ego Ideal. *J. Amer.
Psychoanal. Assn.,* 12:512-516.
Dilthey, W. (1924), Ideen über eine beschreibende und zergliedernde
Psychologie. *Gesammelte Schriften,* 5. Leipzig: Teubner.
Duncker, K. (1945), On Problem-Solving. *Psychological Monographs,*
Vol. 58, No. 5. Washington, D.C.: American Psychological Asso-
ciation.
Eidelberg, L. (1959), The Concept of Narcissistic Mortification. *Int. J.
Psycho-Anal.,* 40:163-168.
Eisnitz, A. J. (1969), Narcissistic Object Choice, Self Representation.
Int. J. Psycho-Anal., 50:15-25.
Eissler, K. R. (1961), *Leonardo da Vinci: Psychoanalytic Notes on the
Enigma.* New York: International Universities Press.
———— (1963a), *Goethe: A Psychoanalytic Study,* 2 Vols. Detroit: Wayne
State University Press.
———— (1963b), Die Ermordung von wievieler seiner Kinder muss ein
Mensch symptomfrei ertragen können, um eine normale Konstitu-
tion zu haben? *Psyche,* 17:241-272.
———— (1965), *Medical Orthodoxy and the Future of Psychoanalysis.*
New York: International Universities Press.
———— (1967), Perverted Psychiatry? *Amer. J. Psychiat.,* 123:1352-1358.
Elkisch, P. (1957), The Psychological Significance of the Mirror. *J.
Amer. Psychoanal. Assn.,* 5:235-244.
Ephron, L. R. (1967), Narcissism and the Sense of Self. *Psychoanal.
Rev.,* 54:499-509.
Erikson, E. H. (1950), *Childhood and Society.* New York: Norton.
———— (1956), The Problem of Ego Identity. *J. Amer. Psychoanal.
Assn.,* 4:56-121.
Federn, P. (1952), *Ego Psychology and the Psychoses,* ed. E. Weiss. New
York: Basic Books, esp. pp. 283-322, 323-364.
Ferenczi, S. (1919), On Influencing of the Patient in Psycho-Analysis.

Further Contributions to the Theory and Technique of Psycho-Analysis. London: Hogarth Press, 1950, pp. 235-237.

Fliess, R. (1942), The Metapsychology of the Analyst. *Psychoanal. Quart.,* 11:211-227.

Frankl, V. E. (1946), *Ein Psychologe erlebt das Konzentrationslager.* Vienna: Verlag für Jugend und Volk. English: *From Death Camp to Existentialism.* Boston: Beacon Press, 1959.

—— (1958), On Logotherapy and Existential Analysis. *Amer. J. Psychoanal.,* 18:28-37.

Freeman, T. (1963), The Concept of Narcissism in Schizophrenic States. *Int. J. Psycho-Anal.,* 44:293-303.

—— (1964), Some Aspects of Pathological Narcissism. *Int. J. Psycho-Anal.,* 12:540-561.

Freud, A. (1951), Obituary: August Aichhorn. *Int. J. Psycho-Anal.,* 32:51-56.

—— (1952), The Mutual Influences in the Development of Ego and Id. *The Psychoanalytic Study of the Child,* 7:42-50.

—— & Burlingham, D. (1942), *Young Children in War-Time.* London: Allen & Unwin.

—— —— (1943), *Infants Without Families: The Case For and Against Residential Nurseries.* London: Allen & Unwin.

—— & Dann, S. (1951), An Experiment in Group Upbringing. *The Psychoanalytic Study of the Child,* 6:127-168.

Freud, S. (1900), The Interpretation of Dreams. *Standard Edition,* 4 & 5. London: Hogarth Press, 1953.

—— (1905), Three Essays on the Theory of Sexuality. *Standard Edition,* 7:125-245. London: Hogarth Press, 1953.

—— (1911), Psycho-Analytic Notes on an Autobiographical Account of a Case of Paranoia (Dementia Paranoides). *Standard Edition,* 12:3-82. London: Hogarth Press, 1958.

—— (1912), The Dynamics of Transference. *Standard Edition,* 12:97-108. London: Hogarth Press, 1958.

—— (1913), On the Beginning of Treatment. *Standard Edition,* 12:121-144. London: Hogarth Press, 1958.

—— (1914), On Narcissism. *Standard Edition,* 14:69-102. London: Hogarth Press, 1957.

—— (1915a), Instincts and Their Vicissitudes. *Standard Edition,* 14:117-140. London: Hogarth Press, 1957.

—— (1915b), Repression. *Standard Edition,* 14:141-158. London: Hogarth Press, 1957.

—— (1915c), The Unconscious. *Standard Edition,* 14:159-204. London: Hogarth Press, 1957.

—— (1917a [1915]), Mourning and Melancholia. *Standard Edition,* 14:237-258. London: Hogarth Press, 1957.

—— (1917b), A Difficulty in the Path of Psycho-Analysis. *Standard Edition,* 17:137-144. London: Hogarth Press, 1955.

—— (1917c), A Childhood Recollection from *Dichtung und Wahr-heit. Standard Edition*, 17:145-156. London: Hogarth Press, 1955.

—— (1921), Group Psychology and the Analysis of the Ego. *Standard Edition*, 18:67-143. London: Hogarth Press, 1955.

—— (1923), The Ego and the Id. *Standard Edition*, 19:3-66. London: Hogarth Press, 1961.

—— (1924a [1923]), Neurosis and Psychosis. *Standard Edition*, 19:149-153. London: Hogarth Press, 1961.

—— (1924b), The Loss of Reality in Neurosis and Psychosis. *Standard Edition*, 19:183-187. London: Hogarth Press, 1961.

—— (1925), Negation. *Standard Edition*, 19:235-239. London: Hogarth Press, 1961.

—— (1926 [1925]), Inhibitions, Symptoms and Anxiety. *Standard Edition*, 20:77-175. London: Hogarth Press, 1959.

—— (1927), Fetishism. *Standard Edition*, 21:149-157. London: Hogarth Press, 1961.

—— (1937a), Analysis Terminable and Interminable. *Standard Edition*, 23:216-253. London: Hogarth Press, 1964.

—— (1937b), Constructions in Analysis. *Standard Edition*, 23:255-269. London: Hogarth Press, 1964.

—— (1940 [1938]), Splitting of the Ego in the Process of Defence. *Standard Edition*, 23:271-278. London: Hogarth Press, 1964.

—— (1969 [1872-1874]), Some Early Unpublished Letters of Freud. *Int. J. Psycho-Anal.*, 50:419-427.

Frosch, J. (1960), The Psychotic Character. Abstr. in: *J. Amer. Psycho-anal. Assn.*, 8:544-548.

—— (1967a), Delusional Fixity, Sense of Conviction, and the Psychotic Conflict. *Int. J. Psycho-Anal.*, 48:475-495.

—— (1967b), Severe Regressive States during Analysis: Introduction and Summary. *J. Amer. Psychoanal. Assn.*, 15:491-507, 606-625.

—— (1970), Psychoanalytic Considerations of the Psychotic Character. *J. Amer. Psychoanal. Assn.*, 18:24-50.

Gedo, J. E. & Goldberg, A. (1969), Systems of Psychic Functioning and Their Psychoanalytic Conceptualization (unpublished manuscript).

—— & Wolf, E. (1970), Die Ichtyosaurusbriefe. *Psyche*, 24:785-797.

Gitelson, M. (1952), Re-evaluation of the Rôle of the Oedipus Complex. *Int. J. Psycho-Anal.*, 33:351-354.

—— (1958), On Ego Distortion. *Int. J. Psycho-Anal.*, 39:245-257.

Gittings, R. (1968), *John Keats*. New York: Little, Brown.

Glover, E. (1939), *Psycho-Analysis*. London, New York: Staples Press, 2nd ed., 1949.

—— (1943), The Concept of Dissociation. *On the Early Development of Mind*. New York: International Universities Press, 1956, pp. 307-327; cf. esp. pp. 316-317.

—— (1945), Examination of the Klein System of Child Psychology. *The Psychoanalytic Study of the Child*, 1:75-118.

334 BIBLIOGRAPHY

Greenacre, P. (1949), A Contribution to the Study of Screen Memories. *The Psychoanalytic Study of the Child*, 3/4:73-84.
—— (1964), A Study on the Nature of Inspiration. *J. Amer. Psychoanal. Assn.*, 12:6-31.
Greenson, R. R. (1965), The Working Alliance and the Transference Neurosis. *Psychoanal. Quart.*, 34:155-181.
—— (1967), *The Technique and Practice of Psychoanalysis*. New York: International Universities Press.
Grinberg, L. (1956), Sobre algunos problemas de técnica psicoanalítica determinados por la identificación y contraidentificación proyectivas. *Rev. Psicoanál.*, 13:507-511.
Grinker, R. R. (1968), *The Borderline Syndrome: A Behavioral Study of Ego Functions*. New York: Basic Books.
Hammett, V. B. D. (1965), A Consideration of Psychoanalysis in Relation to Psychiatry Generally, circa 1965. *Amer. J. Psychiat.*, 122:42-54.
Hart, H. H. (1947), Narcissistic Equilibrium. *Int. J. Psycho-Anal.*, 28:106-114.
Hartmann, H. (1927), Understanding and Explanation. *Essays on Ego Psychology*. New York: International Universities Press, 1964, pp. 369-403.
—— (1939), *Ego Psychology and the Problem of Adaptation*. New York: International Universities Press, 1958.
—— (1947), On Rational and Irrational Action. *Essays on Ego Psychology*. New York: International Universities Press, 1964, pp. 37-68.
—— (1950a), Psychoanalysis and Developmental Psychology. *Essays on Ego Psychology*. New York: International Universities Press, 1964, pp. 99-112.
—— (1950b), Comments on the Psychoanalytic Theory of the Ego. *Essays on Ego Psychology*. New York: International Universities Press, 1964, pp. 113-141.
—— (1952), The Mutual Influences in the Development of Ego and Id. *Essays on Ego Psychology*. New York: International Universities Press, 1964, pp. 155-181.
—— (1953), Contribution to the Metapsychology of Schizophrenia. *Essays on Ego Psychology*. New York: International Universities Press, 1964, pp. 182-206.
—— (1956), The Development of the Ego Concept in Freud's Work. *Essays on Ego Psychology*. New York: International Universities Press, 1964, pp. 268-296.
—— (1960), *Psychoanalysis and Moral Values*. New York: International Universities Press.
—— (1964), *Essays on Ego Psychology*. New York: International Universities Press.

———— & Kris, E. (1945), The Genetic Approach in Psychoanalysis. *The Psychoaanlytic Study of the Child*, 1:11-30.

Hendrick, I. (1942), Instinct and the Ego during Infancy. *Psychoanal. Quart.*, 11:33-58.

———— (1964), Narcissism and the Prepuberty Ego Ideal. *J. Amer. Psychoanal. Assn.*, 12:522-528.

Jacobson, E. (1957), Denial and Repression. *J. Amer. Psychoanal. Assn.*, 5:61-92.

———— (1964), *The Self and the Object World*. New York: International Universities Press.

———— (1967), *Psychotic Conflict and Reality*. New York: International Universities Press.

Jaspers, K. (1920), *Allgemeine Psychopathologie*. Berlin: Springer, 2nd ed., 1946.

Joffe, W. G. (1969), A Critical Review of the Status of the Envy Concept. *Int. J. Psycho-Anal.*, 50:533-545.

———— & Sandler, J. (1967), Some Conceptual Problems Involved in the Consideration of Disorders of Narcissism. *J. Child Psychother.*, 2:56-66.

Jones, E. (1910), The Oedipus Complex as an Explanation of Hamlet's Mystery. *Amer. J. Psychol.*, 21:72-113.

———— (1913), The God Complex. *Essays in Applied Psycho-Analysis*, 2:244-265. London: Hogarth Press, 1951.

———— (1949), *Hamlet and Oedipus*. London: V. Gollancz.

———— (1953), *The Life and Work of Sigmund Freud*, Vol. I. New York: Basic Books.

———— (1957), *The Life and Work of Sigmund Freud*, Vol. III. New York: Basic Books.

Justin (1960), Menschen und Paragraphen: Die Versuchung. *Die Weltwoche*, No. 1395:24 (August 5). As quoted by Eissler, K. R. in: *Medical Orthodoxy and the Future of Psychoanalysis*.

Kanzer, M. (1964), Freud's Uses of the Terms "Autoerotism" and "Narcissism." *J. Amer. Psychoanal. Assn.*, 12:529-539.

Kaplan, S. M. & Whitman, R. M. (1965), The Negative Ego-Ideal. *Int. J. Psycho-Anal.*, 46:183-187.

Kernberg, O. (1966), Structural Derivatives of Object Relationships. *Int. J. Psycho-Anal.*, 47:236-253.

———— (1967), Borderline Personality Organization. *J. Amer. Psychoanal. Assn.*, 15:641-685.

———— (1968), The Treatment of Patients with Borderline Personality Organization. *Int. J. Psycho-Anal.*, 49:600-619.

———— (1969), Factors in the Psychoanalytic Treatment of Narcissistic Personalities. *Bull. Menninger Clin.*, 33:191-196.

———— (1970), Factors in the Psychoanalytic Treatment of Narcissistic Personalities. *J. Amer. Psychoanal. Assn.*, 18:51-85.

Khan, M. M. R. (1960a), Regression and Integration in the Analytic Setting. *Int. J. Psycho-Anal.*, 41:130-146.

——— (1960b), Clinical Aspects of the Schizoid Personality: Affects and Techniques. *Int. J. Psycho-Anal.*, 41:430-437.

——— (1963), Ego Ideal, Excitement and the Threat of Annihilation. *J. Hillside Hosp.*, 12:195-217.

Kleeman, J. (1967), The Peek-a-boo Game. *The Psychoanalytic Study of the Child*, 22:239-273.

Klein, M. (1946), Notes on Some Schizoid Mechanisms. *Int. J. Psycho-Anal.*, 27:99-110.

Kligerman, C. (1953), The Psychology of Herman Melville. *Psychoanal. Rev.*, 40:125-143.

——— (1968), In Panel: Narcissistic Resistance, rep. N. P. Segel. *J. Amer. Psychoanal. Assn.*, 17:941-954, 1969.

Koff, R. H. (1957), The Therapeutic Man Friday. *J. Amer. Psychoanal. Assn.*, 5:424-431.

Kohut, H. (1957), Observations on the Psychological Functions of Music. *J. Amer. Psychoanal. Assn.*, 5:389-407.

——— (1959), Introspection, Empathy and Psychoanalysis. *J. Amer. Psychoanal. Assn.*, 7:459-483.

——— (1961), Discussion of D. Beres's paper: "The Unconscious Phantasie." Meeting, Chicago Psychoanalytic Society. Abstr. in: *Phila. Bull. Psychoanal.*, 11:194-195.

——— (1964), Some Problems of a Metapsychological Formulation of Fantasy. *Int. J. Psycho-Anal.*, 45:199-202.

——— (1965), Autonomy and Integration. *J. Amer. Psychoanal. Assn.*, 13:851-856.

——— (1966a), Forms and Transformations of Narcissism. *J. Amer. Psychoanal. Assn.*, 14:243-272.

——— (1966b), Discussion of M. Schur's paper: Some Additional "Day Residues" of the Specimen Dream of Psychoanalysis. Read to the Chicago Psychoanalytic Society, Sept. 27, 1966.

——— (1966c), Termination of Analysis: Discussion. In: *Psychoanalysis in the Americas*, ed. R. E. Litman. New York: International Universities Press, pp. 193-204.

——— (1967), Chairman, Ad Hoc Committee on Scientific Activities of the American Psychoanalytic Association. Minutes of the Meeting of May 4, 1967.

——— (1968), The Psychoanalytic Treatment of Narcissistic Personality Disorders. *The Psychoanalytic Study of the Child*, 23:86-113.

——— (1970a), Moderator's opening and closing remarks [Discussion of D. C. Levin: The Self: A Contribution to Its Place in Theory and Technique]. *Int. J. Psycho-Anal.*, 51:176-181.

——— (1970b), Scientific Activities of the American Psychoanalytic Association: An Inquiry. *J. Amer. Psychoanal. Assn.*, 18:462-484.

—— & Seitz, P. F. D. (1963), Concepts and Theories of Psychoanalysis. In: *Concepts of Personality*, ed. J. M. Wepman & R. Heine. Chicago: Aldine, pp. 113-141.

Koyré, A. (1968), *Metaphysics and Measurement: Essays in Scientific Revolution in 17th Century Science.* Cambridge: Harvard University Press.

Kramer, M. K. (1959), On the Continuation of the Analytic Process after Psycho-Analysis. *Int. J. Psycho-Anal.,* 40:17-25.

Kris, E. (1950), Notes on the Development and on Some Current Problems of Psychoanalytic Child Psychology. *The Psychoanalytic Study of the Child,* 5:24-46.

—— (1951), Ego Psychology and Interpretation in Psychoanalytic Therapy. *Psychoanal. Quart.,* 20:15-30.

—— (1956a), The Recovery of Childhood Memories in Psychoanalysis. *The Psychoanalytic Study of the Child,* 11:54-88.

—— (1956b), On Some Vicissitudes of Insight in Psycho-Analysis. *Int. J. Psycho-Anal.,* 37:445-455.

Kubie, L. S. (1958), *Neurotic Distortions of the Creative Process.* New York: Noonday Press.

—— (1967), The Relation of Psychotic Disorganization to the Neurotic Process. *J. Amer. Psychoanal. Assn.,* 15:626-640.

—— (1971), The Destructive Potential of Humour in Psychotherapy. *Amer. J. Psychiat.,* 127:861-866.

Lagache, D. (1961), *La Psychanalyse et la Structure de la Personnalité.* Paris: Presses Universitaires de France.

Lampl-de Groot, J. (1947), The Origin and Development of Guilt Feelings. *The Development of the Mind.* New York: International Universities Press, 1965, pp. 126-137.

—— (1953), Depression and Aggression. In: *Drives, Affects, Behavior,* ed. R. M. Loewenstein. New York: International Universities Press, Vol. 1, pp. 153-168.

—— (1954), Problems of Psycho-Analytic Training. *Int. J. Psycho-Anal.,* 35:184-187.

—— (1956), The Role of Identification in Psycho-Analytic Procedure. *Int. J. Psycho-Anal.,* 37:456-459.

—— (1960), On Adolescence. *The Psychoanalytic Study of the Child,* 15:95-103.

—— (1962), Ego Ideal and Superego. *The Psychoanalytic Study of the Child,* 17:94-106.

—— (1963), Superego, Ego Ideal, and Masochistic Fantasies. *The Development of the Mind.* New York: International Universities Press, 1965, pp. 351-363.

Langer, S. (1942), *Philosophy in a New Key.* Cambridge: Harvard University Press, 3rd ed., 1957, p. 248.

Levin, D. C. (1969), The Self: A Contribution to Its Place in Theory and Technique. *Int. J. Psycho-Anal.,* 50:41-51.

Lewin, B. D. (1954), Sleep, Narcissistic Neurosis and the Analytic Situation. *Psychoanal. Quart.*, 23:487-510.

Lichtenstein, H. (1964), The Role of Narcissism in the Emergence and Maintenance of a Primary Identity. *Int. J. Psycho-Anal.*, 45:49-56.

Limentani, A. (1966), A Re-evaluation of Acting Out in Relation to Working Through. *Int. J. Psycho-Anal.*, 47:274-285.

Little, M. (1966), Transference in Borderline States. *Int. J. Psycho-Anal.*, 47:476-485.

Loch, W. (1966), Studien zur Dynamik, Genese und Therapie der frühen Objektbeziehungen. *Psyche,* 20:881-903.

——— (1967), Psychoanalytische Aspekte zur Pathogenese und Struktur depressiv-psychotischer Zustandsbilder. *Psyche,* 21:758-779.

Loewald, H. W. (1960), On the Therapeutic Action of Psycho-Analysis. *Int. J. Psycho-Anal.*, 41:16-33.

——— (1962), Internalization, Separation, Mourning, and the Superego. *Psychoanal. Quart.*, 31:483-504.

——— (1965), On Internalization (unpublished). Quoted in: Schafer, R. (1968), *Aspects of Internalization.* New York: International Universities Press, p. 10 (fn.).

Loewenstein, R. M. (1957), Some Thoughts on Interpretation in the Theory and Practice of Psychoanalysis. *The Psychoanalytic Study of the Child,* 12:127-150.

Lustman, S. L. (1968), The Economic Point of View and Defense. *The Psychoanalytic Study of the Child,* 23:189-203.

Mahler, M. S. (1952), On Child Psychosis and Schizophrenia. *The Psychoanalytic Study of the Child,* 7:286-305.

——— (1968), *On Human Symbiosis and the Vicissitudes of Individuation.* New York: International Universities Press.

——— & Gosliner, B. J. (1955), On Symbiotic Child Psychosis. *The Psychoanalytic Study of the Child,* 10:195-212.

——— & La Perriere, K. (1965), Mother-Child Interaction during Separation-Individuation. *Psychoanal. Quart.*, 34:483-498.

Maier, N. (1931), Reasoning in Humans. *J. Comp. Psychol.*, 12:181-194.

Moser, Tilmann (1969), 26. Internationaler Psychoanalytikerkongress: Bericht aus Rom. Broadcast August 8, 1969.

Murphy, L. (1960), Pride and Its Relation to Narcissism, Autonomy and Identity. *Bull. Menninger Clin.*, 24:136-143.

Murray, J. M. (1964), Narcissism and the Ego Ideal. *J. Amer. Psychoanal. Assn.*, 12:477-511.

Nagera, H. (1964), Autoerotism, Autoerotic Activities, and Ego Development. *The Psychoanalytic Study of the Child,* 19:240-255.

Nemiah, J. C. (1961), *Foundations of Psychopathology.* New York: Oxford University Press.

Niederland, W. G. (1959a), The "Miracled-up" World of Schreber's Childhood. *The Psychoanalytic Study of the Child,* 14:383-413.

——— (1959b), Schreber: Father and Son. *Psychoanal. Quart.*, 28:151-169.

BIBLIOGRAPHY 339

———— (1960), Schreber's Father. *J. Amer. Psychoanal. Assn.*, 8:492-499.

———— (1965), Narcissistic Ego Impairment in Patients with Early Physical Malformations. *The Psychoanalytic Study of the Child*, 20:518-534.

———— (1969), Klinische Aspekte der Kreativität. *Psyche*, 23:900-928.

Nunberg, H. (1932), *Allgemeine Neurosenlehre auf psychoanalytischer Grundlage*. Bern: Hans Huber.

———— (1937), Theory of the Therapeutic Results of Psychoanalysis. *Practice and Theory of Psychoanalysis*, 1:165-173. New York: International Universities Press, 2nd ed., 1961.

Ophuijsen, J. H. W. van (1920), On the Origin of the Feeling of Persecution. *Int. J. Psycho-Anal.*, 1:235-239.

Ostow, M. (1967), The Syndrome of Narcissistic Tranquillity. *Int. J. Psycho-Anal.*, 48:573-583.

Peto, A. (1961), The Fragmentizing Function of the Ego in the Transference Neurosis. *Int. J. Psycho-Anal.*, 42:238-245.

———— (1963), The Fragmentizing Function of the Ego in the Analytic Session. *Int. J. Psycho-Anal.*, 44:334-338.

———— (1967), Dedifferentiations and Fragmentations during Analysis. *J. Amer. Psychoanal. Assn.*, 15:534-550.

Piers, G. & Singer, M. B. (1953), *Shame and Guilt: A Psychoanalytic and Cultural Study*. Springfield, Ill.: Thomas.

Pollock, G. H. (1964), On Symbiosis and Symbiotic Neurosis. *Int. J. Psycho-Anal.*, 45:1-30.

Rangell, L. (1954), The Psychology of Poise. *Int. J. Psycho-Anal.*, 35:313-332.

———— (1955), Panel Report: The Borderline Case. *J. Amer. Psychoanal. Assn.*, 3:285-298.

———— (1968), The Psychoanalytic Process. *Int. J. Psycho-Anal.*, 49:19-26.

———— (1969), The Intrapsychic Process and Its Analysis: A Recent Line of Thought and Its Current Implications. *Int. J. Psycho-Anal.*, 50:65-77.

Rapaport, D. (1950), The Autonomy of The Ego. *Collected Papers*. New York: Basic Books, 1967, pp. 357-367.

Reich, A. (1960), Pathologic Forms of Self-Esteem Regulation. *The Psychoanalytic Study of the Child*, 15:215-232.

Reich, W. (1933), *Character-Analysis*, tr. T. P. Wolfe. New York: Orgone Institute Press, 1945.

Riesman, D. (1950), *The Lonely Crowd: A Study of the Changing American Character* [in collaboration with Reuel Denney and Nathan Glazer]. New Haven: Yale University Press.

Rosen, V. H. (1958), Abstract Thinking and Object Relations. *J. Amer. Psychoanal. Assn.*, 6:653-671.

———— (1960), Some Aspects of the Role of Imagination in the Analytic Process. *J. Amer. Psychoanal. Assn.*, 8:229-251.

——— (1966), Disturbances of Representations and Reference in Ego Deviations. In: *Psychoanalysis—A General Psychology*, ed. R. M. Loewenstein, L. M. Newman, M. Schur, & A. J. Solnit. New York: International Universities Press, pp. 634-654.

Rosenfeld, H. (1964), On the Psychopathology of Narcissism. *Int. J. Psycho-Anal.*, 45:332-337.

——— (1969), On the Treatment of Psychotic States by Psychoanalysis. *Int. J. Psycho-Anal.*, 50:615-631.

Ross, N. (1960), Rivalry with the Product. *J. Amer. Psychoanal. Assn.*, 8:450-463.

——— (1967), The "As If" Concept. *J. Amer. Psychoanal. Assn.*, 15: 59-82.

Sandler, J., Holder, A., & Meers, D. (1963), The Ego Ideal and the Ideal Self. *The Psychoanalytic Study of the Child*, 18:139-158.

——— & Rosenblatt, B. (1962), The Concept of the Representational World. *The Psychoanalytic Study of the Child*, 17:128-145.

Saul, L. (1947), *Emotional Maturity: The Development and Dynamics of Personality*. Philadelphia: Lippincott.

Saussure, R. de (1965), Les sources subjectives de la theorie du narcissisme chez Freud. *Rev. Franç. Psychanal.*, 29:475-483.

Schafer, R. (1968), *Aspects of Internalization*. New York: International Universities Press.

Schreber, D. G. M. (1865), *Das Buch der Erziehung an Leib und Seele*. Leipzig: Fleischer Verlag, 3rd ed., 1891.

Schreber, D. P. (1903), *Memoirs of My Nervous Illness*. London: Dawson, 1955.

Schumacher, W. (1970), Bemerkungen zur Theorie des Narzissmus. *Psyche*, 24:1-22.

Schur, M. (1966), Some Additional "Day Residues" of "The Specimen Dream of Psychoanalysis." In: *Psychoanalysis—A General Psychology*, ed. R. M. Loewenstein, L. M. Newman, M. Schur, & A. J. Solnit. New York: International Universities Press, pp. 45-85.

Schwing, G. (1940), *A Way to the Soul of the Mentally Ill*. New York: International Universities Press, 1954.

Segel, N. P. (1969), Panel Report: Narcissistic Resistance. *J. Amer. Psychoanal. Assn.*, 17:941-954.

Silberer, H. (1909), Report on a Method of Eliciting and Observing Certain Symbolic Hallucinations. In: *Organization and Pathology of Thought*, tr. & ed. D. Rapaport. New York: Columbia University Press, 1951, pp. 195-207.

Spiegel, L. A. (1966), Affects in Relation to Self and Object. *The Psychoanalytic Study of the Child*, 21:69-92.

Spitz, R. A. (in collaboration with K. Wolf) (1949), Autoerotism. *The Psychoanalytic Study of the Child*, 3/4:85-120.

——— (1950), Relevancy of Direct Infant Observation. *The Psychoanalytic Study of the Child*, 5:66-73.

—— (1957), *No and Yes: On the Genesis of Human Communication.* New York: International Universities Press.

—— (1961), Some Early Prototypes of Ego Defenses. *J. Amer. Psychoanal. Assn.,* 9:626-651.

—— (in collaboration with W. G. Cobliner) (1965), *The First Year of Life.* New York: International Universities Press.

Stein, M. (1958), The Cliché: A Phenomenon of Resistance. *J. Amer. Psychoanal. Assn.,* 6:263-277.

Sterba, E. (1960), In Panel: The Psychology of Imagination, rep. H. Kohut. *J. Amer. Psychoanal. Assn.,* 8:159-166.

Sterba, R. F. (1934), The Fate of the Ego in Analytic Therapy. *Int. J. Psycho-Anal.,* 15:117-126.

—— (1960), In Panel: The Psychology of Imagination, rep. H. Kohut. *J. Amer. Psychoanal. Assn.,* 8:159-166.

—— (1969), The First Psychoanalytic Hour. Discussion at 3rd Panamerican Congress for Psychoanalysis, New York.

Stern, A. (1938), Psychoanalytic Investigation of and Therapy in the Borderline Neuroses. *Psychoanal. Quart.,* 7:467-489.

Stone, L. (1967), The Psychoanalytic Situation and Transference. *J. Amer. Psychoanal. Assn.,* 15:3-58.

Sullivan, H. S. (1940), *Conceptions of Modern Psychiatry.* Washington: William Alanson White Psychiatric Foundation, 1947.

Székely, L. (1967), The Creative Pause. *Int. J. Psycho-Anal.,* 48:353-367.

—— (1970), Über den Beginn des Maschinenzeitalters: Psychoanalytische Bemerkungen über das Erfinden. *Schweiz. Z. Psychol.,* 29:273-282.

Tartakoff, H. H. (1966), The Normal Personality in Our Culture and the Nobel Prize Complex. In: *Psychoanalysis—A General Psychology,* ed. R. M. Loewenstein, L. M. Newman, M. Schur, & A. J. Solnit. New York: International Universities Press, pp. 222-252.

Tausk, V. (1919), On the Origin of the "Influencing Machine" in Schizophrenia. *Psychoanal. Quart.,* 2:519-556, 1933.

Tolpin, P. H. (1969), Some Psychic Determinants of Orgastic Dysfunction. Presented to the Chicago Psychoanalytic Society in October, 1969 (unpublished).

Waals, H. G. van der (1965), Problems of Narcissism. *Bull. Menninger Clin.,* 29:293-311.

Waelder, R. (1936), The Problem of the Genesis of Psychical Conflict in Earliest Infancy: Remarks on a Paper by Joan Rivière. *Int. J. Psycho-Anal.,* 18:406-473, 1937.

—— (1939), Kriterien der Deutung. *Int. Z. Psychoanal.,* 24:136-145.

Weiss, J. (1966), Panel Report: Clinical and Theoretical Aspects of "As If" Characters. *J. Amer. Psychoanal. Assn.,* 14:569-590.

Whitman, R. M. & Kaplan, S. M. (1968), Clinical, Cultural and Literary Elaborations of the Negative Ego-Ideal. *Comprehensive Psychiatry,* 9:358-371. Copyright: H. M. Stratton, Inc.

Winnicott, D. W. (1953), Transitional Objects and Transitional Phenomena. *Int. J. Psycho-Anal.,* 34:89-97.

Wulff, M. (1946), Fetishism and Object Choice in Early Childhood. *Psychoanal. Quart.,* 15:450-471.

——— (1957), Therapeutic Alliance in the Psychoanalysis of Hysterical Syndromes (unpublished paper).

Zeigarnick, B. (1927), Über das Behalten von erledigten und unerledigten Handlungen. *Psychol. Forsch.,* 9:1-85.

Zetzel, E. R. (1956), Current Concepts of Transference. *Int. J. Psycho-Anal.,* 37:369-376.

——— (1965), The Theory of Therapy in Relation to a Developmental Model of the Psychic Apparatus. *Int. J. Psycho-Anal.,* 46:39-52.

CONCORDANCE OF CASES

Mr. A. (paradigmatic illustration of idealizing transference), 10, 57-73, 78, 84-85, 168, 170-173, 193, 240, 289

Mr. B. (mirror transference; traumatic state), 80-82, 85, 121, 126-128, 130, 233-235, 237-238

Mr. C. (twinship [alter-ego] transference), 149, 189, 193-196, 249, 257, 326

Mr. D., 149, 257

Mr. E. (mirror transference; sublimation of narcissistic needs), 10, 15, 117-118, 130-132, 136, 158-159, 173, 313-315

Miss F. (mirror transference; analyst's countertransference), 5, 178, 283-293, 312, 314, 326

Mr. G. (borderline [schizophrenia]), 1, 67, 93-94, 126, 135-136, 150

Mr. H., 150, 318

Mr. I. (mirror transference; terminal phase of analysis), 159-161, 167-168

Mr. J. (relationship between "vertical" and "horizontal" split of psyche), 169, 179-183, 226-227, 240-242, 257

Mr. K. (paradigmatic illustration of mirror transference), 25, 139-140, 196, 242-259

Miss L. (analyst's resistance against idealizing transference), 135, 138-139, 260-262

Mr. M., 128-129

Mr. N., 151

Mr. O., 95

Mr. P., 321-324

Mr. Q., 306-307

INDEX

358 INDEX

Mother *(cont'd)*
can maintain relationship with only one child, 253-254
death of, *see* Death
depreciated, 146-147
depressed, 85, 117-118, 196, 284, 288-292
empathy of: 137, 301; faulty, 53, 60-65, 85, 233-234
exerting rigorous control over child, 81-82
merging with, 250
mirror functions of, 124
narcissistic, 65-67, 144, 180-182, 247, 253
narcissistic use of child, 180-185
pathology of, 61-64, 81-82, 85; *see also* Psychopathology
physical illness of, 53, 82
preventing child's internal separation, 80-81
providing narcissistic gratification, 249-250
rejecting child's narcissism, 185
self-preoccupation, 292-293
transference, 257
treats child as extension of herself, 277-278
unpredictability, 53, 60-63
withdrawal from child, 247-253, 258, 301
see also Child-mother interaction, Parent
Motion sickness, 145
Mourning, 50
Murphy, L., 338
Murray, J. M., 338
Music, 118, 318
Mutuality, 219

Nagera, H., 29, 214, 338
Narcissism
acceptance of archaic, 185
of analyst, 260
and autoerotism, 214-216
concept, 24
defensive, 227
definition, 26
development: 27, 40-43, 52, 219-220; follows an independent line, 6
forms of, 213, 258

and hostility, 75-76
idealizing: 54; definition, 42
integration of, 298-328
libidinal aspects, xiii-xvi *et passim*
modes of distribution of, 177-179
and object love, 6
phallic, 146-147, 188
prephallic, 152
primary: 25, 40; defined, 63-64; stage of, 213
and psychosis, 8
stage of, 32, 216
stage of archaic, 11
transformations of: 192, 220, 226, 232, 293; regressive, 7, 9, 296; therapeutic, 296-328
vulnerability of higher forms of, 8
and wisdom, 326-328
Narcissistic configurations (structures), 190, 240-245
analyzable, 218
cohesive therapeutic mobilization, 203
integration of, 224, 295
phallic and prephallic, 152-155
temporary disintegration of, 10-11
transformation of, 164, 184-190
and trauma, 18
weaknesses in, 12-14
see also Grandiose self, Idealized parent imago, Omnipotent object, Self-object
Narcissistic equilibrium, 46, 55, 64-65, 72-73, 85-86, 127, 140, 181, 294, 315-316, 321-322
disturbed, 21, 92-93
primary, 63
Narcissistic homeostasis, 28, 47, 122, 289, 299
Narcissistic injuries, 8, 11-13, 64-65, 92, 155, 244
Narcissistic isolation, 306-307
Narcissistic milieu, 66
Narcissistic personality disturbances
acting "crazy," 235
analysis of, *see* Psychoanalytic therapy and technique
analyzability of, 4, 6, 18, 207
central anxiety in, 152-153
compared to juvenile delinquency, 161-164

Reality (cont'd)
of self, 119
sense of, 287
Reality ego, 3, 79, 84, 96, 108, 145, 148, 156, 176-179, 185-186, 189, 226, 242
Reality testing, 255-256
Reassurance, 88
Rebuff, 2, 17, 160-161, 232, 261-262
Reconstruction, 13-14, 33, 54, 58, 63, 124, 135, 137, 195, 222-223, 227, 238, 252, 283-284, 294-295
of archaic ego states, 224-225
and memories, 231-232, 247, 294
style and form of, 224-225
vs. observation, 219
Regression
in analysis, 1-2, 7, 46, 85-87, 136-137, 159, 245
to bodily tensions, 243-244
chronic, 218
controlled, 277
depth of, 9
of drives, 69
expressed in dreams, 134, 159-161
fears of, 134
flux of, 213-214
hypnagogic, 245
and idealization, 138
and mirror transference, 126, 159
from mirror transference, 121, 159
from narcissism to autoerotism, 216, 253
narcissistic, 41, 86, 215, 247, 301
and narcissistic injuries, 11, 136
of oedipal material, 154
to pathogenic fixation point, 156, 198
pathognomonic, 88-89, 91, 114, 190, 228
and perversion, 69
to preoedipal stage, 153
prevention of, in therapy, 197-199
to primary narcissism, 213
propensity, 11-14
in psychosis, 7-8, 11-14, 217
quasi-religious, 153
resistance against, 148
of speech, 235
spontaneous, 211
to stage of fragmented self, 29-30
to subjectivity, 301

of symbolism, 245
temporary, 1-4, 7, 10, 90, 94-99, 117, 135, 218, 314
therapeutic, 7, 14, 29, 92-93, 115, 138, 141, 151-152, 190, 289
uncontrollable, 12
vicissitudes of, 6
voluntary, 278
Reich, A., xiv, 339
Reich, W., 95, 339
Rejection, 67, 78, 131, 139, 160-161, 230, 298
by analyst, 192, 224, 263, 267
by mother, 121
traumatic, 144, 198
Religion, 27, 164, 261-262; see also God
Religious feelings (preoccupations), 9, 85-88, 97
Repetition, and transference, 206
Repression, 79, 108, 176-178, 192, 196
of animistic tendencies, 302
of archaic self representation, 244
and counterphobia, 191
of grandiose self, 144, 156, 169, 182-183, 257, 289
of idealized parent imago, 83-84
of infantile wish, 197
and mirror transference, 123
and secondary defenses, 75, 242
and transference neurosis, 143
undoing of, 94
Repression barrier, 185, 198, 206, 289
Resistance, 29, 31, 88-90, 98
and acting out, 155-168
against establishment of transference, 87, 134, 166, 189-190
against idealization, 263
against revealing grandiosity, 271-272
of analyst, 148
chronic, 94
circumscribed, 189-190
to communication, 148, 160
correlated to anxiety, 135
ego and superego, 94
and empathy, 305-307
and fantasy, 148-149
and faux pas, 232
idealization as, 84
ingrained, 265
and insight, 285